INTERNATIONAL DEVELOPMENT IN FOCUS

Strengthening Argentina's Integration into the Global Economy

Policy Proposals for Trade, Investment, and Competition

Martha Martínez Licetti, Mariana Iootty,
Tanja Goodwin, and José Signoret

WORLD BANK GROUP

Contents

Figures

Tables

Acknowledgments

This publication was prepared at the request of the government of Argentina and in collaboration with various teams within Argentina's Ministry of Production. The report was prepared by a World Bank Group team led by Martha Martínez Licetti (Investment and Competition Unit, Macroeconomics, Trade, and Investment Global Practice, or MTI) and Mariana Iootty (MTI), under the guidance of Jesko Hentschel (Country Director for Argentina, Paraguay, and Uruguay), Marialisa Motta (Practice Manager, Finance, Competitiveness, and Innovation Global Practice, or FCI), José Guilherme Reis (Practice Manager, MTI), Cecile Fruman (Director, former Trade and Competitiveness Global Practice, or T&C), and Anabel González (Senior Director, former T&C).

Principal authors of the report, all from the MTI Global Practice, are Martha Martínez Licetti, Mariana Iootty, Tanja Goodwin, and José Signoret. The report is based on three individual background papers written by technical teams across the MTI Global Practice. The following team members led work on specific topics and sections of the report. José Signoret coordinated a team working on trade liberalization estimations, analysis of trade policy, and trade in services that included Syud Amer Ahmed, Maryla Maliszewska, Martín Molinuevo, Nadia Rocha, and Marinos Tsigas. Roberto Echandi directed the team working on investment policy and promotion, which included Daniela Gómez Altamirano, Valeria di Fiori, Gabriela Llobet, José Ramón Perea, and Erik von Uexkull. Tanja Goodwin led the team working on markets and competition policy issues that included Marta Camiñas, Seidu Dauda, Soulange Gramegna, Lucas Grosman, Diego Petrecolla, Florencia Saulino, and Lucía Villarán. The report draws on a mapping of the automotive sector prepared by an International Finance Corporation team led by Guillermo Foscarini. Specific inputs were provided by Lourdes Rodriguez Chamussy, Guilherme de Aguiar Falco, Morgane Elise Fouche, Aarre Laakso, and Maria Ana Lugo. Administrative assistance was provided by Flavia Dias Braga, Elena Feeney, Geraldine García, Paula Marcela Houser, Osongo Lenga, and Cara Zappala. Kelly Suzanne Alderson, Carolina Marcela Crerar, Daniel Gomez Gaviria, and Leandro Juan Hernandez provided efficient support with dissemination.

The team is grateful to Andrea Coppola, Calvin Zebaze Djiofack, Ana Alejandro Espinosa-Wang, Sebastián Galiani, Cebreiro Gomez, Graciela Miralles Murciego, Julian Peña, Daniel Saslavsky, and Hector Torres for valuable conversations. The authors also wish to thank the government of Argentina for valuable inputs and feedback throughout the elaboration of the report, in particular, Marina Bidart, Lucio Castro, Germán Coloma, Bernardo Díaz de Astarloa, Martín Goñi, Esteban Greco, Juan Carlos Hallak, Francisco Mango, Gabriel Michelena, Lucas Rusconi Moix, Carlos Gabriel Pallotti, Lucía Quesada, Shunko Rojas, Eduardo Stordeur, Pablo Trevisán, Lorena Triaca, Fernanda Viecens, and Federico Volujewicz, under the leadership of Miguel Braun. Special thanks go to all staff of Sub-Secretaría de Comercio Exterior, Agencia Argentina de Inversiones y Comercio Internacional (AAICI), and Comisión Nacional de Defensa de la Competencia (CNDC) for sharing their views and collaborating with the team during the missions. The team also received thoughtful insights from private-sector representatives and their respective chambers, including Cámara Argentina de Comercio y Servicios, Cámara de Exportadores de la República Argentina, Cámara de Comercio de Córdoba, Unión Industrial de Córdoba, and Cámara de Supermercados y de Autoservicios de Córdoba.

The report has benefited greatly from comments, advice, and guidance from and technical discussions with Tania Begazo, Najy Benhassine, Fernando Giuliano, Lusine Lusinyan, Frank Sader, Alain de Serres, Emily Sinnott, Daria Taglioni, David Tinel, and many others. Anabel González and Marialisa Motta have provided critical guidance to the team on policy advice. On international experience with microeconomic structural reform programs, the team benefited greatly from discussions with Jarosław Beldowski, Mårten Blix, Allan Fels, Eduardo Pérez-Motta, and Paul Phumpiu.

About the Authors

Martha Martínez Licetti is a Global Lead at the World Bank's Macroeconomics, Trade, and Investment Global Practice, where she heads the Markets and Competition Policy Team. During her eight years at the Bank, Licetti has held different positions, including advisor on trade and competitiveness matters, as well as lead economist of the Global Trade Unit, where she has studied the connection between trade agreements and competition-enhancing domestic policies. She has been the technical lead on several projects aimed at improving the investment climate and fostering an efficient private sector through competition reforms across Eastern Europe and Central Asia, Latin America, the Middle East and North Africa, and the Sub-Saharan Africa region. She has led private-sector contributions to Bank-wide initiatives on state-owned enterprises, public procurement frameworks, and improvements to IFC investments. In her current role, she has developed an innovative competition policy offering, and she has built a portfolio of advisory and lending support to more than 60 client countries around the world.

Before joining the Bank, Licetti worked as a practitioner in leading positions in the private and public sectors in areas of antitrust, market and competition analysis, state-owned enterprises, telecom regulation, anti-dumping, and trade negotiations. She is an economist, specializing in industrial organization, applied microeconomics, and antitrust, with more than 15 years of experience in economic regulation, markets, and competition policy. She has given lecture courses in industrial organization, network regulation, antitrust, and economic analysis of law, and she has published articles on antitrust policies in Latin America, Europe, and the United States. She has doctoral, masters, and advanced studies degrees in economics from Northeastern University in Boston, University of Texas at Austin, and the Institute of World Economics in Kiel, Germany. Her current research interests focus on understanding the empirical relationship between competition policy and market regulation, inclusive growths, and shared prosperity.

Mariana Iootty is a Senior Economist at the World Bank working in the Macroeconomics, Trade, and Investment Global Practice, Markets and Competition Policy Team. Iootty is a Brazilian national and has been with the World Bank for six years, during which time she has led projects on innovation financing, regulatory impact assessment, global value chain analysis, trade competitiveness assessment, and productivity analysis in several countries in Eastern Europe and Latin America. Her main area of research is microeconomic analysis of economic development and firm performance. Prior to joining the Bank, Iootty was a tenured assistant professor in Brazil, and a visiting fellow at the University of Reading, United Kingdom.

Tanja Goodwin is a Senior Economist at the World Bank's Macroeconomics, Trade, and Investment Global Practices working with the Markets and Competition Policy Team since 2011. Her work focuses on analytics and technical assistance in pro-competition sectoral regulation, and on the implementation of competition policy with extensive experience in Latin America, as well as Northern Africa and East Asia Pacific. Before joining the World Bank, Goodwin worked at private and public research institutes in Germany and Latin America. She holds a master's degree in economics from New York University. During her time at the Bank, Goodwin has also taught in different graduate programs, including at the Pontificia Universidad Catolica del Peru.

José Signoret is an Economist in the Global Trade and Regional Integration unit in the Macroeconomics, Trade, and Investment Global Practice of the World Bank. His recent research topics include nontariff measures, analysis of preferential trade agreements, and firm-level trade analysis. Before joining the World Bank, he worked in the Research Division at the U.S. International Trade Commission, where he led several research projects, including the recent report on the Trans-Pacific Partnership agreement. From 2007 to 2008, he served as Director for Trade Capacity Building (TCB) at the Office of the U.S. Trade Representative, focusing on TCB efforts in Latin America. Signoret holds a doctorate from the University of California, Berkeley, and a master's degree from the University of Michigan.

Abbreviations

AAICI	Agencia Argentina de Inversiones y Comercio Internacional
ACE	Economic Complementation Agreement
ARSAT	Empresa Argentina de Soluciones Satelitales Sociedad Anónima
AVE	ad valorem equivalent
CES	constant elasticity of substitution
CET	common external tariff
CGE	computable general equilibrium
CNDC	Comisión Nacional de Defensa de la Competencia
ComEx	Sub-Secretaría de Comercio Exterior
DJAI	Declaración Jurada Anticipada de Importación
DNPDP	Dirección Nacional de Protección de Datos Personales
ECI	economic complexity index
ECTR	electricity, communications, and transport
EIU	Economic Intelligence Unit
ENDEI	Encuesta Nacional de Dinámica de Empleo e Inovación
EU	European Union
FADEEAC	Federación Argentina de Entidades Empresarias del Autotransporte de Cargas
FDI	foreign direct investment
FEDCAM	Federación Nacional de Trabajadores Camioneros
FTA	free trade agreement
GCR	Global Competition Review
GDP	gross domestic product
GTAP	Global Trade Analysis Project
GVC	global value chain
ICT	information and communications technology
IMF	International Monetary Fund
INDEC	Instituto Nacional de Estadística y Censos de la República Argentina
IPA	Investment Promotion Agency
IPR	intellectual property rights
IT	information technology
KBS	knowledge-based services
LAC	Latin America and the Caribbean

LAIA	Latin American Integration Association
LCR	local content requirement
MCPAT	Markets and Competition Policy Assessment Tool
MVNO	mobile virtual network operator
NAFTA	North American Free Trade Agreement
NTM	nontariff measure
OECD	Organisation for Economic Co-operation and Development
OLS	ordinary least squares
PCM	price-cost margin
PMR	product market regulation
PPML	Poisson Pseudo-Maximum Likelihood
PPP	purchasing power parity
PROCAMPO	Programa de Apoyos Directos al Campo (Mexico)
PTA	preferential trade agreement
R&D	research and development
RVC	regional value chain
SIMI	Sistema Integral de Monitoreo de Importaciones
SMEs	small and medium enterprises
SOE	state-owned enterprise
TAA	trade adjustment assistance
TFP	total factor productivity
TPSC	Trade Policy Staff Committee
TRIPS	trade-related aspects of intellectual property rights
TiVA	trade in value-added
UNCTAD	United Nations Conference on Trade and Development
UNDP	United Nations Development Programme
USTR	United States Trade Representative
VAT	value-added tax
WBG	World Bank Group
WDI	World Development Indicators
WITS	World Integrated Trade Solution
WTO	World Trade Organization

Executive Summary

The administration of President Mauricio Macri in Argentina faces an economy that is poorly connected with the world economy. Argentina needs to lift and stabilize economic growth to create more and better jobs while reigniting productivity to bring income closer to that of more advanced economies (figure ES.1).[1] Integration into global markets provides opportunities to unleash the country's growth and higher productivity potential by creating conditions and incentives for markets to function better and resources to be used more efficiently. In addition, further integration into the world economy can help deliver inclusive growth, as consumers will gain from the availability of foreign goods and services, greater variety, and prices that are more competitive, while small and medium enterprises (SMEs) can have more opportunities to expand their activities.

ARGENTINA HAS SUBSTANTIAL SCOPE TO INTEGRATE FURTHER INTO THE WORLD ECONOMY

The economy is particularly closed to trade. Partly as a result of policies put in place by previous governments, Argentina's trade flows have fallen by almost half over the last decade. They dropped from 42 percent of gross domestic product (GDP) in 2002 to 26 percent in 2016, slightly above the 1998 level of 23 percent.[2] Trade in services is lower as a share of GDP than in all neighboring countries. Argentina's average import tariff was 13.6 percent in 2015 (figure ES.2),[3] similar to Brazil's (13.5 percent) but well above the level of comparator countries. Nontariff measures (NTMs) further restrict trade flows, with effects similar to those of tariffs as high as 34 percent. As of October 2016, import licenses for around 1,600 tariff lines were still not subject to automatic approval.[4] Countries around the world participate, on average, in about fourteen free trade agreements each; Argentina is a signatory to only one.[5]

Foreign direct investment in Argentina is low. The value of foreign direct investment (FDI) inflows amounted, on average, to only 2 percent of GDP between 2000 and 2015, below the regional average and the average for upper-middle-income countries (3.6 percent and 2.4 percent of GDP, respectively).[6] Consistent with low FDI inflows, stock of FDI is also low, and well

FIGURE ES.1

GDP growth accounting in Argentina, 1992–2016

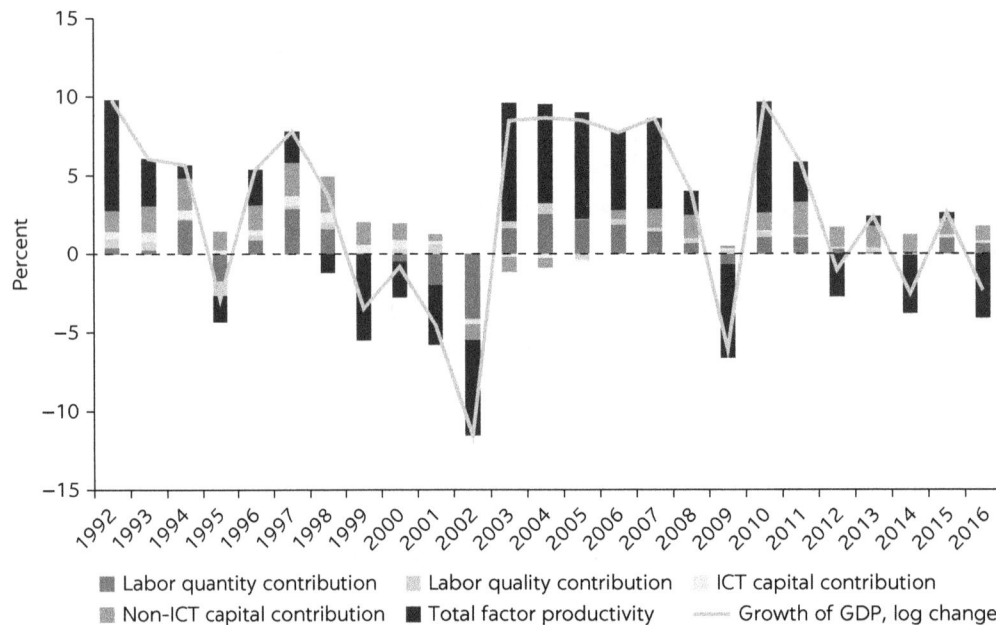

Source: Data from Conference Board database. (https://www.conference-board.org/data/economydatabase/).

FIGURE ES.2

Average import tariff in Argentina vs. comparator countries

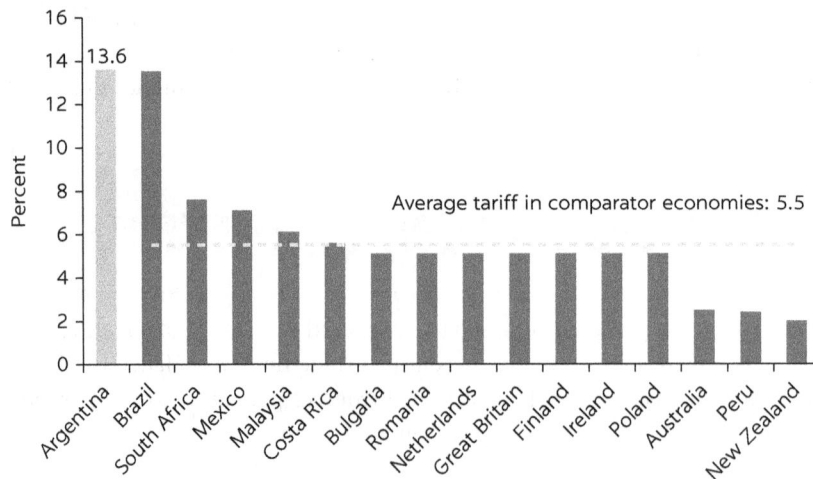

Source: Data from WTO ITC UNCTAD Tariff Profiles, 2016.

below the level of comparator countries (figure ES.3). Weak FDI inflows and stock exacerbate Argentina's already low rate of overall investment, which is critical for closing its infrastructure gap. Gross capital formation in Argentina was 16 percent of GDP in 2016, below the regional average (19 percent) for Latin America and the Caribbean (LAC) in the same year and significantly below the average among upper-middle-income countries (32.3 percent) in 2015.[7]

The lack of integration with global markets is mirrored by a lack of competition in domestic markets. New data collected jointly by the Organisation for Economic Co-operation and Development (OECD) and the World Bank Group (WBG)

FIGURE ES.3

Inward FDI stock over GDP in Argentina vs. comparator countries, 2015

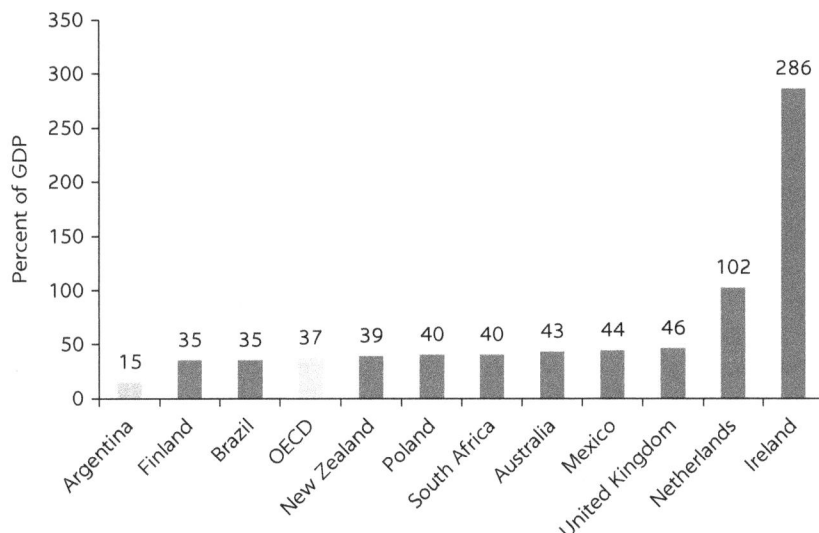

Source: Data from OECD database (https://data.oecd.org/fdi/fdi-stocks.htm).
Note: Inward FDI stock is defined as the value of foreign investors' equity in and net loans to enterprises resident in the reporting economy.

FIGURE ES.4

Product market regulations in Argentina vs. comparator countries, 2013–16

(index scale 0 to 6 from least to most restrictive)

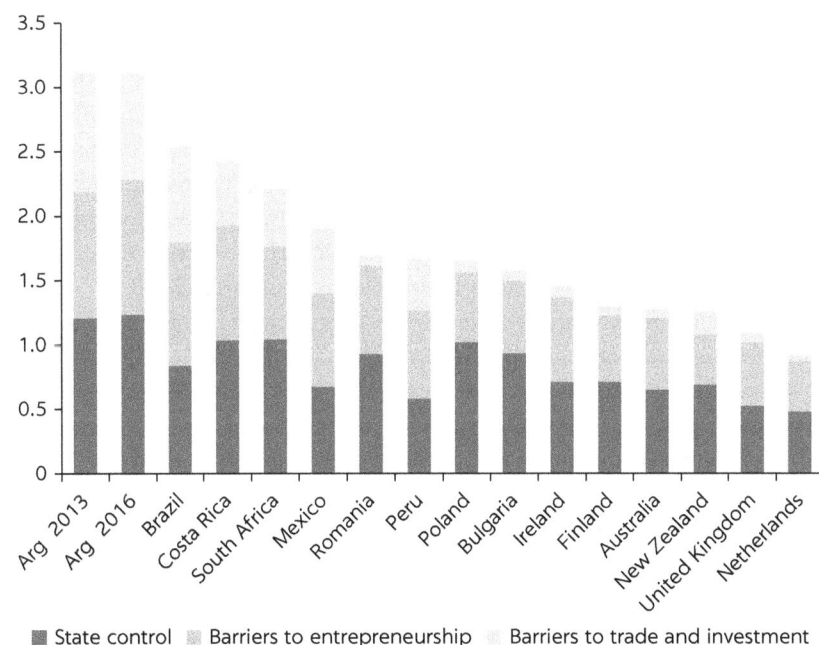

■ State control ▨ Barriers to entrepreneurship ▨ Barriers to trade and investment

Source: OECD Product Market Regulation database, and OECD-World Bank Group Product Market Regulation database for non-OECD countries 2013, 2016, as of March 2018. (http://www.oecd.org/eco/growth/indicatorsofproductmarketregulationhomepage.htm)

suggest that product market regulation (PMR) is not conducive to competition in key sectors of the economy, including transport, energy, and retail. In fact, according to 2016 data, product market regulation is 30 percent more restrictive in Argentina than the average across 19 LAC countries and highest among relevant comparator countries (figure ES.4).

Lack of integration could be associated with the significant price differentials observed among essential food products, sold in relatively concentrated domestic markets. Overall, households in Argentina spend 28 percent of their overall consumption on food products, more than the 14 percent in comparator countries.[8] International price comparisons conducted for this report using panel data for 2010–15 suggest that prices for a series of food products that make up 85 percent of the food consumption basket were, on average, almost 50 percent higher in Argentina when compared to international peers and 35 percent higher than in countries in the Pacific Alliance. Households in Buenos Aires paid, on average, 13 percent more for basic food products than their peers in capital cities worldwide.[9] These results take into account different income levels, import tariffs, and transport costs. Prices for chicken, dairy products, wheat bread, and white rice are significantly higher. This is generally consistent with information on the relatively high concentration in these product markets; however, the level of concentration is only one indicator of the intensity of competition. Further analysis undertaken at specific stages of the supply chain would contribute to identifying specific barriers and constraints that might be affecting competition.[10]

THE CURRENT ADMINISTRATION IS TACKLING THESE CHALLENGES HEAD-ON, WITH NOTABLE EARLY PROGRESS

Complementing macroeconomic and fiscal reforms, the government lifted foreign exchange controls and rolled out reforms to stimulate private investment. The administration approved a new public–private partnership framework and gradual reductions in energy and transport subsidies.[11] Trade-related reforms have included the reduction of export taxes and the establishment of a new import administration system to replace Declaración Jurada Anticipada de Importación (DJAI), the mostly discretionary licensing regime in place until 2015, with a simpler monitoring system, Sistema Integral de Monitoreo de Importaciones (SIMI).[12] Even just this import licensing reform is expected to boost GDP by at least 0.14 percent over baseline projections by 2020.[13]

Argentina is displaying a renewed interest in engaging in trade negotiations and taking a more active role in the international policy arena. Argentina has accelerated negotiations for new free trade agreements (FTAs) with the European Union (EU) and countries of the Pacific Alliance and has bid successfully for the G20 presidency and the hosting of the Eleventh World Trade Organization (WTO) Ministerial Conference.

The government has taken steps to restructure and strengthen its institutions for investment promotion and competition policy. The renewed investment promotion agency (IPA), Agencia Argentina de Inversiones y Comercio Internacional (AAICI), has already facilitated investment in at least 539 cases. This contributed to the announcement of 778 new investment projects in the first 24 months of President Macri's administration, totaling US$102 billion in new investment.[14] This is more than double the annual amount between 2012 and 2015. The new head and staff at the competition authority, Comisión Nacional de Defensa de la Competencia (CNDC), have already reduced the time required for merger reviews by almost 50 percent, sanctioned one price-fixing cartel, presented a new competition bill to the National Congress, and promoted changes to strengthen competition in the card payment market.[15]

ARGENTINA HAS MUCH TO GAIN FROM CONTINUING TO PURSUE ITS STRATEGY OF OPENING MARKETS AND INTEGRATING INTO THE WORLD ECONOMY BY BOOSTING TRADE, COMPETITION, AND INVESTMENT

Partial and general equilibrium analyses suggest that trade, competition, and investment policy reforms will boost growth and productivity. This report presents a set of robust empirical analyses to assess the potential impacts from such reforms.

Argentina's strategy of pursuing unilateral trade policy reforms and regional trade integration will yield permanent gains, if implemented successfully. Using a computable general equilibrium (CGE) model tailored specifically to Argentina, this report assesses the effects of several trade reform measures (see box ES.1).

BOX ES.1

Economic impact of trade reforms: A CGE analysis

The CGE analysis conducts a comparison between economic outcomes (including GDP, exports, imports, output, and others) that would accrue from policy reforms and the baseline projection of the economy with current policies in place through the medium and long terms (2020 and 2030). Figure BES.1.1 illustrates how to interpret the CGE results. The estimated impact of the reform in the long run, for example, is represented by the vertical distance (α) in the figure between a baseline projection of the economy through 2030 without reform and the alternative scenario reflecting the policy changes. Certain effects, such as the potential effect on GDP, can accumulate over time (as represented by the area between the curves). Overall, the simulated effects of potential trade-opening scenarios using CGE models may underestimate the actual impact.[a] The results for Argentina are similar in percentage terms to those for CGE simulations of comparable trade reforms for other countries, such as Brazil.[b]

FIGURE BES.1.1

Interpreting CGE results

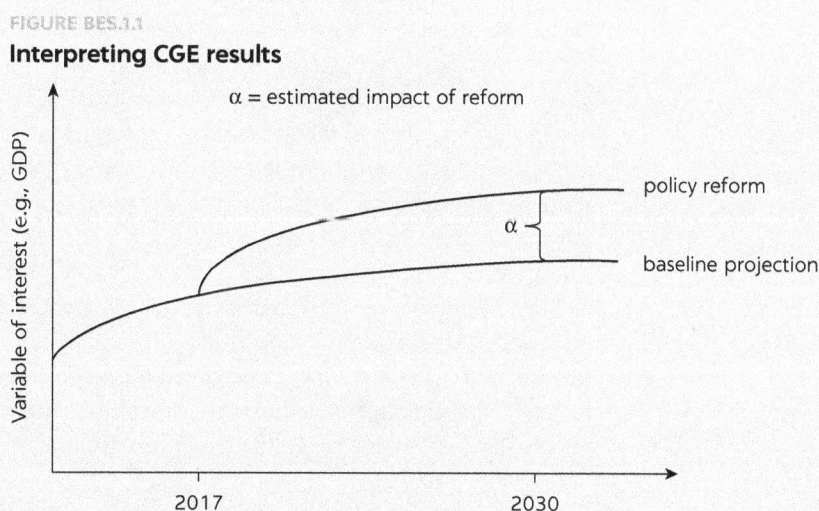

α = estimated impact of reform

Variable of interest (e.g., GDP)

policy reform

α

baseline projection

2017   2030

[a] The CGE model does not include some possible dynamic factors proposed in the literature, such as productivity increases from endogenous growth effects via technological spillovers and "learning by doing" or FDI and foreign technology inflows that may be induced by the reform. Moreover, certain policy changes that are often difficult to quantify, such as reforms related to NTMs in goods and services, and restrictions on investment, present analytical challenges that may affect the estimated economic effects. CGE results may underestimate the likely impacts due to these limitations. Ex post evidence in the trade reform literature tends to suggest larger gains than ex ante analysis, such as that presented here. See, for example, Casacuberta, Fachola, and Gandelman (2011); Wacziarg and Welch (2008); Salinas and Aksoy (2006); Felbermayr, Prat, and Schmerer (2011); and Falvey, Foster, and Greenaway (2012).
[b] See, for instance, Petri and Plumer (2016), as well as Araujo and Flaig (2016).

Conservative simulations of the potential gains from unilateral trade policy reform suggest that:

- Removing all export taxes would expand GDP by at least 1 percent over baseline projections by 2020. The potential fiscal implications of this measure need to be taken into consideration, however.[16]
- Expanding the import licensing reform (initiated at the end of 2015) would boost the GDP gains already achieved through the removal of the DJAI to at least 0.22 percent over baseline projections by 2020.[17]

Conservative simulations of the potential gains from successful trade negotiations suggest that:

- A more integrated Mercosur—with lower external tariffs and streamlined internal NTMs—would expand Argentina's economy by at least 1 percent over baseline projections by 2030.[18]
- A Mercosur–EU FTA would boost Argentine exports to the EU by 80 percent over baseline projections by 2030.[19]
- A Mercosur–Pacific Alliance FTA would boost Argentine exports to Pacific Alliance countries by 25 percent over baseline projections by 2030.[20]

GIVEN THAT THE GAINS WOULD ACCUMULATE OVER TIME, ARGENTINA FACES THE COST OF NOT PURSUING THESE REFORMS WITH EVERY YEAR THAT PASSES

Trade liberalization reforms would involve the reallocation of labor across sectors; employment would shrink relative to the baseline in certain sectors and would need to be absorbed by expanding activities relative to the baseline. Simulations drawn from the CGE model suggest that certain sectors would be more susceptible to losing jobs in response to trade reforms. Overall, for most of the trade integration scenarios modeled, sugar, metal products, footwear, auto parts, and other manufacturing sectors are expected to be more susceptible to experiencing large or moderate losses in formal employment. On the other hand, some sectors emerge as formal employment generators, regardless of the trade integration scenario under consideration. These include services and other agriculture and meat sectors.

Argentina can gain even more from "deeper" trade agreements and complementary regulatory reforms that foster domestic competition. Partial equilibrium analysis suggests that "deep provisions," such as commitments with regard to competition and investment in regional trade agreements, as well as reforms that tackle anticompetitive business practices, remove entry barriers, and modify product market regulations that restrict competition, would translate into tangible gains:[21]

- With a Mercosur agreement as deep—in terms of the number of enforceable provisions—as the agreement among the EU, Colombia, and Peru, Argentina would export between 1 percent and 9 percent more parts and components to Mercosur members.
- Increasing competition in the manufacturing sector would increase the annual growth rate of labor productivity by 7 percent, on average, with all else being equal.

- Reducing the regulatory restrictiveness of competition in Argentine service sectors (such as energy, transport, professional services, and telecommunications) would translate into an additional 0.1 percent to 0.6 percent growth in annual GDP, with all else being equal.

THE NEW GLOBAL TRADE LANDSCAPE OPENS UP THREE SPECIFIC OPPORTUNITIES FOR ARGENTINA: CONNECTING TO CERTAIN REGIONAL AND GLOBAL VALUE CHAINS THROUGH FOREIGN DIRECT INVESTMENT, TRADING SERVICES, AND EXPANDING E-COMMERCE

Trade is not growing as quickly as before, and its nature has been evolving rapidly, leading to the emergence of new opportunities. Setting global economic integration as a priority may seem to be an unusual choice in light of protectionist threats worldwide and slower growth in total trade volumes, but the changing *nature* of trade over the past decade opens up specific opportunities for Argentina. As a result of technological changes, the content and mode of trade have shifted. First, trade in intermediate goods has grown faster than trade in final goods, and FDI has played a crucial role in such global value chains (GVCs).[22] Second, services can be traded by virtually connecting provider and consumer or by one or the other moving across borders. Today, trade in services makes up over 20 percent of global trade.[23] Third, information communications technology (ICT) tools can facilitate cross-border e-commerce and the participation of smaller and new entrants in global markets by boosting their ability to reach a sufficient scale.

One opportunity these changes open up for Argentina is the opportunity to connect to specific segments of regional value chains (RVCs) and GVCs by facilitating trade in intermediate goods, attracting strategic FDI, and building on existing capabilities in specific industries. Trade in parts and components is higher, on average, for countries that have signed deeper agreements with provisions on investment, competition, and others.[24] As mentioned above, evidence provided in this report suggests that a deeper Mercosur agreement would boost Argentina's trade in parts and components with its regional partners. Foreign investors who seek efficiencies in Argentina—as opposed to resources or market access—offer the opportunity to connect domestic firms and, in particular, SMEs, to GVCs. For example, building on existing capabilities in specific market segments (such as auto and food processing), Argentina can attract FDI in these sectors while strengthening linkages with local suppliers in order to reorient the production structure and integrate into GVCs and/or RVCs.[25]

Second, Argentina can leverage comparative advantages in services to increase FDI and exports. Argentina is competitive in knowledge-based services, such as software and information technology services, business services, and audiovisual services. Twenty-eight clusters already host 1,000 companies and employ 37,000 workers, and Argentina has attracted some of the world's leading information technology (IT) companies.[26] Proper interinstitutional coordination across federal and provincial governments may help to attract more FDI into the knowledge-based service sectors, but investment incentives need to be well coordinated, applied in a (fiscally) conservative manner, balanced, competitively assigned, and properly monitored.

Third, Argentina can foster inclusive trade by facilitating cross-border e-commerce for SMEs. Retail e-commerce in Argentina grew by 50 percent between 2010 and 2015, displaying much stronger progress than selected peer economies in the region and the average in Latin America.[27] However, its share in world retail e-commerce is one-fifth that of Australia and Brazil, which points to untapped potential. Updating legislation on electronic transactions and signatures, privacy and data protection, and consumer protection for online purchases could enhance the growth of e-commerce. By the same token, trade facilitation efforts (in particular, in cross-border procedures) need to be enhanced significantly to facilitate e-commerce and trade more broadly.

ARGENTINA CAN IMPLEMENT MITIGATION MEASURES TO OFFSET THE TRANSITION COSTS OF OPENING UP TO THE GLOBAL ECONOMY

Integrating into the global economy and taking advantage of available opportunities will entail transition costs in some segments of the economy. Microeconomic reforms, trade integration, and the associated changes in relative prices would trigger a reallocation of production factors (within and between firms and sectors) that entail efficiency gains but also adjustment costs. Some segments of Argentina's manufacturing sector are susceptible to adjustment costs. According to data from the Argentine Chamber of Commerce and Services, the total number of workers in the private sector in sensitive sectors such as automobiles, home appliances, and textiles represents close to 1.7 percent of Argentina's total labor force, and these industries are concentrated mainly in Buenos Aires and the central region, particularly in Córdoba and Santa Fe.[28]

International experience suggests that there is no one-size-fits-all strategy for effective mitigation measures, but that protecting workers instead of jobs is good practice. When well-designed and tailored to the country context, both active labor-market policies (such as job search assistance and training) and passive policies (including income support and social insurance programs) have proved effective. Complementary policies and reforms in other markets (such as housing, credit, and infrastructure) play a crucial role in facilitating mobility, thereby reducing adjustment frictions.[29]

Argentina has recently put in place adjustment programs to help domestic workers and companies become more competitive, which is a step toward facilitating the reallocation of labor in a context of trade opening and technological changes. Argentina launched the Programa de Transformación Productiva at the end of 2016. This adjustment program is designed to help companies enhance their competitiveness through mechanisms that facilitate improving productive processes; implementing jumps in scale or technology; developing new products; and reorienting production toward more competitive and dynamic activities that demand long-term, high-quality employment. Within three months of the launch of this program, about 20 firms had presented expansion or conversion projects with the potential to add up to 1,000 more workers. The government has also launched the Programa "111 mil, aprende a programar," an initiative that seeks to train "100,000 programmers, 10,000 professionals, and 1,000 technological entrepreneurs" in the next four years to meet the demand from companies in the knowledge-based service sector.[30] Additional programs of this kind, together with policies to protect workers and reduce adjustment frictions, will increase the social benefits of trade integration.

INTERNATIONAL EXPERIENCE IN STRUCTURAL MICROECONOMIC REFORMS REVEALS POTENTIAL GAINS; HOWEVER, PRIOR EXPERIENCE HAS ALSO SHOWN THAT PROPER SEQUENCING AND MONITORING ARE ESSENTIAL TO SUCCESS

The economy-wide benefits of trade liberalization are well established, and studies of countries that have executed more comprehensive structural reform packages suggest that FDI and competition policy improvements are complementary. A microeconomic reform program to open markets to competition in Australia complemented unilateral trade liberalization and added 2.5 percent to GDP.[31] Substantial structural reforms that opened Sweden up to FDI in the early 1990s encouraged private-sector participation and strengthened competition, and these reforms were followed by the highest productivity growth rate in the OECD (aside from the United States) during the period from 1995 to 2011, together with wage increases. Mexico complemented its early moves toward trade openness with important domestic market reforms beginning in the early 1990s, before accessing NAFTA.[32] These country case studies are discussed in this report and can inform not only the sequence and nature of reforms, but also successful compensation mechanisms to support the adjustment process and mitigate social costs.

Based on international experience, such ambitious reform programs require a long-term national commitment and interinstitutional coordination. Comprehensive reform programs in Australia, Mexico, and Sweden were gradual and took a decade or more. Argentina's new strategy should, therefore, aim at results beyond the current legislative period. Argentina could consider establishing a national policy and respective institutional setup that could sustain a comprehensive reform package to integrate into the global economy over the coming decade.

TO SCALE UP AND SUSTAIN REFORM EFFORTS FOR A SUCCESSFUL TRANSITION TOWARD A MORE COMPETITIVE, OPEN, AND INCLUSIVE ECONOMY, THIS REPORT HIGHLIGHTS BEST PRACTICES IN TERMS OF INSTITUTIONAL SETUP AND POLICY IMPLEMENTATION

Institutions in charge of trade, investment, and competition policy are key to implementing a broad national policy of integration into the global economy. Successful institutions are typically structured efficiently and allow complementarity and coordination among them:

• According to international experience, successful institutions in charge of promoting FDI have certain good practices in common: a precise mandate that allows effective interaction with investors, separate regulatory and promotional functions, and a clear sector strategy. Activities related to trade promotion and investment promotion have, by nature, different needs in terms of staff expertise, skills, target audiences, clients, and stakeholders. Best practices point, in general, to a split between trade promotion and investment promotion, although some IPAs with joint mandates have been successful in attracting FDI. Ireland's IDA and the Republic of Korea's KOTRA are good examples of IPAs with separate and joint mandates, respectively. Particularly potent are investment promotion agencies that have some semiautonomous status, either as an autonomous public body, a joint public private or private entity, or a semiautonomous agency that reports to a ministry rather than merely being the subunit of a ministry. Another feature of the most effective investment promotion agencies is that they focus on promoting specific locations and do not have regulatory roles. A precise mandate to serve investors, to focus on foreign investors and not just domestic investors, and to target strategic sectors—as in the case of knowledge-based services in Argentina—is also key to a conducive investment climate. To address these responsibilities, IPAs can benefit from staff with a private sector–minded culture and deep business knowledge.

- Effective competition agencies design and implement enforcement and advocacy tools to ensure the greatest impact on market outcomes, work to embed competition principles in broader public policies, and operate under technical and functional autonomy. Autonomy can be critical to applying effective sanctions and issuing recommendations based on objective criteria alone and without political interference. More than half of the world's 120 competition agencies are institutionally independent from ministerial control. Of these independent agencies, 22 are in developing and transition economies.[33] To use scarce public resources effectively, effective competition authorities also typically focus on the most harmful violations of competition—cartel agreements—and use other antitrust tools, such as merger control, as residual tools. Agencies set appropriate thresholds for merger notifications to be able to focus on transactions that are large and may reduce competition significantly in the medium term. A comparative review across 82 countries suggests that these thresholds are generally aligned with the size of the economy. Through dedicated competition advocacy units, agencies also identify and recommend changes to rules and regulations that may have facilitated anticompetitive practices in the first place. Authorities also develop joint programs and/or collaboration mechanisms with sector regulators in order to foster procompetition economic regulation.

- Preparation and conduct of negotiations, as well as implementation of their outcomes, are the core responsibilities of trade institutions. To ensure effective trade negotiation, best practices highlight three main responsibilities: analysis, communication and coordination, and representation. Trade institutions should have institutional capacity to collect, analyze, utilize, and disseminate trade-related information and to ensure independent assessment of the negotiated agreement. Communication and coordination with all stakeholders is also important. Countries such as the United States have set up sophisticated interagency coordination processes to ensure the flow of information among all involved government agencies. In terms of consultation and legitimization of internal negotiations with the private sector during trade negotiations, countries like Mexico, through the Coordinating Body of Foreign Trade Business Associations, have successfully established a recognized consultation process that channels the participation of the private sector and strategic social groups. These functions are best served by representatives who are fully trained in trade policy and negotiation techniques and institutions that are equipped with crucial resources and skills that ultimately guarantee the predictability of trade agreements.

AGAINST THIS BACKDROP, THE REPORT MAPS KEY CHALLENGES THAT FIRMS HAVE BEEN FACING IN ARGENTINA AS THEY ATTEMPT TO INTEGRATE INTO THE GLOBAL ECONOMY. TO ADDRESS THESE CHALLENGES, THIS REPORT PROPOSES MEASURES IN THE AREAS OF TRADE, INVESTMENT, AND COMPETITION POLICY

Successful integration into the global economy relies on the following four conditions faced by firms: (1) opportunities to enter and invest; (2) access to efficient input markets; (3) ability to compete on a level playing field; and (4) capacity to expand and thrive in global markets (figure ES.5).

Specific measures designed under trade, investment, and competition policy areas can influence these conditions and have positive effects on market and productivity dynamics while boosting shared prosperity. Figure ES.6 illustrates how particular policy measures under these three policy areas are associated with each of the four conditions firms face in integrating into the global economy. If implemented in a coherent way, these measures can have positive effects on productivity dynamics and consumer welfare and generate more and better jobs. For example, opportunities to enter may depend on licenses (which might be

FIGURE ES.5

Essential conditions for successful integration into global markets

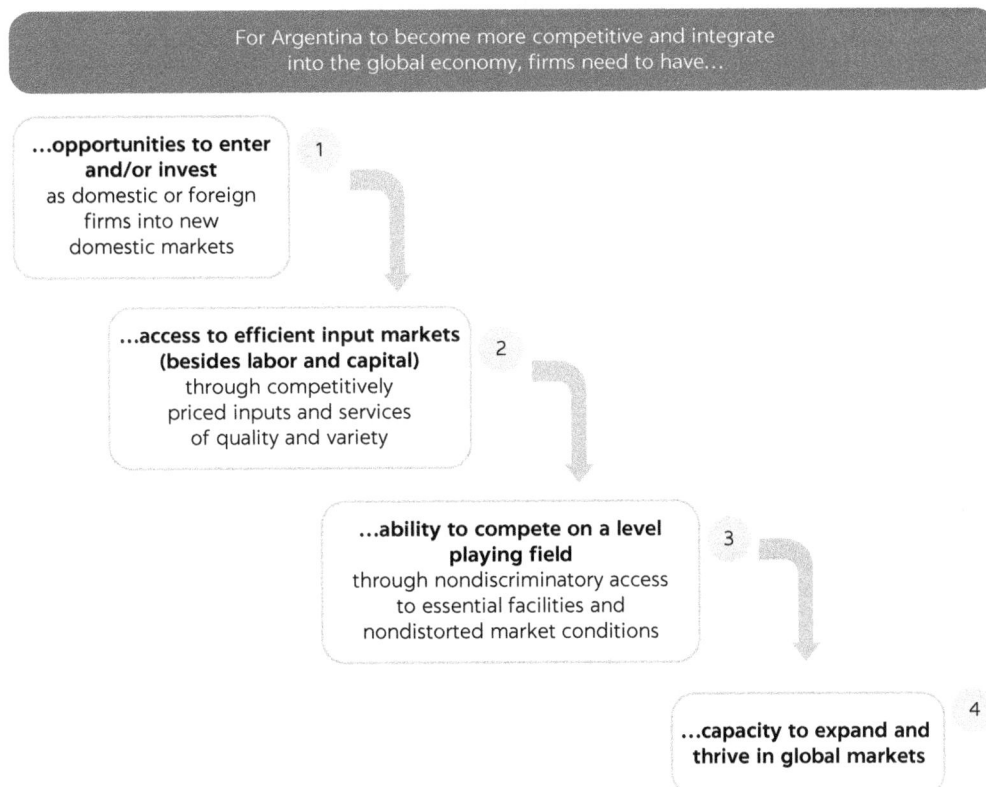

For Argentina to become more competitive and integrate into the global economy, firms need to have…

…opportunities to enter and/or invest
as domestic or foreign firms into new domestic markets
1

…access to efficient input markets (besides labor and capital)
through competitively priced inputs and services of quality and variety
2

…ability to compete on a level playing field
through nondiscriminatory access to essential facilities and nondistorted market conditions
3

…capacity to expand and thrive in global markets
4

FIGURE ES.6

Associations between trade, investment, and competition policy areas and conditions for successful integration into global markets

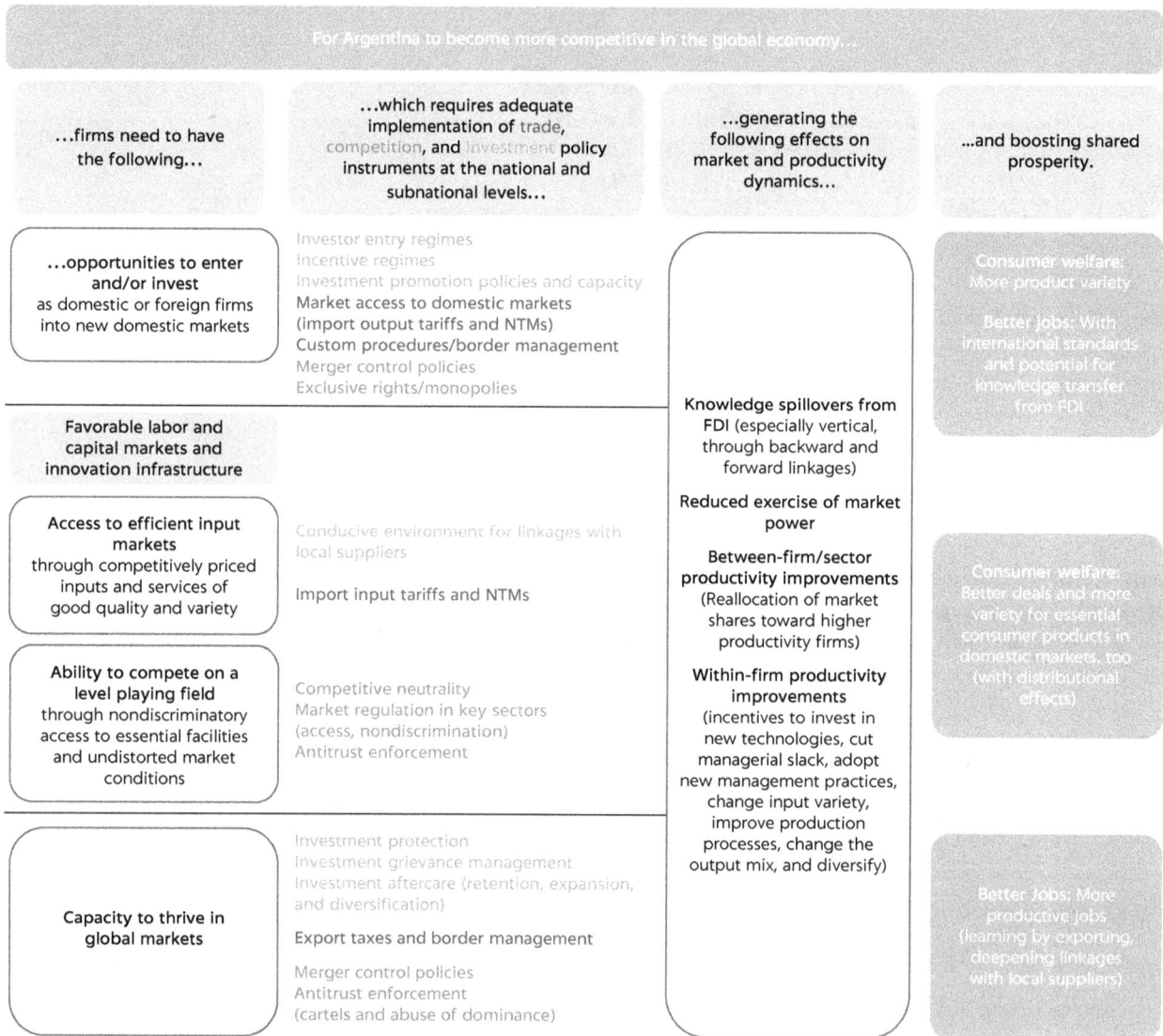

For Argentina to become more competitive in the global economy...

...firms need to have the following...	...which requires adequate implementation of trade, competition, and investment policy instruments at the national and subnational levels...	...generating the following effects on market and productivity dynamics...	...and boosting shared prosperity.
...opportunities to enter and/or invest as domestic or foreign firms into new domestic markets	Investor entry regimes Incentive regimes Investment promotion policies and capacity Market access to domestic markets (import output tariffs and NTMs) Custom procedures/border management Merger control policies Exclusive rights/monopolies	Knowledge spillovers from FDI (especially vertical, through backward and forward linkages) Reduced exercise of market power Between-firm/sector productivity improvements (Reallocation of market shares toward higher productivity firms) Within-firm productivity improvements (incentives to invest in new technologies, cut managerial slack, adopt new management practices, change input variety, improve production processes, change the output mix, and diversify)	Consumer welfare: More product variety Better jobs: With international standards and potential for knowledge transfer from FDI
Favorable labor and capital markets and innovation infrastructure **Access to efficient input markets** through competitively priced inputs and services of good quality and variety	Conducive environment for linkages with local suppliers Import input tariffs and NTMs		Consumer welfare: Better deals and more variety for essential consumer products in domestic markets, too (with distributional effects)
Ability to compete on a level playing field through nondiscriminatory access to essential facilities and undistorted market conditions	Competitive neutrality Market regulation in key sectors (access, nondiscrimination) Antitrust enforcement		
Capacity to thrive in global markets	Investment protection Investment grievance management Investment aftercare (retention, expansion, and diversification) Export taxes and border management Merger control policies Antitrust enforcement (cartels and abuse of dominance)		Better Jobs: More productive jobs (learning by exporting, deepening linkages with local suppliers)

Note: Purple-colored policy instruments refer to trade instruments, blue to competition policy instruments, and green to investment policy instruments.

general or sector specific), approval from the CNDC to acquire or merge with a local company—potentially an incentive (especially for foreign companies) from investment promotion agencies to cover the risk and cost of investment— approval to import (import licenses and tariffs) inputs, and so on. When this condition is met, the domestic markets are more contestable, can benefit from knowledge spillovers, and can generate new and better jobs.

Based on this framework, this report highlights potential reforms across these policy areas to address business and market challenges in Argentina. Evidence collected for the report suggests that firms that already operate or seek to invest in Argentina have faced challenges across all four conditions, and that the solutions to these challenges lie in all three policy areas (trade, investment, and competition) across the four conditions. That is, no one policy alone can ensure that these conditions are fulfilled and firms can integrate into the global

FIGURE ES.7

Proposed policy actions for Argentina and how they relate to the policy areas of trade, investment, and competition

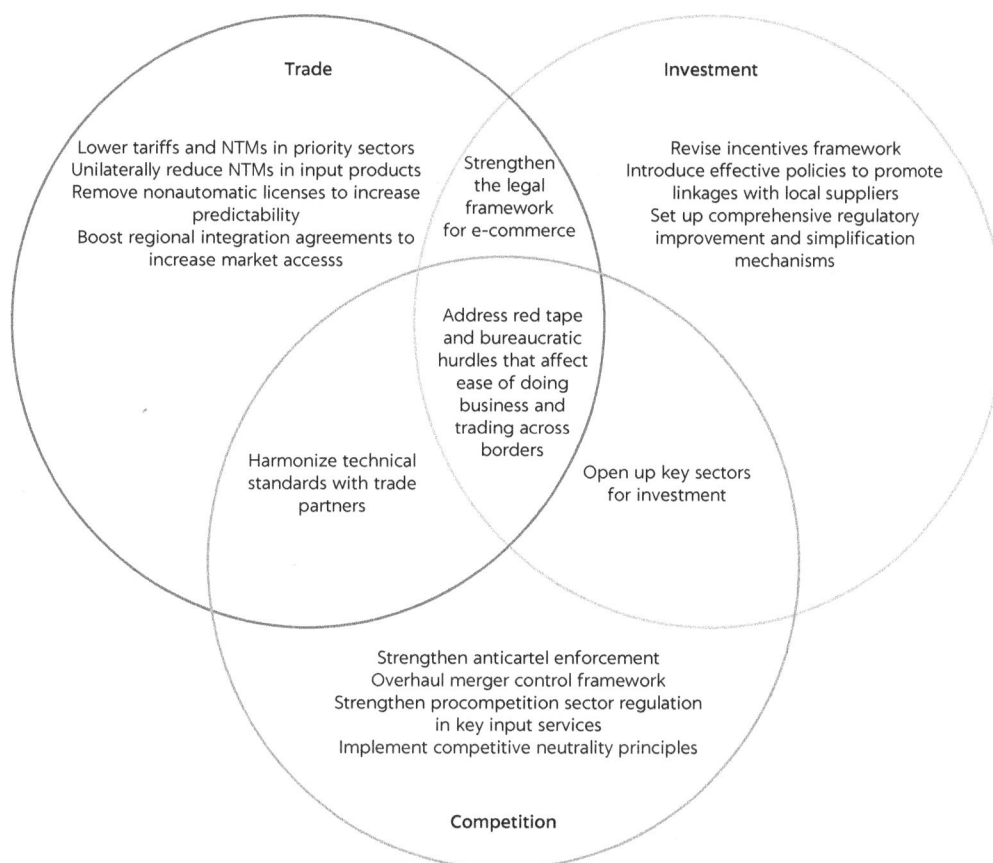

Trade

Lower tariffs and NTMs in priority sectors
Unilaterally reduce NTMs in input products
Remove nonautomatic licenses to increase predictability
Boost regional integration agreements to increase market accesss

Strengthen the legal framework for e-commerce

Investment

Revise incentives framework
Introduce effective policies to promote linkages with local suppliers
Set up comprehensive regulatory improvement and simplification mechanisms

Address red tape and bureaucratic hurdles that affect ease of doing business and trading across borders

Harmonize technical standards with trade partners

Open up key sectors for investment

Strengthen anticartel enforcement
Overhaul merger control framework
Strengthen procompetition sector regulation in key input services
Implement competitive neutrality principles

Competition

economy (figure ES.7). A summary of policy recommendations is presented in the matrix at the end of this summary (table ES.1). It reflects a systematic review of all policy areas and regulatory frameworks in key sectors, as well as the prioritization process described below.

Rather than sequencing reforms among policy areas, this report suggests sequencing specific reform options within each policy area so as to advance in all three areas simultaneously. When assessing the potential sequence of reforms, priority should be given to reforms that are feasible in the short term and can achieve tangible results. Argentina should focus first on policy steps that remove key bottlenecks and yield results in the short term and later on those that require significant resources or comprehensive legal reforms. Table ES.1 organizes the recommendations along these lines. For example, removing import bans on used machinery and equipment would, arguably, benefit in particular smaller businesses that cannot afford new machinery and equipment. Setting up a systematic inventory of incentives is a small but necessary step toward conducting a thorough evaluation and streamlining of incentive programs. Raising merger notification thresholds is an urgent step toward more efficiently using the scarce resources of the competition authority. Strengthening the capacity to investigate cartels is a critical prerequisite for an effective leniency program, under which the first cartel member to come forward can seek exemption from fines in return for assistance in pursuing the rest of the cartel. In addition, ensuring the autonomy of the competition agency is key to addressing the most harmful private and public barriers to competition.

ARGENTINA CAN OPEN UP OPPORTUNITIES TO ENTER AND INVEST BY ADDRESSING CHALLENGES IN THE BUSINESS-ENABLING ENVIRONMENT

Currently, entrepreneurs generally face difficulties in starting businesses, registering property, and paying taxes. Obtaining a construction permit, for example, takes almost a full year. Argentina ranks at 117th out of 190 countries in terms of the overall ease of doing business (World Bank Group 2018). Some firms cannot invest at all because of absolute barriers to entry, such as limits on foreign investments in air transport. Where firms want to invest, there is little predictability in terms of which incentives they can access, and they are often required to negotiate with several levels of government.

Argentina can address the red tape and bureaucratic hurdles by setting general procedures for regulatory simplification and establishing a broad application of the silence-is-consent rule. The government can further open up key sectors for investment and eliminate barriers that limit market entry (for example, in the air transport sector) and improve the incentive framework by setting up systems to help adjudicate, monitor, and evaluate incentive schemes. Finally, the government can facilitate entry of firms that organize their activities around imports of final goods rather than investment in production by lowering tariffs and NTMs in protected sectors, such as furniture and home appliances, as was recently done with computers.[34] The large number of measures related to product standards reveals opportunities to streamline regulations to lower trade costs.

ARGENTINA CAN PROVIDE INVESTORS WITH ACCESS TO MORE EFFICIENT INPUT MARKETS BY STRENGTHENING PROCOMPETITION REGULATIONS

Improved regulatory design in key service input markets could achieve higher contestability in communications technologies, allow for price signals to attract investment in electricity generation, and reduce the risk of collusion among transport providers. Currently, only 40 percent of broadband connections in Argentina provide speeds above 4 megabits per second, compared to 67 percent of top performers in the region. SMEs lost, on average, 2.4 percent of sales due to outages, which is double the amount in comparator countries. Logistics costs have increased by 40 percent since 2003 in real terms (Castro, Szenkman, and Lotitto 2015).

In industrial input markets, investors seeking more competitive inputs from abroad face nonautomatic licenses and other NTMs, as well as local content requirements. Since 2005, Argentina has increased its use of temporary barriers to trade (for example, putting antidumping measures in place) more rapidly than many other middle-income countries.[35] A review of the market characteristics of products affected by these temporary measures suggests that these barriers may often reinforce market dominance.

Argentina can strengthen procompetition regulation in key network sectors, such as transport, electricity, and telecommunications. It can further strengthen anticartel enforcement, in particular in homogeneous input markets, and simultaneously reduce NTMs, including nonautomatic licenses for input products. Finally, Argentina can actively promote linkages with domestic firms by setting up online databases of national suppliers, redesigning performance requirements, and avoiding local content requirements.

ARGENTINA CAN FURTHER LEVEL THE PLAYING FIELD AND ENSURE UNDISTORTED MARKET CONDITIONS TO ALLOW THE MOST PRODUCTIVE AND EFFICIENT FIRMS TO GROW

Argentine state-owned enterprises (SOEs) operate in 17 sectors without a clear set of rules that guarantee competitive neutrality relative to private investors. These and other direct government interventions in the market (such as the price control system) can generate business risk and reduce investor confidence.

To ensure that government interventions in the market do not reduce predictability for potential market entrants, Argentina can establish rules that set the right incentives for SOEs to compete in the markets or that simulate competitive outcomes. For example, it can incorporate SOEs under the same regime as joint-stock companies and introduce tax and regulatory neutrality principles for SOEs. In addition, it can fully revoke instruments that can—even if gradually being phased out—eventually allow for discretionary application, such as the Supply Law that enables price control.[36]

ARGENTINA CAN PROMOTE FIRMS' CAPACITY TO EXPAND AND THRIVE IN GLOBAL MARKETS AND TO FULLY INTEGRATE INTO THE GLOBAL ECONOMY BY REDUCING NONTARIFF MEASURES, BOOSTING INVESTOR CONFIDENCE, AND FACILITATING MORE EFFICIENT REVIEW OF PROPOSED MERGERS AND ACQUISITIONS

In the past, adverse government interventions have prevented investment from expanding and thriving. Participation in global production networks has been stifled by high tariff and nontariff barriers on parts and components. As of October 2016, over 1,600 tariff lines were still subject to import licenses not subject to automatic approval, and other NTMs and procedural obstacles remained. Existing import bans on used capital goods constrain expansion, potentially more so for SMEs that are less able to afford new machines.[37] Furthermore, Argentina has an unfavorable track record on investor–state disputes, even though most of these arose under previous governments.

Argentina can reduce NTMs and harmonize technical standards with trade partners and, thereby, facilitate both exports and imports. It can establish clear protocols to address problems faced by foreign investors and proactively create a legal obligation for regulatory agencies to publish proposed regulations before they are enacted. A systematic investor response mechanism could also increase investor confidence. Finally, Argentina can overhaul the framework for reviewing mergers and acquisitions to accelerate efficient firm consolidation.

TO ACHIEVE THE FULL POTENTIAL OF ARGENTINA'S REINTEGRATION INTO THE GLOBAL ECONOMY, INSTITUTIONS WILL NEED TO COORDINATE EFFECTIVELY SO THAT REFORM INITIATIVES ARE CONCURRENT, COHERENT, AND INTEGRATED IN DESIGN AND IMPLEMENTATION

Reforms in these areas need to be implemented in a coherent way to ensure that positive payoffs stemming from reforms on one front are not curtailed by inappropriate (or lack of) reforms on the other two fronts. In this way, firms can enter and invest in the market, access inputs to their products, compete on a level playing field, and expand and thrive in global markets. In line with figure ES.7, the AAICI will not be able to promote FDI in GVCs successfully if trade in parts and components is obstructed by NTMs involving other government institutions. By the same token, the CNDC's objective of ensuring a level playing field among domestic and foreign competitors could be hampered by potential discretionary and selective investment incentives relevant to AAICI. Similarly, attempts by the Ministry of Production's Undersecretariat for Foreign Trade (Sub-Secretaría de Comercio Exterior) to expand market access for Argentine exporters could be impaired by distortive regulation of input services (such as logistics, telecommunications, and energy). The CNDC can also act as a market intelligence institution, providing recommendations and analysis on market structure and dynamics to other public bodies in order to foster more contestable markets. This can positively influence a better economy-wide regulation agenda.

Ultimately, Argentina can design better policies and regulations to break down barriers to competition. In some cases, this will involve jointly removing or overriding rules that hinder competition; in other cases, it means designing different rules and regulations that achieve public policy objectives while minimizing market distortions and preventing firms from engaging in anticompetitive behavior. A comprehensive regulatory reform agenda with clear prioritization, improvement mechanisms, and monitoring can tackle this systematically. Given the connections among trade, investment, and competition policy—in theory and in practical application—all institutions will need to coordinate to ensure that integrating Argentina into the world economy elicits the greatest possible gains in terms of increasing the welfare of the broader population.

Looking forward, Argentina could benefit from a comprehensive strategy to improve data availability—especially at the firm level—as well as further analytical work. Systematic data collection and statistics are key for detailed design of reform options and estimations of the potential impact of further reform. While individual surveys, such as the Pilot Survey on Innovation and Employment Dynamics (Encuesta Nacional de Dinámica de Empleo e Innovación, or ENDEI, in Spanish) yield valuable information, Argentina could aim to collect firm-level panel data in a consistent manner and make it publicly available to academia, specialized government units, and private think tanks, making sure to adhere to the usual data protection standards. This information can also be complemented by market-level information stemming from competition enforcement and advocacy implementation. This would allow a broader body of research to become available as an input into effective, evidence-based policy design and as a means to help identify policy changes that could foster additional reform momentum.

TABLE ES.1 **Matrix of policy recommendations**

SHORT TERM	MEDIUM TERM	LONG TERM
QUICK WINS: URGENT POLICY ACTIONS WITH SHORT-TERM IMPACT THAT ARE RELATIVELY FEASIBLE	IMPORTANT MILESTONES: POLICY ACTIONS WITH SUBSTANTIAL IMPACT THAT REQUIRE MORE SUBSTANTIVE LEGAL REFORMS, NEGOTIATIONS, OR INSTITUTIONAL EFFORTS	POLICIES THAT REQUIRE HIGH-LEVEL, COMPLEX INSTITUTIONAL REFORMS AND COULD ENCOUNTER SUBSTANTIAL POLITICAL OPPOSITION AND/OR INVOLVE SIGNIFICANT EXTERNAL CONSTITUENCIES
Open up further opportunities to enter and invest		
Lower tariffs and NTMs in priority sectors		
Limit nonautomatic licenses to the minimum (such as hazardous imports)	Unilaterally reduce tariffs for highly protected sectors	Harmonize standards among Mercosur parties
	Pursue FTA with EU	Pursue "community reforms" at Mercosur
Improve incentive framework to attract efficiency-seeking FDI more effectively		
Introduce a systematic inventory of incentives	Create a procedural mapping of steps to adjudicate incentives	
	Strengthen monitoring and evaluation of incentives	
Open key sectors for investment and eliminate barriers that limit market entry		
Limit government's liability for losses of Aerolineas Argentinas	Eliminate "public hearing" for granting new licenses for air transport services	Open domestic air transport market to foreign carriers
Address red tape and bureaucratic hurdles that affect ease of doing business, particularly in the entry phase		
Improve regulation efforts to facilitate doing business in key areas	Apply broadly the "silence is consent" rule	Devise a general procedure for regulatory simplification
Enhance access to more efficient input markets for firms		
Unilateral NTM reduction in input products		
Remove import ban on used machinery, equipment, instruments, devices, and parts	Reduce NTMs for key industrial inputs	
Introduce effective policies to promote linkages with domestic firms		
Develop a central (online) database of national suppliers	Redesign performance requirements and local content rules—for example, revise tax benefits in auto industry	
	Introduce behavioral incentives for firms to enhance capacities	
Strengthen anticartel enforcement, especially in homogeneous input products		
Strengthen cartel investigation techniques (IT forensic capabilities)	Elevate sanctions for cartels	
	Introduce leniency program	
Strengthen procompetition sector regulation in key input services		
Implement rules to protect competitive neutrality in the telecom sector	Fully enforce Mobile Virtual Network Operator (MVNO) framework	Allow pay-TV companies to offer telecommunication services
Guarantee effective nondiscriminatory access in rail freight	Review toll exemption rules for private ("self") cargo transport and public cargo transport (to third parties)	
Enhance predictability and a level playing field for the private sector		
Implement competitive neutrality principles and eliminate instruments that can limit competition		
Eliminate the government's ability to control prices	Incorporate state-owned enterprises (SOEs) under the same regime as private joint-stock companies	Introduce regulatory and tax-neutrality principles for SOEs

continued

TABLE ES.1, *continued*

SHORT TERM	MEDIUM TERM	LONG TERM
QUICK WINS: URGENT POLICY ACTIONS WITH SHORT-TERM IMPACT THAT ARE RELATIVELY FEASIBLE	IMPORTANT MILESTONES: POLICY ACTIONS WITH SUBSTANTIAL IMPACT THAT REQUIRE MORE SUBSTANTIVE LEGAL REFORMS, NEGOTIATIONS, OR INSTITUTIONAL EFFORTS	POLICIES THAT REQUIRE HIGH-LEVEL, COMPLEX INSTITUTIONAL REFORMS AND COULD ENCOUNTER SUBSTANTIAL POLITICAL OPPOSITION AND/OR INVOLVE SIGNIFICANT EXTERNAL CONSTITUENCIES
Enhance the capacity of firms to thrive and expand		
Remove nonautomatic licenses to increase predictability		
	Ensure that nonautomatic licenses are set to the minimum	
Reduce regulatory and legal uncertainty through broad regulatory improvement mechanisms		
Introduce a clear procedural protocol to solve problems faced by foreign investors and arising from regulatory conduct	Create legal obligation for regulatory agencies to publish text or proposed regulations before enactment	Establish a systemic investor response mechanism
Strengthen the legal framework for e-commerce		
Remove exemptions to e-signatures and e-documents; give validity to all types of e-signatures	Strengthen consumer protections specific to electronic consumers	
Overhaul merger control framework		
Raise notification threshold for mergers	Introduce fast-track procedures for mergers unlikely to have anticompetitive effects	
	Improve procedural effectiveness in reviewing mergers	

Note: While this table identifies short-, medium-, and long-term priorities based on the binding constraints, medium- and long-term priorities should be addressed simultaneously with short-term priorities if they require changing the same law. The reforms may also involve other third parties (such as regulators, *cancillería*, parliament, and others), which this table does not highlight.

NOTES

1. As seen from the growth accounting exercise, total factor productivity has, in fact, been dragging down growth rather than boosting it over the past few years.
2. All values are from the World Bank's World Development Indicators (WDI) database.
3. Simple average of most favored nation (MFN) rate for 2015.
4. More recently, in January 2018, the Ministry of Production issued a resolution (No. 5-E/2018) that eliminates 314 products from the list of nonautomatic import licenses.
5. Argentina is party to five partial-scope agreements, according to the World Trade Organization's regional trade agreements database.
6. World Bank Group (WBG) analysis using data from the Argentine Central Bank shows that, between 2012 and 2015, half of this FDI constituted reinvestment of earnings artificially boosted, at least in part, by restrictions on repatriation of investors' profits.
7. See WDI database. Low (private and public) investment has led to a declining capital stock in Argentina, with direct effects on infrastructure quantity and quality. According to the World Bank (2015), Argentina dropped 62 positions in the worldwide ranking of infrastructure quality between 2006 and 2015, as per the World Economic Forum survey. Investing more in infrastructure would be a key driver to increase the country's competitiveness by enabling firms to reap the benefits of further integration with the global economy. FDI can play a pivotal role in this area.
8. Percentage of household final consumption expenditures spent on food that was consumed at home (in 2016), as computed by Economic Research Services of the US Department of Agriculture. The comparator countries are the same as used throughout this report. When considering only the developing economies in this comparator group, the average share is 18 percent. Data are available at https://www.ers.usda.gov/data-products/food-expenditures.aspx.

9. Estimations based on Numbeo data for 2010–15.

10. Argentina's competition authority has initiated market studies in some of these product markets.

11. The exception is the social tariff for transport services targeted to poor people.

12. The elimination of the DJAI and introduction of the SIMI, at the end of 2015, eliminated the preapproval process. This new regime maintained about 1,400 tariff lines subject to nonautomatic licenses. Subsequent resolutions have modified the list of nonautomatic licenses, with the end result of increasing tariff lines to 1,626 in October 2016.

13. With the removal of the DJAI, the NTM *ad valorem* equivalent is reduced by five percentage points for many goods sectors. The Computable General Equilibrium (CGE) exercise compares the resulting economic outcomes accrued by the introduction of SIMI/replacement of DJAI versus a baseline projection through 2020 without the reform. CGE results show that real GDP would be 0.14 percent higher than the baseline value by 2020.

14. Based on Télam (2017) and AAICI (2018).

15. The competition authority (CNDC) had determined that the payment card acquirer, processor, and point-of-sale operator Prisma (owned by Visa and 14 Argentine banks) had a dominant position in the market and recommended changes to the legal framework for payment cards, many of which have since been implemented. In September 2017, CNDC accepted a divestment plan by Prisma that also obliges the firm to offer its payment processing services to competitors in a nondiscriminatory way. In March 2017, banks, payment card companies, and chambers of commerce in Argentina agreed on a plan to reduce interchange fees gradually from 3 percent to 1.8 percent by 2021.

16. See discussion on the fiscal implications in the main report.

17. As mentioned above, CGE results show that the removal of DJAI and introduction of SIMI at the end of 2015 would increase real GDP by 0.14 percent above the baseline value by 2020. This "elimination of DJAI" scenario is considered a partial reform in the sense that nonautomatic import licenses still cover a share of trade in certain sectors; as of October 2016, about 1,600 tariff lines remained with import licenses that were not subject to automatic approval. CGE simulations suggest that expanding this reform to eliminate all remaining nonautomatic licenses would bring the GDP gains from 0.14 percent to 0.22 percent above the baseline projections for 2020.

18. This scenario includes a reduction in tariffs in all Mercosur countries for world imports by 50 percent (tariffs within Mercosur are essentially zero), a 15 percent cut in NTMs within the borders of Mercosur, and the elimination of export controls among Mercosur parties.

19. This scenario includes reciprocal tariff reductions, where the average tariff applied to EU products by Argentina would fall from about 11 percent to about 3 percent by full implementation in 10 years, while the average tariff in the EU for Argentine products would fall from about 3 percent to close to zero. Also, NTMs would be streamlined by 15 percent and export controls eliminated among the parties.

20. This scenario is similar to the Mercosur–EU agreement, but with lower tariff reductions. The average tariff applied by Argentina to products from the Pacific Alliance would fall from about 1 percent to 0.3 percent, and the average tariff in the Pacific Alliance on products from Argentina would fall from 2.3 percent to 0.3 percent.

21. Empirical estimations used as inputs for these results include a gravity model on trade in parts and components, a panel-data estimation with firm-level data on price–cost margins and firm-level productivity, and a panel-data estimation of the link between regulatory restrictiveness in service sectors and growth in industries that use such services intensively among OECD and additional developing economies.

22. Trade in intermediate goods contributed more than trade in final goods to the growth of total manufacturing trade in 2001–08 and 2009–14 (World Bank et al. 2017).

23. The share of service exports increased from around 9 percent in 1970 to around 20 percent in 2014 (Loungani et al. 2017).

24. Most modern-day trade agreements contain provisions that cover a wide array of NTMs, both at the border and behind the border—for example, technical barriers to trade (TBTs) and sanitary and phytosanitary (SPS) measures, rules on investment and intellectual property rights protection, provisions on competition policy, and so on. Recent FTAs tend to go beyond multilateral rules. The literature refers to these new trade agreements as "deep" to distinguish them from traditional FTAs that focus only on market access commitments—sometimes referred to as "shallow" (Osnago, Rocha, and Ruta 2015).

25. A more detailed GVC analysis could offer insights into the potential for upgrading and diversifying these exports.

26. See Nahirnak 2016 for further details.

27. According to data from eMarketer.

28. See Camara Argentina de Comercio y Servicios 2017 for further details.

29. Evidence suggests that adjustment frictions can reduce the gains from trade. In the case of Mexico, Kambourov (2009) finds that a lack of flexibility in the labor market slowed the reallocation of labor in response to trade reform, so that the benefits of the reform were as much as 30 percent less than would have been achieved under a more flexible labor market. Similarly, Dix-Carneiro (2014) finds that the reallocation in the labor market following trade liberalization in Brazil would accelerate from fourteen years to four years if capital were completely mobile.

30. See Ministry of Production, Argentina website: https://www.argentina.gob.ar/111mil.

31. See Productivity Commission (2005) for further details.

32. See Dougherty (2015) for further discussion.

33. See UNCTAD (2011) for further discussion.

34. Import tariffs for certain computer items were brought down to zero in March 2017.

35. Estimations based on the World Bank's Global Antidumping Database (Bown 2016) measuring the stock of antidumping measures (antidumping investigation resulting in antidumping measures, minus measures revoked over time) in Argentina and 32 other economies. The average number of measures in place in Argentina in 2005–09 was 79, which increased to 103 by 2010–14 (a 30 percent increase). Middle-income countries in the database accounted for 936 measures in place in 2005–09, which increased to 1,070 measures by 2010–14 (a 14 percent increase). High-income countries accounted for 565 measures in 2005–09, which decreased to 532 measures by 2010–14 (a 6 percent decrease). By 2010–14, Argentina would be the top-seven user of antidumping measures, after India, the United States, Turkey, Brazil, China, and the EU.

36. Although the Macri administration initially reduced the number of products included under the *"Precios Cuidados"* program, in September 2017 it extended it again until January 2018, maintaining 325 products on the list and adding 151 new products.

37. Argentina generally restricts or prohibits the importation of used and remanufactured goods, including agricultural machinery, auto parts, and medical equipment. Capital goods that may be imported are subject to higher duties than new ones. Recently, in December 2016, the government introduced a program to facilitate imports of used production lines as part of investment projects, subject to approval under certain conditions, including that these production lines are complete and autonomous (decree 1174/2016).

REFERENCES

AAICI. 2018. *Agencia Argentina de Inversiones y Comercio Internacional.* http://www .investandtrade.org.ar/mapadelainversion.php (accessed August 23, 2017).

Araujo, S., and D. Flaig. 2017. "Trade Restrictions in Brazil: Who Pays the Price?" *Journal of Economic Integration* 32 (2): 283–23.

Bown, C. 2016. *Global Antidumping Database.* Washington, DC: World Bank.

Cámara Argentina de Comercio y Servicios. 2017. "Informe CAC: Costo Argetnino Agosto de 2017." http://www.cac.com.ar/data/documentos/11_CAC%20-%20Informe%20Costo%20 Argentino%20-%20Agosto%202017.pdf.

Casacuberta, C., G. Fachola, and N. Gandelman. 2011. "Employment, Capital and Productivity Dynamics: Trade Liberalization and Unionization in the Uruguayan Manufacturing Sector." *The Developing Economies* 49 (3): 266–96.

Castro, L., P. Szenkman, and E. Lotitto. 2015. "¿Cómo puede cerrar el próximo gobierno la brecha de infraestructura?" Centro de Implementación de Políticas Públicas para la Equidad y el Crecimiento. Documento de políticas públicas no. 148. https://www.cippec.org/wp -content/uploads/2017/03/1241.pdf.

Dix-Carneiro, R. 2014. "Trade Liberalization and Labor Market Dynamics." *Econometrica* 82 (3): 825–85.

Dougherty, S. 2015. "Boosting Growth and Reducing Informality in Mexico." OECD Economic Department Working Papers. OECD (Organisation for Economic Co-operation and Development), Economics Department Working Papers, no. 1188. http://www.oecd-ilibrary .org/docserver/download/5js4w28dnn28-en.pdf?expires=1520534212&id =id&accname=guest&checksum=31D4E67FCB48CFC6B2A2B27223590885.

Falvey, R., N. Foster, and D. Greenaway. 2012. "Trade Liberalization, Economic Crises, and Growth." *World Development* 40 (11): 2177–93.

Felbermayr, G., J. Prat, and H. Schmerer. 2011. "Trade and Unemployment: What Do the Data Say?" *European Economic Review* 55 (6): 741–58.

Kambourov, G. 2009. "Labour Market Regulations and the Sectoral Reallocation of Workers: The Case of Trade Reforms." *Review of Economic Studies* 76 (4): 1321–58.

Loungani, P. M., and K. Wang. 2017. "World Trade in Services: Evidence from a New Dataset." IMF (International Monetary Fund) Working Paper No. 17-77. https://www.imf.org/en /Publications/WP/Issues/2017/03/29/World-Trade-in-Services-Evidence-from-A-New -Dataset-44776.

Nahirñak, P. 2016. *Informes de Cadenas de Valor: Software y Servicios Informáticos* (10.13140/ RG.2.2.21708.82567 ed.). Buenos Aires, Argentina: Ministerio de Hacienda y Finanzas Públicas.

Osnago, A., N. Rocha, and M. Ruta. 2015. "Deep Trade Agreements and Vertical FDI: The Devil Is in the Details." World Bank Policy Research Working Paper No. 7464 (no. WPS 7464), World Bank, Washington, DC.

Petri, P., and M. Plummer. 2016. "The Economic Effects of the Trans Pacific Partnership: New Estimates." Peterson Institute for International Economics Working Paper No. 16-2. https:// piie.com/publications/working-papers/economic-effects-trans-pacific-partnership-new -estimates.

Productivity Commission. 2005. "Review of National Competition Policy Reforms." Productivity Commission Inquiry Report No. 33, World Bank, Washington, DC.

Salinas, G., and A. Aksoy. 2006. Growth Before and After Trade Liberalization. World Bank Policy Research Working Paper No. 4062, World Bank, Washington, DC.

Télam. 2017. *Télam S. E. Agencia Nacional de Noticias.* http://www.telam.com.ar/notas /201705/188892-gobierno-lanzo-mapa-inversiones.html (accessed August 23, 2017).

UNCTAD. 2011. *Foundations of an Effective Competition Agency.* Geneva: UNCTAD.

Wacziarg, R., and K. H. Welch, 2008. Trade Liberalization and Growth: New Evidence. *World Bank Economic Review* 22 (2): 187–231.

World Bank. 2015. *Argentina: Notas de políticas públicas para el desarrollo.* Report no. 106122. http://documents.worldbank.org/curated/en/899411467995396294/pdf/106122-WP -P156046-PUBLIC-SPANISH-NotasdePol%C3%ADticas-ARGENTINA.pdf.World Bank, IDE-Jetro, OECD, and WTO. 2017. *Global Value Chain Development Report: Measuring and Analyzing the Impact of GVCs on Economic Development.* Washington, DC: World Bank.

World Bank Group. 2018. *Doing Business 2018: Reforming to Create Jobs.* Economy Profile: Argentina. http://documents.worldbank.org/curated/en/899411467995396294/pdf /106122-WP-P156046-PUBLIC-SPANISH-NotasdePol%C3%ADticas-ARGENTINA.pdf.

1 *Quo Vadis,* Argentina? Context, Outlook, and Possible Scenarios

NEW PRIORITIES: STRENGTHENING THE ARGENTINE ECONOMY'S INTEGRATION INTO GLOBAL MARKETS

The government of Argentina is undertaking a major transition in its economic policies, moving beyond correcting urgent macroeconomic imbalances to prioritizing reintegration of the Argentine economy in global markets to ensure a return to sustainable growth. Following President Mauricio Macri's inauguration in 2015, substantial economic reforms were undertaken in 2016. Argentina removed foreign exchange controls, tightened monetary policy, reached a major deal with holdout creditors, and reduced subsidies on utility prices and transport services to narrow the fiscal imbalance (box 1.1). The government improved supply-side policies for connecting with international markets. Export taxes on most crops, beef, and most industrial manufacturing products were eliminated, while export taxes on soy were reduced by 5 percentage points. In addition, Argentina officially replaced its previous Declaración Jurada Anticipada de Importación (DJAI) import licensing system with a new, simpler monitoring system, Sistema Integral de Monitoreo de Importaciones (SIMI), thus moving, in line with World Trade Organization (WTO) procedures, from de facto nonautomatic to automatic import licenses for the majority of products and facilitating imports. The government also sent a new competition bill to Argentina's congress,[1] created a new investment promotion agency, and removed prohibitions on repatriating profits.

Integration into global markets can improve the efficiency of the Argentine economy, providing opportunities for private investment to flourish and for the associated benefits to accrue to consumers. Productivity growth remains critical in Argentina, and its insufficiency lies at the heart of the country's lack of income convergence with most developed economies.[2] Policies that support further integration into the global economy have the potential to boost productivity gains, both economy-wide and within sectors and firms.[3] Economic integration would open several sources of efficiency simultaneously. First, firms would have access to larger markets with higher elasticity of demand. Second, entering such markets would allow Argentina to exploit economies of scale without encountering large declines in prices. Third, it would spur competition, as domestic

Main reforms to date

- Foreign exchange controls lifted and exchange rates unified (December 2015). Exporters, importers, and the public could now buy foreign currency freely at a unique exchange rate without authorization from the Federal Tax Agency, resulting in the unification of the official and unofficial exchange rates.
- Restrictions on the repatriation of profits removed (December 2015). A successful tax amnesty program was implemented to encourage repatriation of undeclared funds held abroad. It resulted in additional tax revenues amounting to 1.6 percent of gross domestic product (GDP).
- Credibility of the national statistical system restored (December 2015). As a result, the International Monetary Fund (IMF) lifted its Declaration of Censure on Argentine official statistics.
- New imports administration system implemented (December 2015). To facilitate imports, Argentina replaced its licensing system for authorizing imports (DJAI), which had been mostly subject to a nontransparent preapproval process, with a simpler import monitoring system (SIMI).
- Export taxes reduced (December 2015). Argentina eliminated export taxes on agricultural goods (including beef, wheat, and corn) while cutting the tariff on soybeans by 5 percentage points (from 35 percent to 30 percent).
- New investment promotion agency created (March 2016). By a decree of the Ministry of Production (Resolution 83/2016), the statutes of Fundación Exportar—a private entity dedicated exclusively to export promotion—were amended to create the Argentina Investment and Trade Promotion Agency (Agencia Argentina de Inversiones y Comercio Internacional, or AAICI) and dedicate it not only to export promotion but also to investment promotion and facilitation.
- Return to international financial markets (March–April 2016). Argentina reached a major deal with holdout creditors and successfully returned to international capital markets with

a bond issuance of US$16.5 billion in April 2016, the largest single bond issuance in history for an emerging economy.
- Energy and transport subsidies reduced, with a social tariff maintained for low-income users (March–April 2016). Electricity and gas tariffs were increased, although they had to be revised following a Supreme Court ruling based on the lack of mandatory public hearings. Transport subsidies were also reduced (with the exception of the social tariff for poor people). Energy subsidies will continue to decrease gradually until they are eliminated by 2019, except for social tariffs.
- Social safety net expanded (April 2016). Family allowances were expanded to reach 4.1 million children, up from 2.9 million.
- Income tax reform implemented (April 2016 and December 2016). The income tax floor was raised from Arg$15,000 gross per month to Arg$30,000. In December 2016, the Congress approved another reform to the income tax that raised all tax brackets and decreased the minimum income tax rate.
- Monetary policy adopted (September 2016). The Central Bank formally adopted an inflation-targeting regime with a floating exchange rate (target of 2 to 25 percent by the end of 2016, falling to 5 percent by 2019). It committed to decreasing financial assistance to the central government gradually.
- International relations normalized. In November 2016, the IMF conducted its first Article IV consultation with Argentina in a decade. Moreover, Argentina held the WTO Ministerial Conference in 2017 and will hold the G20 presidency in 2018.
- Inflation-indexed accounting unit (Unidad de Valor Adquisitivo, in Spanish) introduced by the Central Bank to support the development of the market for mortgages in Argentina. Mortgages are growing but from negligible levels.
- Framework for public–private partnerships approved. Congress approved a new public–private

continued

Box 1.1, *continued*

partnership framework to help address the country's existing infrastructure deficit and to stimulate private investment in major sectors of the economy, such as infrastructure, housing, services, production, applied research, and technological innovation.

- Transparency promoted in government. President Macri declared his intention to place Argentina among the top countries in the world in terms of transparency. The primary measures included passing the Access to Public Information Law in 2016 (which entered into force in September 2017), ongoing reforms in procurement for public infrastructure (contrat.ar portal) and

public procurement (via compr.ar portal), and a renewed commitment to open government with the open data portal (datos.gob.ar) and the implementation of the second open government action plan.

- New export regime for SMEs established. The Ministry of Production and the Federal Tax Authority published Joint General Resolution No. 4049-E/2017 in the *Official Gazette*. It set out the framework of a simplified export regime called "Exporta Simples," which implements a fast track procedure for SMEs to make it easier to export their products via private postal service providers (couriers).

firms are pushed to face fiercer pressure from either import competition or the entry of foreign companies and as those who enter export markets face competition from international peers. Fourth, it would relax technological constraints through access to better-quality and competitively priced inputs, which increase returns to investment and innovation while allowing firms to join the growth platform provided by international production networks. Finally, consumers would benefit from the availability of foreign goods and services, greater variety, and more competitive prices. For a detailed review of these effects identified in the theoretical and empirical literature, refer to appendix A. Spurring integration into the global economy can also help create more and better jobs (see box 1.2 for further discussion).

Among many policies that are important for integrating into the global economy, particularly relevant—and also challenging—are trade, investment, and competition policies. Adequate macroeconomic policies, labor market policies, credit and financial policies, innovation policies, and business regulations can all shape the incentives and opportunities for economic agents at home and abroad (appendix B). As documented in the empirical literature (see appendix A) and suggested by international evidence covered in this report, investment and competition policy reforms are important complements to trade liberalization. They are particularly important, in fact, for integration into the 21st century's global, interconnected, and competitive world economy. These three policies are often shaped and determined by diffuse rules, policies, and regulations in many individual markets and sectors. In such specific segments of the economy, particular interest groups can block reforms that would benefit the overall economy.

Trade, investment, and competition policies are not set in one law or one institution alone. While there is often one investment law and one competition law, many sector-specific laws or public policy programs have effects on the attractiveness of the economy for investment and the intensity of competition. This has two implications. First, policy improvement requires detailed analysis of sector-specific laws, regulations, and their implementation; and, second, no

BOX 1.2

Implementing product market reforms can help create better-quality jobs and has the potential to increase aggregate employment in the long term

Creating new (and better) jobs is essential in Argentina, owing to high unemployment and underemployment rates. Of Argentina's workforce, 11.2 percent are underemployed, meaning that employees work part-time jobs because they cannot get full-time positions (INDEC 2017).

By boosting productivity growth—among other mechanisms, through labor reallocation toward more productive firms and sectors—reforms in the area of trade, investment, and competition can help improve the quality of jobs by increasing demand for highly skilled workers or by allowing workers to learn while working and be deployed to higher-value-added tasks. Making jobs more productive typically generates higher wages. From a trade perspective, a set of (strong) stylized facts helps to support this view: first, exporters are more productive than nonexporters (see, for instance, Bernard and Jensen 1999 and Melitz 2003, among many others), and, second, exporters tend to pay higher wages than nonexporters (see, for instance, Brambilla, Depetris Chauvin, and Porto 2016, who show that Argentine exporters pay 31 percent higher wages than nonexporters).

The impact on aggregate employment will depend on macroeconomic conditions and labor market institutions. Empirical evidence on the impact of product market reforms on employment points to overall positive gains in the long term. A comprehensive literature review presented by Schiantarelli (2016) shows that procompetitive product market reforms generate significant employment in the long term in Organisation for Economic Co-operation and Development (OECD) countries by stimulating firms' demand for labor and their willingness to invest. Favorable long-term employment effects are more likely if labor markets are rigid and tend to be enhanced by product market deregulations that encourage labor market reforms. In addition, the empirical literature using cross-country data suggests that countries that are more open to trade have lower unemployment (see, for instance, Felbermayr, Prat, and Schmerer 2011). Additional empirical evidence provided by Hollweg, Lederman, and Mitra (2014) suggests that pro-opening reforms increase both employment and wages.

one institution alone can change trade, investment, or competition policy. For all three to be coherent and efficient in achieving their objectives, institutional cooperation and coordination are indispensable.

Effective trade, investment, and competition policies reinforce each other in fostering firms to source, produce, and sell across borders. From a microeconomic perspective, there are multiple, nonexclusive contractual modes for integrating domestic firms into global markets: exporter, importer, outsourcer, outsourcee, foreign owner, and foreign direct investor.[4] The success of firm internationalization through any combination of these modes depends on how policies shape incentives and rules. While foreign investment policy encourages or discourages entry of new international actors, trade policy influences the size of the output market and the range of input sources available to firms, and competition affects "behind the border" market entry and the contestability of both input and output markets while providing incentives to innovate and increase productivity (figure 1.1).

Based on robust empirical analysis for Argentina and a comprehensive review of international experience in this regard, this report develops recommendations for each institution in charge of the three respective policy areas, together with a roadmap of specific reforms that all institutions can promote jointly. This report and its recommendations build on the results of a robust set of empirical analyses

FIGURE 1.1

Trade, investment, and competition policies: Attributes, synergies, and complementarities

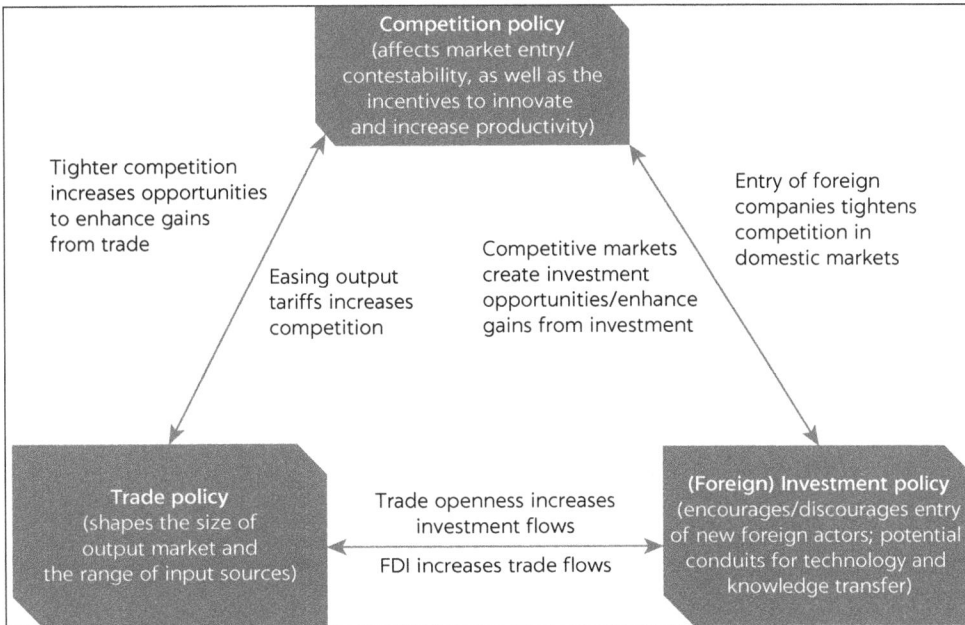

comprising a tailor-made computable general equilibrium (CGE) model for Argentina that allows for simulations of different trade liberalization scenarios; a partial equilibrium exercise based on a gravity framework to estimate the average effect of deeper integration on trade within global value chains (GVCs); firm-level analysis of potential productivity gains from enhanced competition; simulation of a reform of product market regulation and its effect on growth in service-intensive industries; and a cross-country price comparison using panel-level data. Furthermore, this report draws on worldwide comparative analysis of institutional characteristics of trade, investment promotion, and competition authorities. A new comparative review of international experience with structural microeconomic reform programs yields insights for Argentina's design and sequencing of such reforms. Competition policy reform opportunities are developed following the WBG's Markets and Competition Policy Assessment Tool (MCPAT). Finally, the individual reform recommendations are presented in an integrated step-by-step framework from the firm perspective to illustrate the critical challenges to investment and internationalization for Argentine firms.

HOW INTEGRATED IS ARGENTINA WITH THE GLOBAL ECONOMY?

Argentina trades little, and its share in world exports has been declining since the 2008 global financial crisis. Trade openness, as measured by exports and imports over GDP, has been below the level that Argentina's per-capita income would predict, with no signs of improvement (figure 1.2; figure 1.3). Trade openness in Argentina fell from 40.5 percent in 2005 to 23 percent in 2015.[5] Aided by strong commodity prices in international markets, Argentina's exports

FIGURE 1.2

Trade openness and GDP, 2000–11

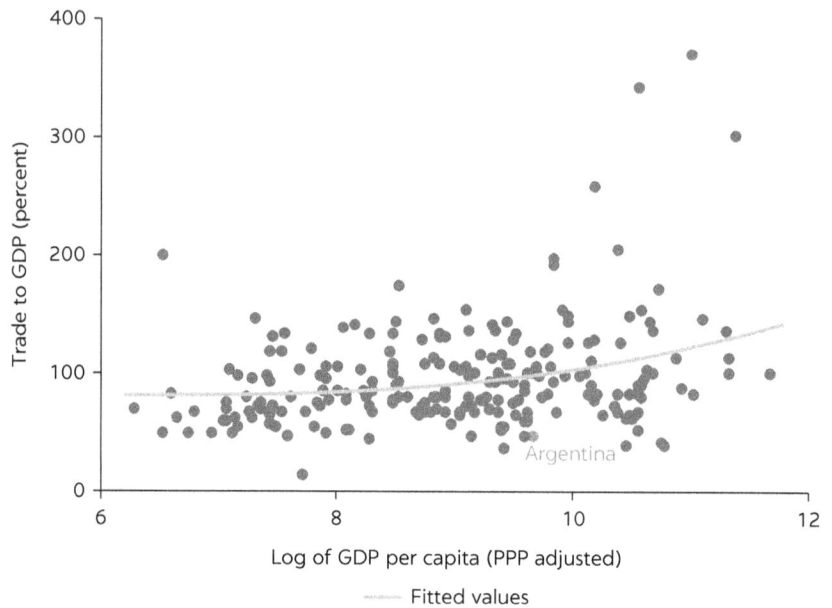

Source: Data from World Development Indicators (WDI) dataset (http://wdi.worldbank .org/tables).

FIGURE 1.3

Trade openness and GDP, 2012–15

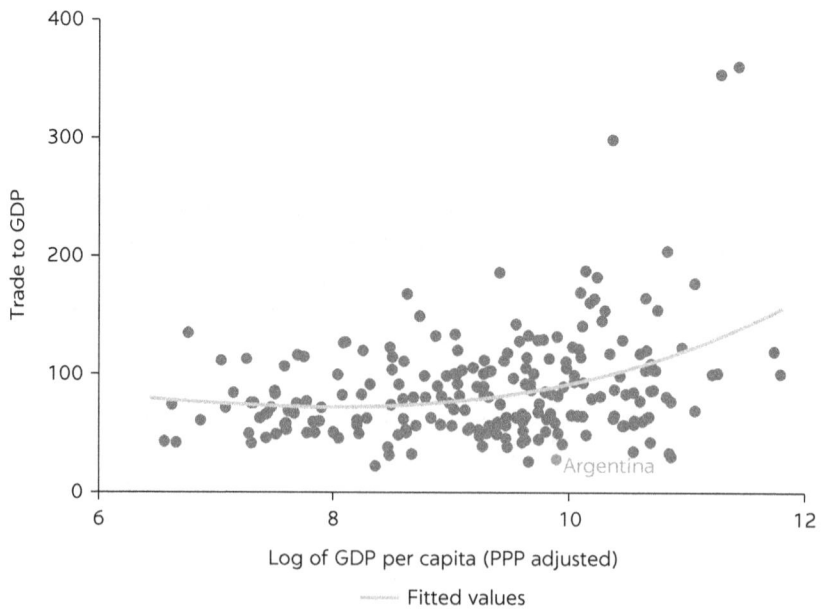

Source: Data from World Development Indicators (WDI) dataset (http://wdi.worldbank .org/tables).

grew above the world average before the global economic collapse of 2008, with an average rate of 20 percent per quarter between the first quarter of 2006 and the fourth quarter of 2008. As a result, Argentina gained market share, as indicated by the green area in figure 1.4. Since the crisis, Argentina's exports have been retrenching by 2.6 percent each quarter, on average, resulting in losses of world market share for Argentina, as indicated by the red area in figure 1.4.

FIGURE 1.4

Export growth and change in market share: Argentina vs. world, 2006 Q1-2016 Q1

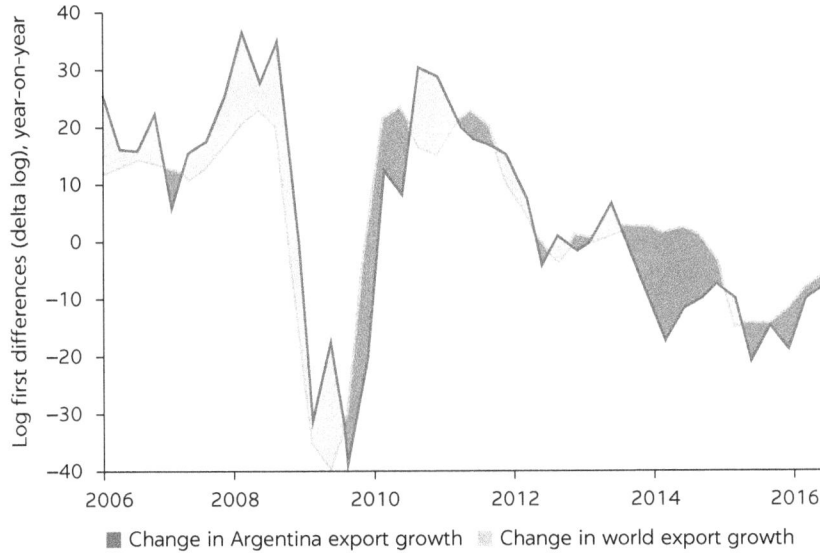

■ Change in Argentina export growth ░ Change in world export growth

Source: Data from Measuring Export Competitiveness (https://mec.worldbank.org/).
Note: The numbers in the figure are log first differences. They approximate the percentage change in the variable of interest. Strictly speaking, the percentage change in a variable Y at period t is defined as $(Y(t)-Y(t-1))/Y(t-1)$, which is approximately equal to $\log(Y(t))-\log(Y(t-1))$.

FIGURE 1.5

New exporting firm entry density in Argentina, 1998-2015

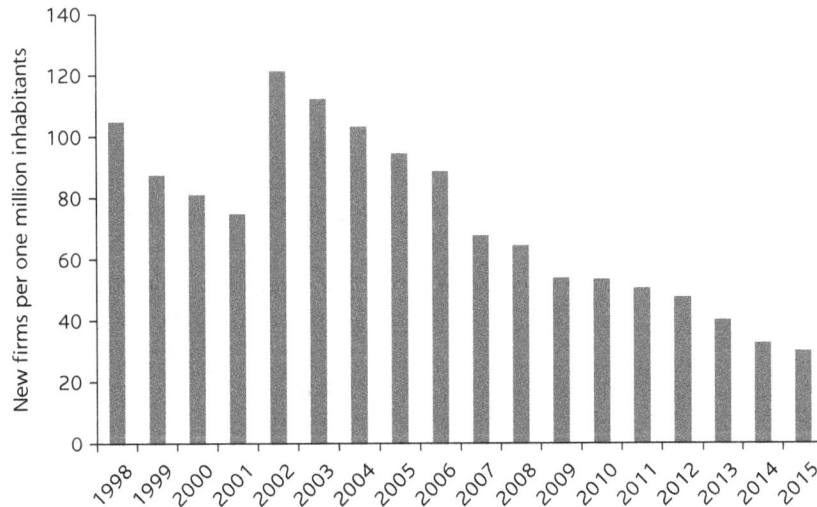

Source: Data from World Development Indicators (WDI) dataset (http://wdi.worldbank.org /tables) and *GPS de Empresas, Ministerio de Producción, Argentina* (http://www .produccion.gob.ar/gpsempresas/).

Contrary to global trends, trade in services is declining in Argentina, and fewer firms start to export each year than one or two decades ago. Argentina's export sector is not very dynamic; the entry density of new exporting firms in the country has been declining since the peso devaluation in 2002, falling from 121 new exporting firms per one million habitants in 2001 to less than 30 in 2014 (figure 1.5). Argentina may also be forgoing a major source of efficiency and an

FIGURE 1.6

Trade in services: Argentina vs. comparator countries, 2007–15

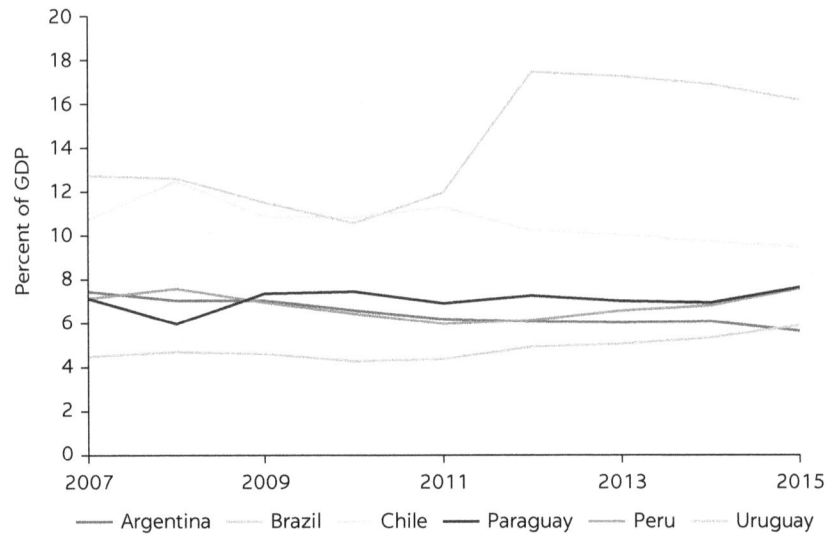

Source: Data from World Integrated Trade Solutions (WITS) dataset (https://wits.worldbank .org/).

enabler of trade in higher-value-added goods, as trade in services fell to merely 5.5 percent of GDP in 2015, the lowest among neighboring countries (figure 1.6).

In addition, Argentina's integration into GVCs, the 21st century mode of trade, is somewhat limited and is relatively stronger on the seller (forward) side than on the buyer (backward) side. The production of export goods is becoming increasingly unbundled; global trade in parts and components has grown faster than trade in final goods over the last 20 years.[6] In GVCs, a country does not need the capability to produce an entire export good but instead contributes a segment of its production process. The latest Trade in Value Added (TiVA) data from OECD, for 2011, suggest that Argentina could participate more strongly in GVCs, especially in buying goods produced abroad and using them as inputs for production of higher-value export goods. Backward GVC participation— measured as the share of foreign value added embodied in Argentina's gross exports—amounted to 14.1 percent in 2011,[7] less than in comparator countries such as Bulgaria, Costa Rica, Malaysia, Mexico, Poland, and Romania (box 1.3).[8] Forward GVC participation—measured as the share of Argentina's value added embodied in foreign countries' gross exports—was higher when compared to the backward participation measure, amounting to 16.8 percent, and essentially reflected Argentina's export of agribusiness commodities (for example, the use of Argentine soy in soy products). Argentina's forward GVC integration was still lower than in Australia, Brazil, and Peru, however (figure 1.7).

Overall, Argentina's limited integration into GVCs relates to its low participation in free trade agreements (FTAs). Worldwide, more and more countries participate in FTAs,[9] but Argentina is an exception to this pattern. Part of this may be explained by the fact that, as part of the Mercosur customs union, Argentina cannot negotiate bilateral trade agreements on its own. Instead, it must seek consensus and coordination with all Mercosur members. As of 2015, countries participated in an average of 14 agreements. The European Union (EU) participated in the largest number of agreements (37), followed by European Free Trade Association members (between 31 and 29), Singapore (21),

FIGURE 1.7

GVC participation: Argentina vs. comparator countries, 2011

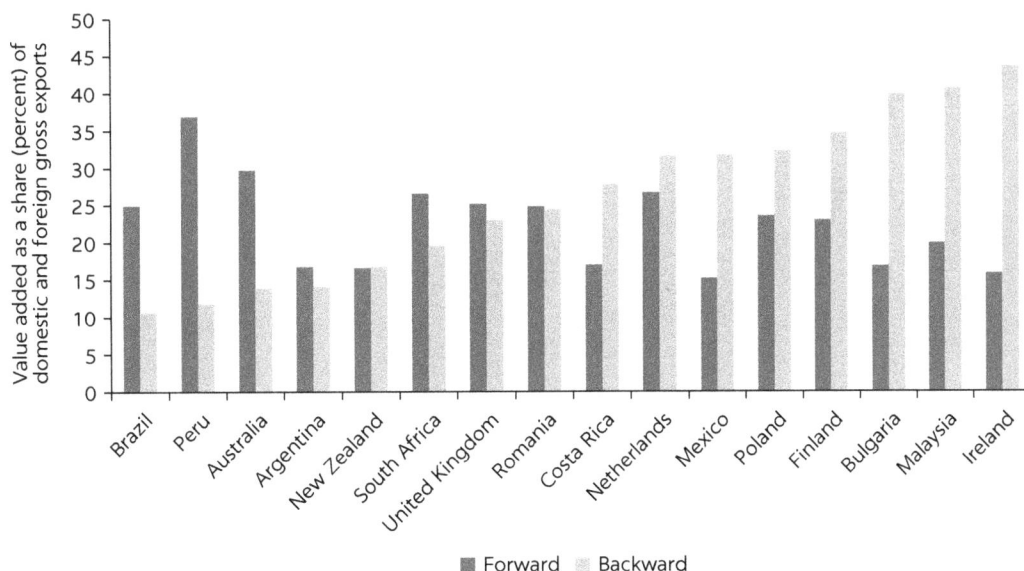

Source: Data from OECD/WTO TiVA dataset (https://stats.oecd.org/index.aspx?queryid=75537).
Note: Countries are ranked by backward participation ratios.

BOX 1.3

Comparator countries

Throughout the report, Argentina is benchmarked against a consistent set of countries: Australia, Brazil, Bulgaria, Costa Rica, Finland, Ireland, Malaysia, Mexico, the Netherlands, New Zealand, Peru, Poland, Romania, South Africa, and the United Kingdom.

This set of peers was selected on the basis of three criteria. The first relies on an algorithm that identifies peer countries that are similar in economic development and/or size, competitors with similar export baskets, or "neighboring" countries within the region, as well as benchmark countries. The algorithm employs five specific economic dimensions: (1) export basket composition (measured as product share in exports, using Standard International Trade Classification (SITC Rev2) with one digit and using products 0 to 8,

based on data from the World Integrated Trade Solution (WITS); (2) GDP per capita, using WDI data; (3) population as a measure of size, using WDI data; (4) human capital, measured as average of years of schooling among the population aged 15 years or more in 2010; and (5) physical capital, measured as capital stock per capita in 2010, using WDI data. Per this first criterion, the following set of comparator countries was selected: Brazil, Bulgaria, Costa Rica, Malaysia, Peru, Poland, South Africa and Romania.[a] The second criterion draws from a selected set of OECD countries: Finland, Great Britain, Ireland, Netherlands and New Zealand. The third includes Australia, a country whose economy bears similarities to the Argentine economy, and Mexico, to enlarge the subset of LAC comparators.

a. The algorithm calculates the Manhattan distances among all countries (Argentina and potential peers) for each dimension. For two points with coordinates $(x_1, ..., x_n)$ and $(y_1, ..., y_n)$, the Manhattan distance between the two is defined as $|x_1 - y_1| + |x_2 - y_2| + ... + |x_n - y_n|$. The five coordinates are not on the same scale, which calls for standardization. Countries with weighted smallest distances are selected as final comparators.

Chile (22), Turkey (18), Mexico (10), and Egypt (5) (map 1.1). Argentina had only one preferential trade agreement in force, the Mercosur.[10]

According to WDI data, Argentina receives little foreign direct investment (FDI) in comparison to small or large Latin American economies. FDI in Argentina amounts to only 2 percent of GDP and has consistently been below the

MAP 1.1

Number of active agreements by country, 2015

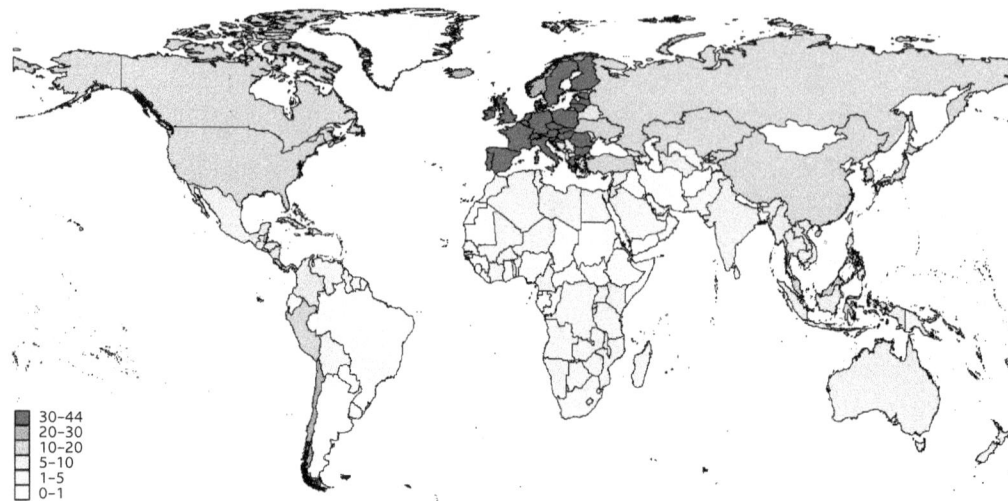

Source: Data from World Bank Preferential Trade Agreement (PTA) Content dataset (https://wits.worldbank.org/gptad/trade _database.html).

FIGURE 1.8

FDI inflows as a share of GDP: Argentina vs. comparator countries, average 2000–15

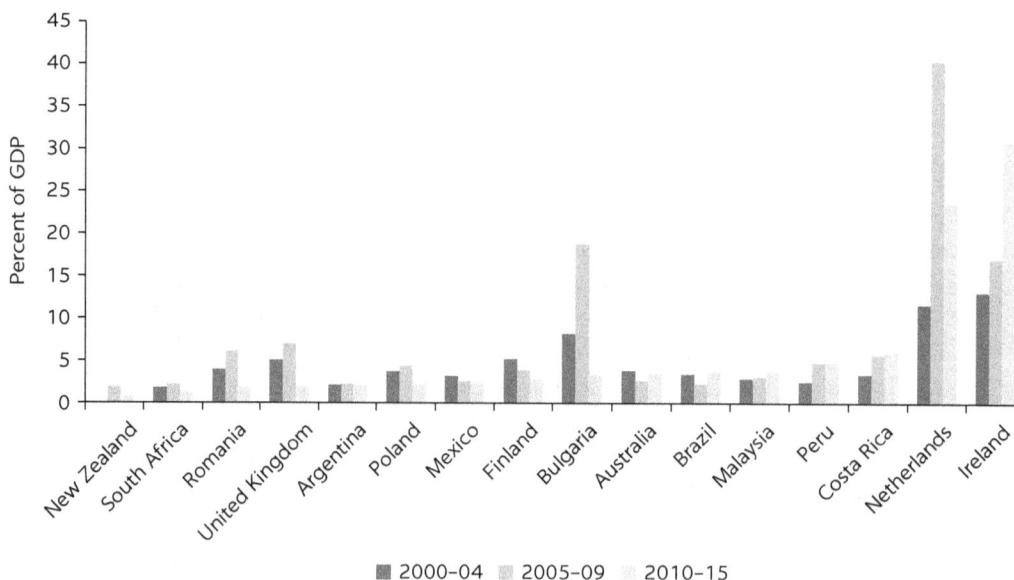

■ 2000–04 ▪ 2005–09 ▫ 2010–15

Source: Data from World Development Indicators (WDI) database (http://wdi.worldbank.org/tables).
Note: Countries are ranked by 2010–15 values.

average for LAC. Global FDI flows rose by 38 percent in 2015, reaching US$1.76 trillion—their highest level since the global economic and financial crisis of 2008. An intense wave of cross-border mergers and acquisitions, mainly in developed countries, accounted for this recent growth of global FDI. Argentina shared this upward trend in FDI accruals during 2015, reaching almost US$12 billion, after enduring an intense downward trend during the preceding years. The share of FDI inflows in Argentina's GDP is among the lowest across a selected group of advanced and emerging markets (figure 1.8). This share has

FIGURE 1.9

Inward FDI stock as a share of GDP: Argentina vs. comparator countries, 2015

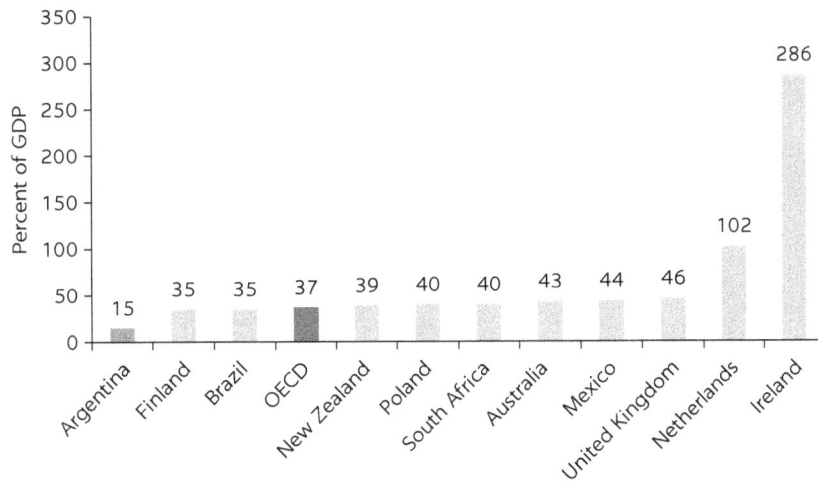

Source: Data from OECD database (https://data.oecd.org/fdi/fdi-stocks.htm).
Note: Inward FDI stock is defined as the value of foreign investors' equity in and net loans to enterprises resident in the reporting economy.

stayed systematically at around 2 percent, below not only the best performers in Latin America (such as Costa Rica) but also the largest regional economies (such as Brazil and Mexico). Argentina's performance is no better when compared to countries outside the region; Argentina has had one of the lowest FDI-to-GDP ratios in the world since 2000. Consistent with low FDI inflows, stock of FDI is also low, and well below the level of comparator countries (figure 1.9).

While FDI flows into many sectors, it does not translate into higher export complexity. Overall, FDI inflows have been quite diversified across sectors; data for 2010 to 2015 suggest that the chemicals (15 percent), mining (11 percent), and financial (10 percent) sectors accounted for the largest individual shares of FDI (figure 1.10). Meanwhile, several smaller sectors contributed to a substantial portion of FDI inflows; besides food and beverages (8 percent) and communication (7 percent), sectors such as automotive, machinery and equipment, wholesale, and others also accounted for some FDI inflows. This diversification in foreign investment has not translated into higher economic and export complexity, however (figure 1.11). Unsophisticated, unprocessed products—primarily in the agricultural sector—still dominate Argentina's export portfolio, leading to a relatively low economic complexity index (ECI).[11] Argentina's ECI was −0.502 (ranking 72nd out of 107 countries) in 2014.[12] FDI complexity[13] in Argentina was also low, at −0.39 (ranking 78th) in the same year. This value falls below the global average and below other Latin American countries (such as Brazil and Costa Rica) with similar ECI standings.

Argentina has both the most restrictive product market regulations in the region and more restrictive regulations than other countries of similar size and income level. The OECD's product market regulation (PMR) indicators measure the degree to which policies or regulatory measures promote or inhibit competition in areas of the product market where competition is viable.[14] Data collected jointly by the World Bank Group (WBG) and OECD suggest the existence of significant regulatory constraints on competition in Argentina. Compared to other

FIGURE 1.10

Sectoral composition of FDI inflows in Argentina, 2010–15

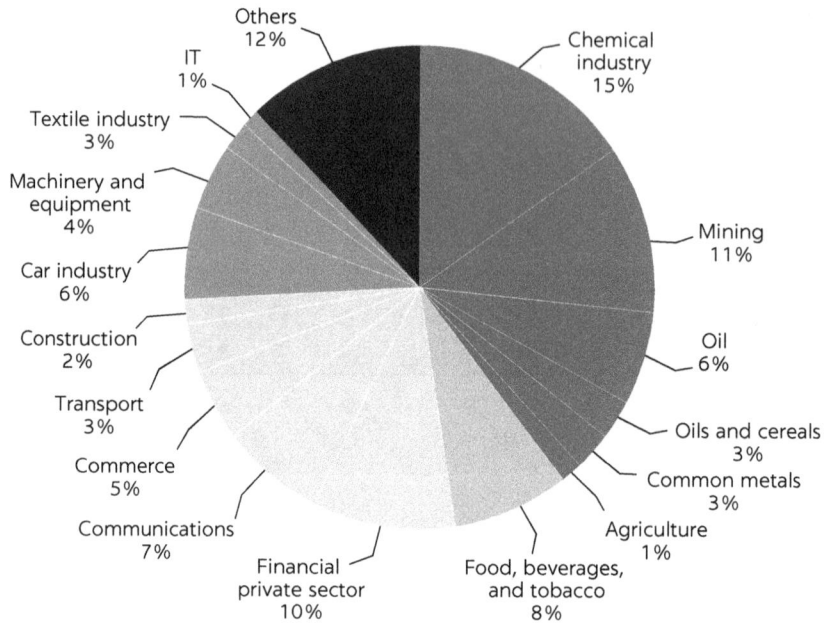

Source: Data from Central Bank of Argentina.

FIGURE 1.11

FDI complexity and economic complexity index: Argentina vs. comparator countries, 2014

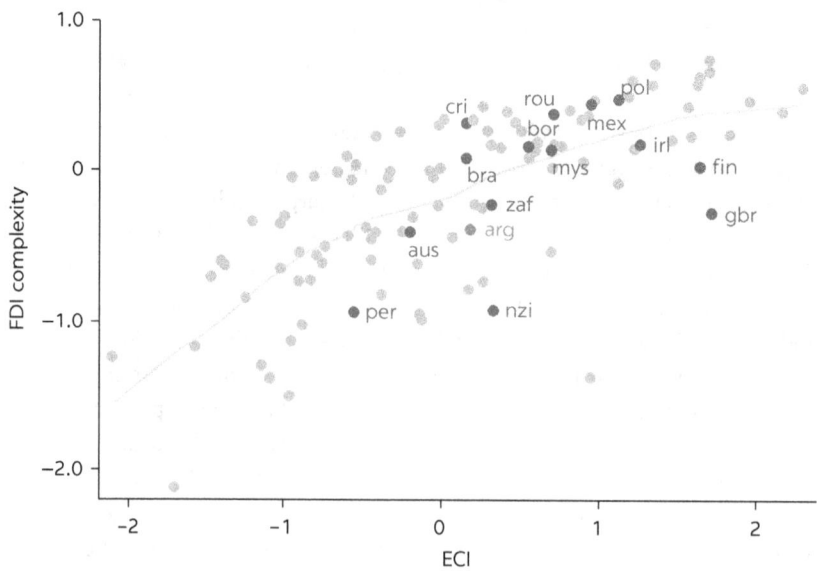

Source: Data from MIT observatory of economic complexity (https://atlas.media.mit.edu /en/rankings/country/eci/).

LAC countries and countries outside the region with similar market characteristics, PMR in Argentina is restrictive (figure 1.12). In fact, the PMR scores assigned according to the restrictiveness of legal and regulatory provisions in each country indicate that product market regulation is 30 percent more restrictive in Argentina than across 19 Latin American countries, on average.

FIGURE 1.12

PMR indicator: Argentina vs. comparator countries, 2013–16

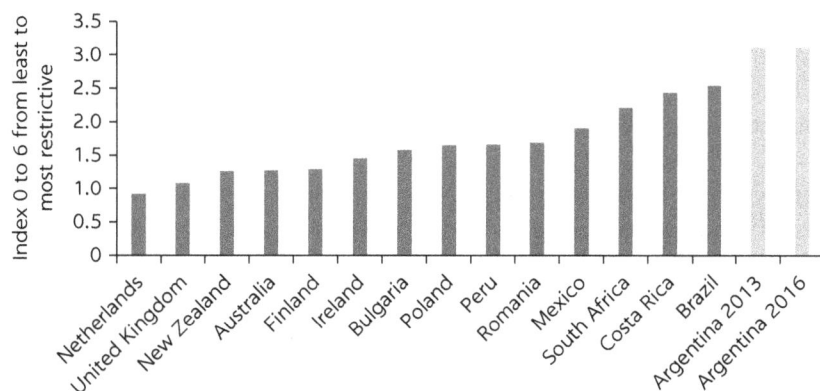

Source: OECD Product Market Regulation database, and OECD-World Bank Group Product Market Regulation database for non-OECD countries 2013, 2016, as of March 2018. (http://www.oecd.org/eco/growth/indicatorsofproductmarketregulationhomepage.htm).

FIGURE 1.13

Decomposition of PMR indicator: Argentina vs. comparator countries, 2013–16

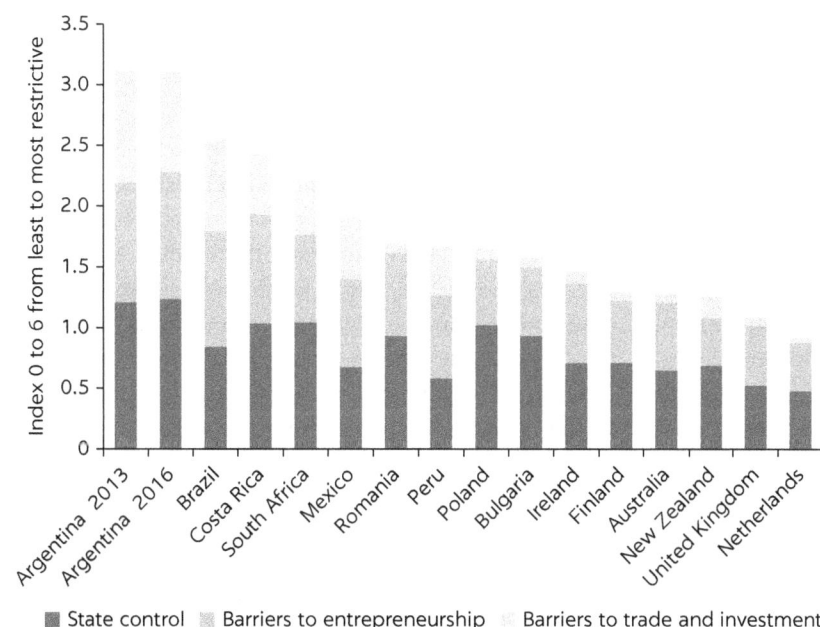

■ State control   ▓ Barriers to entrepreneurship   ░ Barriers to trade and investment

Source: OECD Product Market Regulation database, and OECD-World Bank Group Product Market Regulation database for non-OECD countries 2013, 2016, as of March 2018. (http://www.oecd.org/eco/growth/indicatorsofproductmarketregulationhomepage.htm).

The extent to which Argentine government interventions in markets restrict competition in product markets is driven in particular by the degree of state control and barriers to trade and investment (figure 1.13). In key sectors, private investors face both state-owned enterprises (SOEs) and private national incumbents that appear to benefit from regulatory protection. Investors face business risks as a result of a policy that regulates prices for over 400 specific consumer goods.

This policy, "Precios Cuidados," is being phased out by the current administration but has not yet been revoked, and in September 2017 the number of products included was extended.[15] Furthermore, investors are exposed to the potential for discretionary application of unusually complex administrative procedures. Lack of competition in input markets, such as professional services, can limit the competitiveness of downstream firms.

The prevalence of anticompetitive business practices and government-imposed barriers to competition can affect the price level of basic tradable consumer goods. International evidence shows that a lack of competition is associated with higher prices for homogeneous staple goods.[16] High concentration in specific segments of the supply chain, lack of effective antitrust enforcement, and low market contestability due to regulatory barriers to foreign or domestic market entry can reduce the intensity of competition and allow firms to raise prices above the competitive level on international markets.

In Argentina, basic food product markets exhibited prices that were nearly 50 percent higher, on average, than those of international peers in 2010–15. The underlying empirical analysis used different panel-level data sources for the

---

BOX 1.4

Price comparison analysis: Are prices higher in Argentina?

The price comparison analysis uses two data sources to explore whether food prices in Argentina are higher than in comparator countries: (a) "Numbeo" database, and (b) the EIU database. The sample was restricted to products with yearly data available in both Numbeo and EIU. The sample covers yearly information on prices for 11 products from 2010 to 2015. Both databases apply a common methodology in gathering price data across countries, thus strengthening the comparability of price information used in this analysis.

The baseline empirical specification for the price comparison analysis follows the equation,

$$Ln(price_{ijt}) = \beta_1 GDP_{it} + \beta_2 Ln(X_{it}), + \beta_3\ Argentina + \eta_j + \delta_t + \varepsilon_{ijt},$$

where i = country; j = product; t = year; X_{it} = GDP per capita, cost of imports, tariffs; δ_t = year fixed effects, and η_j = product fixed effects. The Argentina dummy variable captures the relative difference between price levels in Argentina and the average across other countries after adjusting for differences in per-capita GDP PPP, import costs, customs duties, and product type, as well as time-specific effects. The variable to capture costs to import (taken from the Trading Across Borders dataset) accounts for domestic transport costs. Other sources of transport costs (overseas shipping) depend on the origin and destination of each product, for which data are not consistently available. In the case of Argentina, many of these goods come from domestic production.

The food products were selected based on availability across databases,[a] relevance in the Argentine consumption basket, and product characteristics. For example, products that are relatively similar (or homogeneous) across countries were selected to minimize the differences associated with product differentiation. The analysis uses different sets of comparator jurisdictions to account for potential distortions in markets of other countries.[b]

a. The analysis uses the following products: milk (regular, 1 liter), loaf of fresh white bread (500g), rice (white, 1kg), eggs (12), local cheese (1kg), chicken breasts (boneless, skinless, 1kg), beef round (1kg, or equivalent back leg red meat), apples (1kg), bananas (1kg), oranges (1kg), tomatoes (1kg), potatoes (1kg), onions (1kg), and lettuce (1 head).
b. The comparator countries in Latin America with available data include Belize, Bolivia, Brazil, Chile, Colombia, Costa Rica, Ecuador, Guatemala, Mexico, Panama, Peru, Uruguay, and Venezuela. The comparator countries in the OECD with available data are Australia, Canada, the Czech Republic, Denmark, Hungary, Iceland, Israel, Japan, Korea, Latvia, Mexico, New Zealand, Norway, Poland, Sweden, Switzerland, Turkey, the United Kingdom, and the United States.

FIGURE 1.14

Product share in food consumption basket

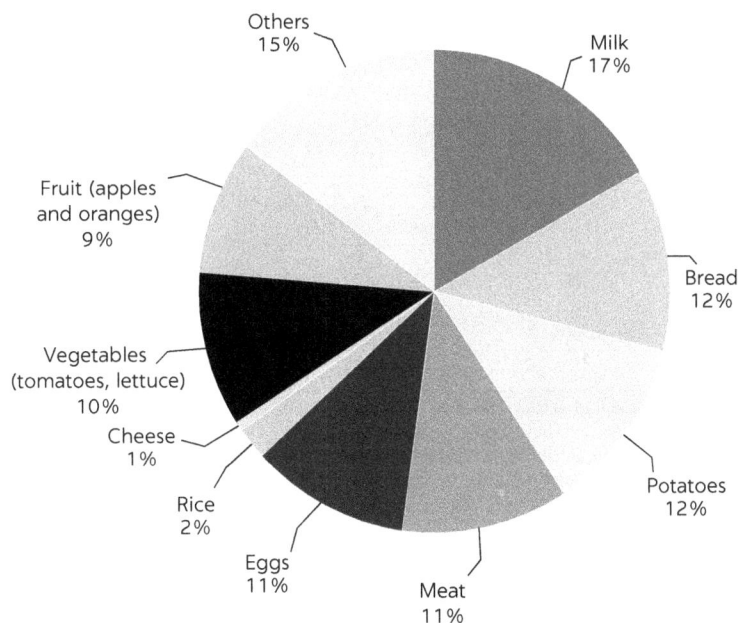

Source: Data from INDEC (2016).

TABLE 1.1 **Price comparison analysis: Argentina vs. comparator countries in the OECD**

	(1)	(2)	(3)
Argentina	0.667***	0.693***	0.487***
	(0.126)	(0.160)	(0.084)
Log of GDP per capita PPP (2011 international $)	0.971***	0.972***	1.100***
	(0.133)	(0.136)	(0.150)
Log of cost of import	—	−0.038	−0.047
		(0.147)	(0.109)
Tariff rate, applied	—	—	0.071***
			(0.024)
Number of observations	1,242	1,242	1,242
R-squared	0.817	0.817	0.827

Source: An elaboration using Numbeo data.
Notes: Results are from an ordinary least squares (OLS) regression using data from Numbeo. All regressions include product and year fixed effects. Standard errors clustered at the country level are in parentheses. Significance is indicated by ***, **, and * at 1 percent, 5 percent, and 10 percent, respectively. — = not available.

2010–15 period and estimation techniques to compare the average prices of 11 basic food items for which there was comparable information at the international level (for details on the methodology, see box 1.4). These food items make up 85 percent of the food consumption basket (figure 1.14).[17] The results suggest that the prices for these products in that period were 49 percent higher than in OECD countries,[18] after accounting for differences in income per capita, cost of import (which captures domestic transport costs), and tariff rates (table 1.1, specification (3)).

TABLE 1.2 **Price comparison analysis: Argentina vs. comparator countries in the Pacific Alliance**

	(1)	(2)	(3)
Argentina	0.391***	0.461***	0.347***
	(0.032)	(0.028)	(0.053)
Log of GDP per capita PPP (2011 international $)	0.193	0.092	−0.045
	(0.111)	(0.047)	(0.061)
Log of cost of import	—	−0.166**	−0.546***
		(0.046)	(0.115)
Tariff rate, applied	—	—	0.103**
			(0.035)
Number of observations	300	300	300
R-squared	0.904	0.910	0.921

Source: An elaboration using Numbeo data.
Notes: Results are from an ordinary least squares (OLS) regression using data from Numbeo. All regressions include product and year fixed effects. Standard errors clustered at the country level are in parentheses. Significance is indicated by ***, **, and * at 1 percent, 5 percent, and 10 percent, respectively. — = not available.

Prices were 35 percent higher in Argentina than in Pacific Alliance countries. Drawing on Numbeo data[19] and comparing the simple level of food product prices across countries in 2010–15, prices in Argentina appeared to be 21 percent higher than in a large set of comparator countries in Latin America.[20] However, this difference can be explained in part by other factors, such as the tariff rate. Arguably, there are many other countries in Latin America where prices may not be competitive due to government interventions or lack of effective competition law enforcement. A more appropriate benchmark is countries in the Pacific Alliance (namely Chile, Colombia, Mexico, and Peru), which have generally more open regulatory and trade regimes than other Latin American countries. The country-level regression results comparing prices in Argentina to those in the Pacific Alliance are reported in table 1.2. They show that food prices were about 35 percent higher in Argentina than in Pacific Alliance countries, after controlling for income levels and potential cost drivers (table 1.2, specification (3)).[21]

Even when comparing food prices among the typically more expensive capital cities, results suggest that, in 2010–15, households in Buenos Aires paid 13 percent more, on average, for basic food products than their peers in capital cities worldwide. Within countries, there is often substantial price-level variation.[22] Hence, the country-level average price level might not be representative across all households in the economy. Economist Intelligence Unit (EIU) data for food prices in capital cities around the world suggest that, after taking into consideration differences in purchasing power and trade costs, prices were still 13 percent higher in Buenos Aires (table 1.3, specification (4)). The difference in countrywide estimations suggests that the wedge between domestic and international price levels may be more accentuated outside the Argentine capital.

Even after controlling for an overvalued exchange rate, price differentials remain. Price differences may be explained in part by an overvalued exchange rate, but even after accounting for available proxies for differences in purchasing power, several of the comparisons presented above still find

TABLE 1.3 **Price comparison analysis: Buenos Aires, Argentina, vs. cities in all other countries**

	(1)	(2)	(3)	(4)
Argentina	0.018	0.087***	0.097***	0.134***
	(0.029)	(0.028)	(0.035)	(0.042)
Log of GDP per capita PPP (2011 international $)	—	0.199***	0.196***	0.149***
		(0.029)	(0.030)	(0.036)
Log of cost of import	—	—	−0.020	−0.002
			(0.049)	(0.050)
Tariff rate, applied	—	—	—	−0.023*
				(0.012)
Number of observations	11,684	11,433	11,433	11,433
R-squared	0.626	0.678	0.678	0.682

Source: An elaboration using EIU data.
Notes: Results are from an ordinary least squares (OLS) regression using EIU data. All regressions include product and year fixed effects. Standard errors clustered at the city level are in parentheses. Significance is indicated by ***, **, and * at 1 percent, 5 percent, and 10 percent, respectively. — = not available.

a significant wedge in prices. The differences in income level and exchange rate may affect price levels and are accounted for in this analysis.[23] Given that there may still be differences in purchasing power that are not captured (for example, in the case of an overvalued exchange rate), we also convert the unit values in local currency into U.S. dollars using a purchasing power parity (PPP) conversion factor. Even though these specifications do not explain the variation as well,[24] and the PPP conversion factor for Argentina may be endogenous to the price differentials analyzed,[25] several specifications still point to a statistically significant price difference of over 10 percent (appendix F). More importantly, evidence that there is no statistically significant difference in prices for some food products suggests that the results of these regressions are not affected by general currency overvaluation or inflation trends (table 1.4).

While there is broad evidence that the price level for basic food products is higher, on average, in Argentina, results vary among specific product markets and may reflect different degrees of intensity of market competition. The results suggest that the prices for certain individual products are significantly higher in Argentina than in comparator countries in the OECD and the Pacific Alliance. Chicken breasts, eggs, dairy products, wheat bread, and white rice had significantly higher prices. The analysis of tariff equivalence of nontariff measures (NTMs) suggests that this is not necessarily due to protection from imports. The price differences are more consistent with information on a relatively high degree of concentration in these product markets: one bread company makes up 80 percent of production,[26] and out of one thousand milk companies, four process 40 percent of the entire market.[27] The level of concentration is only one indicator of the intensity of competition, and further analysis would need to be undertaken at specific stages of the supply chain, as other factors also determine effective competition.[28] Argentina's competition authority has selected several food product markets for in-depth market studies, including meat and dairy products, as well as the supermarket sector.

TABLE 1.4 **Market structure information for individual food products**

PRODUCT	LEVEL OF PRICES IN ARGENTINA/BUENOS AIRES ...			CONCENTRATION	NUMBER OF FIRMS	MARKET SHARE OF LARGEST PLAYER	VERTICAL INTEGRATION	PRODUCT DIVERSITY	NTM TARIFF EQUIVALENT	IMPORTANCE OF IMPORTS
	...vs. OECD	...vs. COMPARATOR CITIES (NUMBEO)	...vs. COMPARATOR CITIES (EIU)							
Oranges	—	—	Lower	Low	36 major firms	30% (exports)	High	Low	Low	Low
Apples	—	—	—	Low (medium only in exports)	42 major firms	24% (exports)	Medium	Low	High	Low and increasing
Potatoes	—	Higher	—	Medium	4 major processing firms	75% (potato chips), 60% (frozen potatoes)	Low	Medium	Low	—
Tomatoes	Higher	Higher	N/A	Medium	40 firms	—	Low	Low	Low	Low
White bread	—	Higher	N/A	High	200 (industrial bakeries)	80%	High	High	Medium	Low
White rice	Higher	Higher	N/A	Medium	40	18%	Low	Low	Medium	High
Chicken	Higher	Higher	Higher	Medium	60	—	High	—	N/A	Low
Eggs	Higher	Higher	Higher	Medium	13 (industrial)	40%	High	—	N/A	Low
Cheese	Higher	Higher	N/A	Medium	20 (in 2008)	—	—	High	Medium	Low
Milk	Higher	Higher	Higher	High	900	>40%	—	Low	N/A	Low

Source: Author's own summary based on publicly available information. Note that the data may refer to specific segments of the value chain (for example, processing rather than production). Cells with "—" in columns 2 to 4 suggest that the difference is not statistically significant.

HOW MUCH COULD ARGENTINA GAIN FROM FOSTERING CONTESTABLE MARKETS AND INTEGRATING INTO THE WORLD ECONOMY?

Boosting competition intensity can increase productivity growth. Competition enhances productivity by improving allocative efficiency, enhancing productive efficiency, and boosting innovation. Empirical studies have linked the intensity of competitive pressures—proxied by price-cost margins (PCMs)—to the increase in labor and total factor productivity growth in developed economies[29] as well as developing countries, such as Turkey, Tunisia, and China.[30] An early study from the United Kingdom shows that an increase of 10 percentage points in PCMs is associated with, on average, a 1.3–1.6 percent loss in total factor productivity growth.[31] For Tunisia, World Bank (2014) estimated in 2013 that a decrease of 5 percentage points in PCMs was associated with an additional 5 percent growth in labor productivity.

In Argentina, more competition in manufacturing sectors could add almost 7 percent to annual labor productivity growth. Empirical analysis using data from over 3,500 firms surveyed in the 2010–12 Encuesta Nacional de Dinámica de Empleo e Innovación (ENDEI) suggests that higher PCMs (implying that firms face lower levels of competition intensity) are significantly associated with lower growth in labor productivity in the following year (box 1.5). The coefficients further suggest that increasing competition intensity (using a 10 percent decrease

Estimating the association between the intensity of competition and productivity growth in the Argentine manufacturing industry

Following the standard in the literature, we approximate market power using the price–cost margin, which is derived from the Lerner Index. The PCM measures margins (that is, the difference between price and marginal cost) as a proportion of price. In the absence of information on price and marginal cost, the extent of pricing power in an industry is proxied by the difference between value added and labor costs as a proportion of sales (all measured in current prices), as follows:

$$PCM_{jt} \approx \frac{(value\,added)_{jt} - (salaries)_{jt}}{sales_{jt}}, \quad (1)$$

where j denotes the firm and t denotes the respective year (varying from 2010 to 2012). Sales, valued added, and salaries are all taken from the ENDEI enterprise survey. Owing to a lack of data, financial costs of capital are not included in the average costs. However, Aghion et al. (2005) show that

excluding costs of capital from the Lerner measure does not affect the results, given that these costs are relatively small and constant over time. Changes in PCM within a sector drive changes in productivity, while the different levels of PCMs across sectors are not indicative of differences in productivity levels. Typically, the capital stock or cost and the capital rent as a fraction of value added do not change dramatically from year to year within one sector.

We use real labor productivity growth as our measure of productivity growth. We calculate real labor productivity by firm j as real value added per worker, as recorded in the ENDEI survey.

Using contemporaneous values of the measures to evaluate the relationship between market power and productivity growth could be problematic. Higher margins could be the result, rather than a cause, of innovation and changes in productivity growth.

continued

Box 1.5, *continued*

Similarly, the cost advantage gained from innovation could translate into higher margins. We address this problem, therefore, by relating PCMs from the preceding year (denoted as "[t-1]") with changes in contemporaneous productivity growth, as done in other studies (for example, Aghion et al. 2008). Exceptional growth in labor productivity can occur independently from firms' innovation efforts. The analysis therefore accounts for productivity shocks that occur economy-wide at specific points in time and for differences across firms in the growth rates of productivity that are unrelated to competition levels and do not change over time by including firm and year fixed effects. (For robustness, we also include estimations with sector- instead of firm-level effects. However, this is less conservative since it allows firm-specific effects to influence the results.) Recent studies (for example,

Aghion et al. 2005, 2008) have shown that the relationship between market power and productivity growth could be nonlinear, and so we allow for that by including the squared term of PCM in the regression analysis.

Based on Aghion et al (2008), we estimated the following fixed effect regression:

$$ln\left(LP_{j,t} / LP_{j,t-1}\right) = \alpha + \beta PCM_{jt-1} + \gamma \left[PCM_{jt-1}\right]^2$$
$$+ \sum_{j} \theta_j \, firm_j + \sum_{t} \delta_t \, time_t + \in_{jt} \quad (2)$$

where $\Delta LP_{i,j,t,t-1}/LP_{i,j,t-1}$ is defined as the growth rate of real labor productivity of firm j, from year t-1 to t. The term PCM_{jt-1} denotes the one-year-lagged markup in firm j, as computed in equation (1). If competition spurs productivity growth, we would expect a negative coefficient for PCM.

TABLE 1.5 **Relationship between competition (PCMs) and labor productivity**

	(1)	(2)	(3)	(4)
	(LINEAR)	(NONLINEAR)	(LINEAR)	(NONLINEAR)
PCM[t-1]	−2.471***	−2.661***	−0.249***	−0.619***
	(0.234)	(0.307)	(0.013)	(0.062)
PCM[t-1] squared	—	0.427	—	0.472***
		(0.279)		(0.070)
Constant	0.832***	0.807***	0.211***	0.230***
	(0.065)	(0.065)	(0.009)	(0.008)
Firm fixed effects	Yes	Yes	No	No
Sector fixed effects	No	No	Yes	Yes
Year fixed effects	Yes	Yes	Yes	Yes
Number of observations	6,675	6,675	6,675	6,675
R-squared	0.571	0.575	0.038	0.063

Source: An elaboration using ENDEI data.
Notes: Results are from a fixed effects ordinary least squares (OLS) regression. The dependent variable is the real labor productivity growth; PCM = (value added − salaries)/sales. Standard errors (clustered at either firm or sector level) are in parentheses. Significance is indicated by ***, **, and * at 1 percent, 5 percent, and 10 percent, respectively. — = not available.

from the average PCM as a proxy) would be expected to generate additional growth in labor productivity of 7 percent per year, on average (table 1.5, specifications (1) and (2)).[32] Productivity growth may accelerate to a much greater extent in individual sectors and up to 10 percent for wood products, basic metals, and paper industries (figure 1.15).

Reducing regulatory restrictiveness in the service sectors can strengthen competition and accelerate growth. Product market regulation that limits entry, distorts the level playing field, or does not enable more efficient producers to

FIGURE 1.15

Expected gains in labor productivity following a 10 percent decrease in mean PCMs for 2011–12

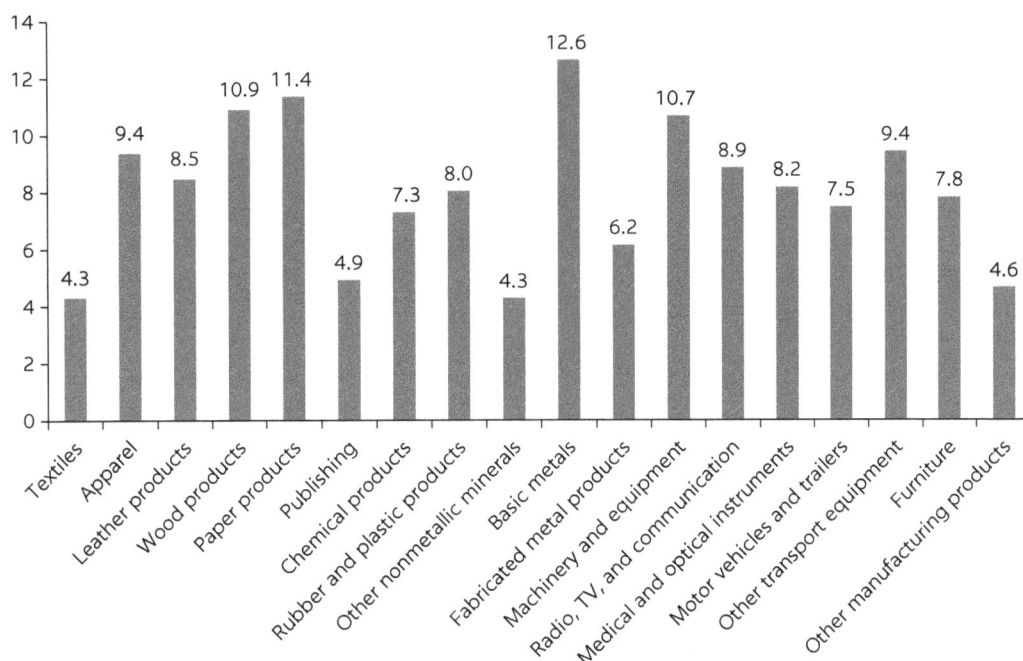

Source: World Bank calculation using ENDEI data.

gain market share can lead to higher prices, lower quality, and less availability.[33] PMR data suggest that, in Argentina, this affects transport, communications, electricity, and professional services (such as legal, accounting, and architectural services). These sectors provide inputs to firms in other sectors. Hence, structural reforms and competition-driven market outcomes could translate into benefits for other sectors that use such services intensively.[34] A simulated scenario in which Argentina undergoes reforms that decrease the regulatory restrictiveness of service sectors suggests that such reforms would translate into additional growth of 0.1 percent to 0.6 percent in annual GDP, with all else being equal.[35]

Easing barriers to trade in Argentina would also improve the overall economy; in sum, the greatest gains in terms of economic growth can be achieved from a Mercosur-wide reduction in tariff and nontariff measures. Reducing tariffs on world imports by 50 percent in all Mercosur countries, cutting NTMs within the borders of Mercosur by 15 percent, and eliminating export controls within Mercosur could boost GDP by at least 1 percent compared to baseline projections to 2030. This would open Argentina to all world trade and allow importers to source from the most efficient producers worldwide. While the greatest gains would be achieved in this scenario, the current political economy context makes this an elusive goal in the short term. A Mercosur–EU FTA would boost Argentina's exports to the EU by a remarkable 80 percent by 2030, relative to the baseline. Argentina's companies would still benefit from access to more efficient inputs, but only from Europe, so gains for the overall economy would be smaller than in the case of a 50 percent tariff cut by all Mercosur members for worldwide imports. Unilaterally, Argentina could pursue NTM reforms, such as eliminating all nonautomatic licenses and export taxes to the world, which could boost GDP notably in the medium term (by about 0.22 percent and 0.97 percent

TABLE 1.6 **Unilateral liberalization scenarios and economy-wide effects**

	TARIFF LIBERALIZATION		NTM LIBERALIZATION: IMPORT LICENSING REGIME		NTM LIBERALIZATION: EXPORT TAXES	
	ONE SECTOR AT A TIME	SIMULTANEOUS	ELIMINATION OF DJAI	REMOVAL OF REMAINING NONAUTOMATIC IMPORT LICENSES	ELIMINATION/ REDUCTION OF EXPORT TAXES APPLIED TO SEVERAL PRODUCTS	ELIMINATION OF ALL REMAINING EXPORT TAXES
Assumptions						
	Target the top protected sectors. Focus on tariff lines that can be lowered to zero in each targeted sector; this would reduce the average tariff for each sector.		Already implemented (end of 2015)		Already implemented (end of 2015, early 2016): trade-weighted average export tax fell from about 14 percent to 8 percent.	Average export tax is brought down from 8 percent to 0 percent.
Deviations from the baseline by 2020 (percent)						
GDP	0.05 (furniture)	0.16	0.14	0.22	0.27	0.98
Exports	16.1* (footwear)	26.8* (footwear)	3.00	4.50	8.20	16.80
Imports	129* (furniture)	121.8* (furniture)	2.50	3.50	7.10	14.50

Source: Estimates from CGE analysis.
* Estimated numbers refer to trade effects for the sectors in parentheses only.

above baseline projections, respectively, to 2020). Sectoral effects are likely to be heterogeneous in these scenarios, with particular gains for agriculture and food products and for services.

Argentina also has options for unilateral trade liberalization. Three types of unilateral reforms can be modeled using a CGE framework customized for Argentina (table 1.6; box 1.6). The first option is a unilateral tariff reform. In principle, the scope for unilateral tariff liberalization is limited, given Mercosur commitments. One way to lower tariffs, however, would be to make use of national exceptions to the common external tariff (CET). Against this backdrop, the first scenario targets the liberalization of the most protected sectors as of 2015 (including, among others, footwear, furniture, and textiles and apparel);[36] in this case, the number of tariff lines that could be lowered to zero in each sector is identified,[37] and the associated tariff reduction at the sector level is computed.[38] Two hypothetical variants of tariff reforms are simulated: liberalizing one sector at a time, and simultaneous sector liberalization.[39] A second type of scenario comprises the reform of the nonautomatic import license system. Two variants are modeled: the elimination of DJAI (already implemented in 2015),[40] and the hypothetical expansion of this reform to eliminate all remaining nonautomatic import licenses. Finally, the third type of scenario comprises reforming export taxes. Two (complementary) settings are considered: the recent (by early 2016) elimination of export taxes applied to several products, and the hypothetical expansion of this reform to eliminate all remaining export taxes.

A unilateral tariff liberalization reform targeting highly protected sectors would increase GDP, with different impacts across sectors. Argentina imposes relatively high tariffs on its imports from the rest of the world on a most-favored nation basis; the simple average tariff in 2015 was about 14 percent.[41] Liberalizing the 10 highest tariff sectors[42] one at a time would have a negligible impact on the overall economy; the largest individual effect would result from eliminating the tariff on furniture, and this would increase real GDP by at least 0.05 percent over baseline projections to 2020 (figure 1.16).[43] A combined and simultaneous tariff

Brief description of the CGE analysis

A dynamic CGE analysis assesses several implications of trade integration for Argentina. The analysis uses economic data and an economic model to simulate how an economy would react to exogenous policy changes. The model used is the LINKAGE model, a dynamic, multisector, multiregion model with economy-wide coverage for each region. For each economy, the model tracks the linkages between sectors through input–output transactions, as well as various sources of final demand, including private and government consumption, imports, exports, and investment.

The CGE analysis uses data based on the Global Trade Analysis Project (GTAP) database,[a] modified to update the data and identify subsectors of interest for Argentina. Starting from the GTAP database 9.2, the base year of 2011 was updated to 2015 and the input–output structures for Argentina were updated to reflect the latest official tables from the National Institute of Statistics and Censuses (Instituto Nacional de Estadística y Censos de la República Argentina, or INDEC). The sectoral dimension in GTAP was expanded to include several new sectors of interest in Argentina. These included beef, soybeans, soybean products, wine, footwear, furniture, home appliances, and auto parts that are part of more aggregated

GTAP sectors. Appendix C displays the CGE model's final sector aggregation.

The potential economic effect of a policy change can be measured at any point in time relative to a baseline projection absent the reform. The dynamic analysis starts from the development of a long-term baseline scenario, which reflects a projection of the Argentine and global economies with current policies in place (figure B1.6.1). This baseline is used to compare alternative scenarios under which policies are changed (or "shocked") to reflect the reform in question (whether it is a unilateral or reciprocal liberalization). The construction of the baseline targets certain economy-wide variables based on available forecasts—for example, real GDP per capita and labor supply. These include macroeconomic projections by the World Bank's Global Economic Prospects dataset and working-age population growth by the United Nations World Population Prospects dataset.

The economic effects of trade agreements would have a permanent impact on trade, production, and employment. The regional integration scenarios considered provide economy-wide increases in trade and output. To the extent that these reforms are not rescinded, trade and output values would remain

FIGURE B1.6.1

Annualized real GDP growth in Argentina under the baseline

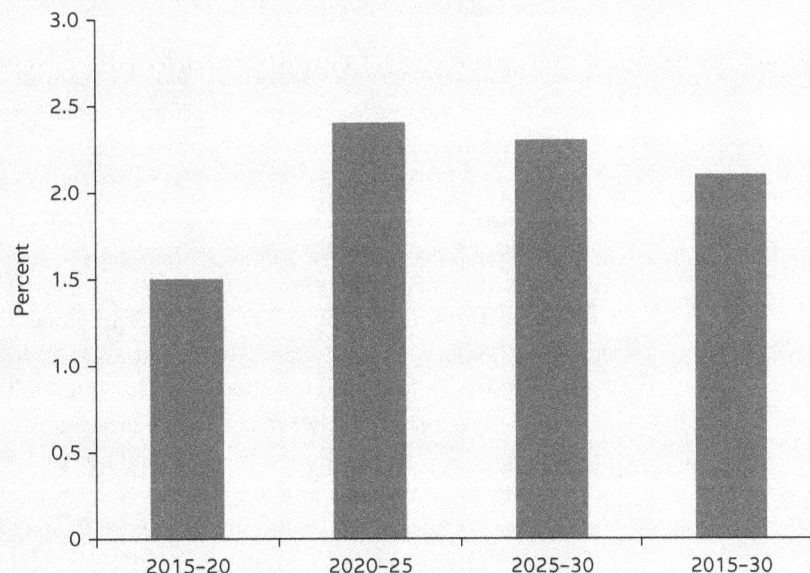

continued

Box 1.6, *continued*

above their baseline levels over time. Effects on real GDP, for example, are found to be positive, but are modest on a percentage basis. This reflects in part the relatively large size of the economy and its domestic orientation, as well as the specifics of the liberalization (whether it is full versus partial, unilateral versus reciprocal, or preferential versus most-favored nation). Yet the small GDP effects are in perpetuity and can translate into significant cumulative real income gains over time.

Estimated results from the CGE analysis may be interpreted as partial effects. The ability to assess comprehensively the impact of policy changes depends on the extent to which all changed conditions can be measured. While the model is dynamic in the sense that the capital stock can change over time, the model does not include other dynamic factors proposed in the literature, such as productivity increases from endogenous growth effects via technological spillovers, "learning by doing," or inflows of foreign technology and FDI induced by liberalization. These effects, while potential, are difficult to measure and incorporate in this type of analysis. Moreover, certain policy changes that are often difficult to quantify—such as reforms related to NTMs in goods and services and restrictions on investment—present analytical challenges that may affect the estimated economic effects. Owing to these limitations, the CGE results presented in this report are likely to be conservative.

CGE analyses are best thought of as tools for understanding the implications of different scenarios. Thanks to their rich structure, they capture complex linkages between sectors and long-term developments in demand and supply. They provide a rigorous framework that is most useful in helping to understand the underlying and contradicting economic forces and mechanisms at play and in comparing different scenarios in ex ante policy analysis.

a. GTAP is a network of researchers coordinated by the Center of Global Trade Analysis in Purdue University's Department of Agricultural Economics. For further details, see https://www.gtap.agecon.purdue.edu/.

liberalization of these highly protected sectors would have greater benefits for the economy (expanding GDP by at least 0.16 percent above baseline projections to 2020) but would require Mercosur-wide changes.[44] While the overall Argentine economy would grow following tariff liberalization, import competition would reduce the real output of all sectors for which tariffs were liberalized. Figure 1.17 shows how much real output would change by 2020 and by 2030—relative to projected values without the reform—under both scenarios: opening all sectors simultaneously or opening one at a time.

A unilateral NTM reform with a focus on a less restrictive licensing regime would bring permanent effects on total trade and economic activity. The 2015 elimination of prior approval for many imports (through the replacement of the DJAI with the SIMI) was a key reform in reducing nontariff barriers to trade.[45] CGE estimations show that this change will permanently accelerate trade, increasing both imports and exports by at least 2.5 to 3 percent, respectively, by 2020, compared to baseline projections to 2020 without this reform. Real GDP will also be 0.14 percent higher than baseline projections to 2020 (figure 1.18). Expanding this reform to eliminate remaining nonautomatic licenses would bring even greater benefits; total imports would be at least 3.5 percent higher than baseline projections to 2020, and total exports would be at least 4.5 percent higher. Similarly, economic activity would be higher, boosting GDP at least 0.22 percent over baseline projections to 2020.

FIGURE 1.16

Real GDP deviations from the baseline due to unilateral tariff liberalization, 2020–30

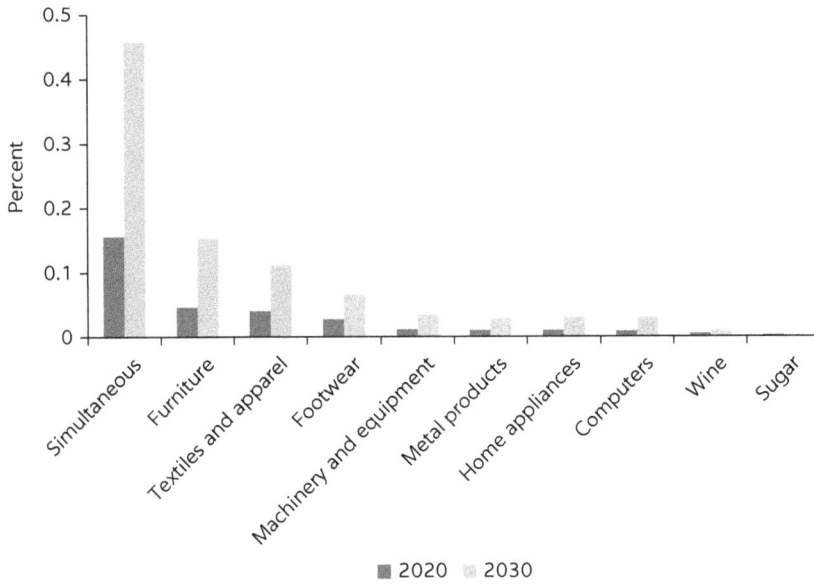

Source: Estimates from CGE analysis.

FIGURE 1.17

Sectoral output deviations from the baseline due to unilateral tariff liberalization, 2020

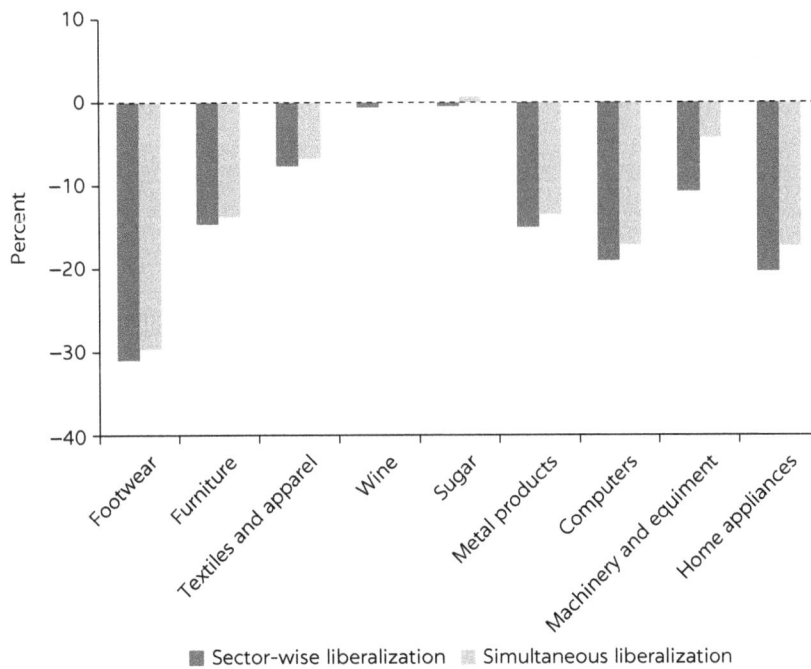

Source: Estimates from CGE analysis.

FIGURE 1.18

Trade and GDP deviations from the baseline due to import license reforms, 2020

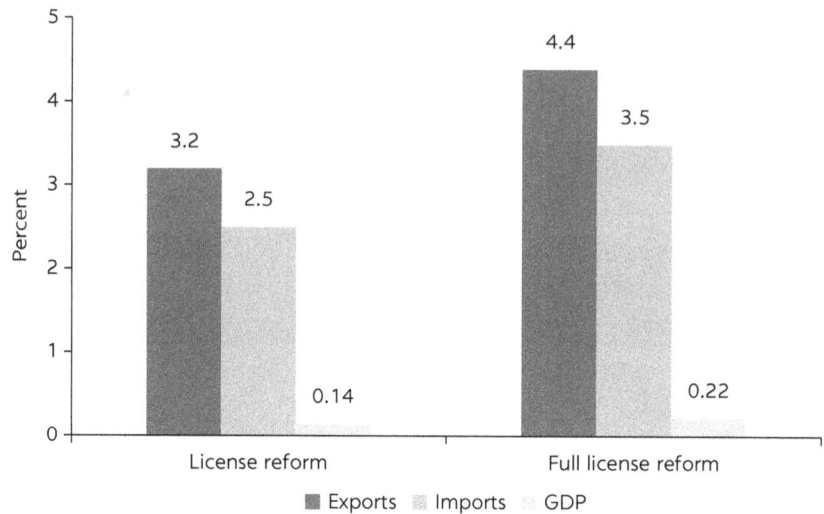

Source: Estimates from CGE analysis.

FIGURE 1.19

Sectoral output deviations from the baseline due to import license reforms, 2020

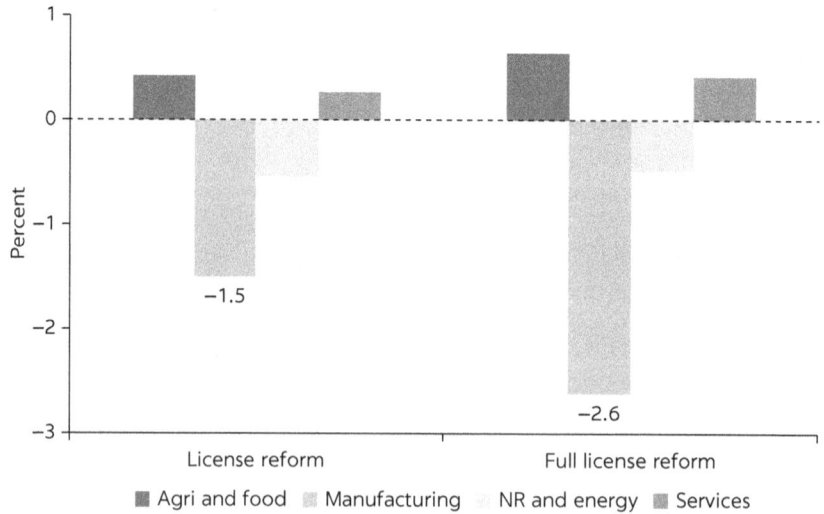

Source: Estimates from CGE analysis.

While output as a whole would expand, the effect would vary by sector. Simulations suggest that real output in the manufacturing sector would be 1.5 percent lower than if DJAI had continued; this contraction would be led by retrenchments in pharmaceuticals, auto parts, and other manufacturing sectors (figure 1.19). Not all manufacturing sectors would shrink, however. In the vehicle sector, for example, imports would increase, but real output would still expand from higher sales in the domestic and foreign markets, owing to cheaper imported parts. Real output in the food and agriculture sector, on the other hand,

FIGURE 1.20

Trade and GDP deviations from the baseline due to export control reforms, 2020

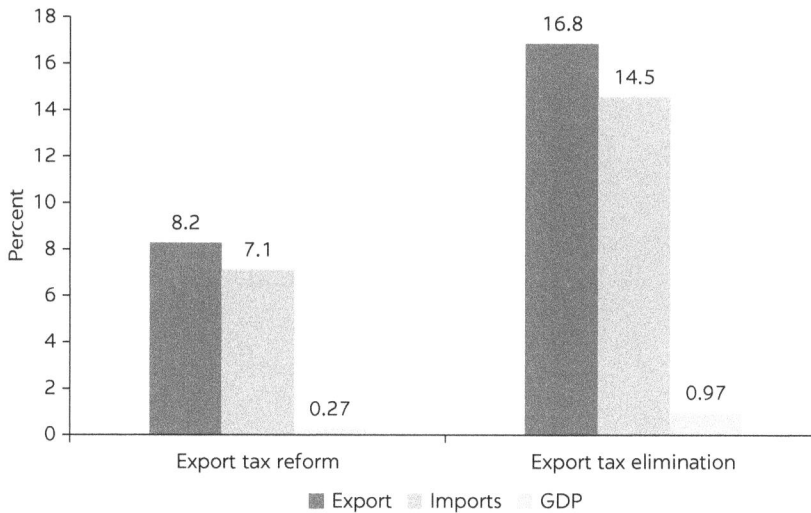

Source: Estimates from CGE analysis.

would grow above the baseline; this expansion would be led by higher exports of soybeans and soybean products, partly compensating for the increase in net imports in other sectors. These sectoral patterns hold in the scenario where all nonautomatic licenses are removed. However, the contraction in real output for manufacturing is accentuated because the remaining nonautomatic licenses are concentrated in these sectors.

Trade and economic activity would expand in response to a unilateral NTM reform focused on easing export taxes, and, again, different sectors would face distinct impacts. In 2015, export taxes were the predominant form of export control and accounted for 7 percent of total tax revenue for the country. By early 2016, Argentina had mostly eliminated export taxes, but certain products were still taxed, including soybeans and soybean products.[46] CGE estimations suggest that, as a result of the export tax reduction implemented in 2016, exports will be 8 percent higher and imports about 7 percent higher in 2020 than under a scenario without reforms. Real GDP will be 0.27 percent higher than baseline projections to 2020 (figure 1.20). If all export taxes were eliminated, the (weighted) average export tax would decrease from the current 8 percent to zero, the impact on both exports and imports would double, and the effect on real GDP would more than double to 0.98 percent above baseline projections to 2020.[47] The elimination of all export taxes would have the strongest impact on the agricultural sector, with real output being almost 16 percent above baseline projections to 2020 (figure 1.21). Growth in the real output of the food and agriculture sector would be driven largely by a drastic expansion in soybean products, soybeans, and other food and agriculture products.[48]

Argentina has taken up trade negotiations with various potential partners, and this could result in substantial reciprocal trade liberalization. Up to now, Argentina has sat at the margins of regional integration trends in other parts of the world. Recently, however, there has been a renewed interest in deepening integration with the global economy. Three prospective trade agreements are

FIGURE 1.21

Sectoral output deviations from the baseline due to export control reforms, 2020

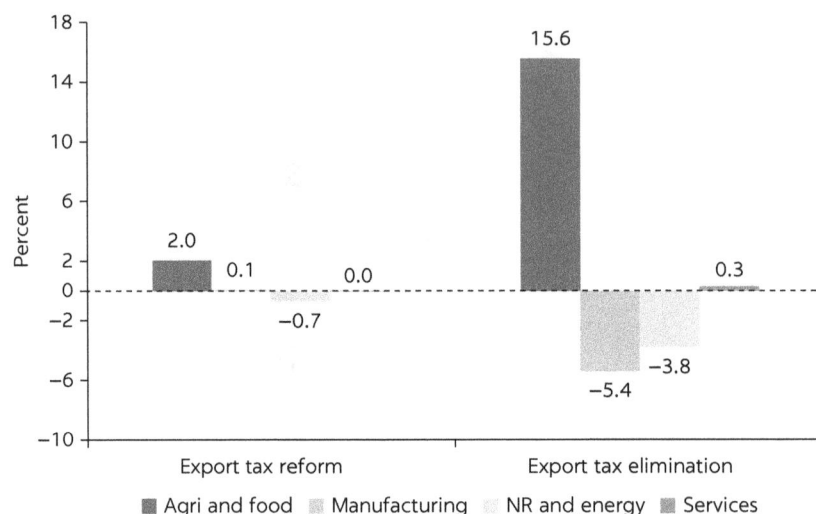

Source: Estimates from CGE analysis.

TABLE 1.7 **Regional liberalization scenarios and economy-wide effects**

	"COMMUNITY REFORMS" AT MERCOSUR	EU-MERCOSUR FTA	EU27-MERCOSUR FTA	PACIFIC ALLIANCE-MERCOSUR FTA
Assumptions				
Tariffs	Tariffs in all Mercosur countries reduced by 50%	Bilateral tariffs: in Argentina from 11.0% to 3.0%; in the EU from 2.7% to nearly 0%	Bilateral tariffs: in Argentina from 11.0% to 3.0%; in the EU from 2.7% to nearly 0%	Bilateral tariffs: in Argentina from 1.0% to 0.3%; in the Pacific Alliance from 2.3% to 0.3%
NTMs	Reduced by 15% intra-Mercosur; export controls eliminated	Reduced by 15% among parties; export controls eliminated	Reduced by 15% among parties; export controls eliminated	Reduced by 15% among parties; export controls eliminated
Deviations from the baseline by 2030 (percent)				
GDP	0.94	0.37	0.35	0.19
Exports	5.9	7.0	6.5	3.5
Imports	4.6	5.8	5.4	3.0

Source: Estimates from CGE analysis.

particularly relevant. Four major trade negotiation scenarios are modeled (table 1.7).[49] In the first scenario, each Mercosur country unilaterally reduces tariffs by 50 percent with respect to non-Mercosur countries.[50] The second scenario considers a reciprocal preferential trade agreement between Mercosur and the EU, under which the average tariff applied by Argentina to EU products would fall from about 11 percent to about 3 percent by full implementation in 10 years, while the average tariff in the EU for Argentine products would fall from about 3 percent to close to zero.[51] In the third scenario, a potential EU agreement is assessed with the exclusion of the United Kingdom as part of the EU.[52] The final scenario considers a preferential trade agreement between Mercosur and the Pacific Alliance, under which Mercosur countries and Pacific Alliance countries gradually reduce tariffs over 10 years. For Argentina, the trade-weighted average tariff applied to products from countries in the Pacific

Alliance would fall from about 1 percent to 0.3 percent. The average tariff faced by Argentina in the Pacific Alliance would fall from 2.3 percent to 0.3 percent.[53]

A free trade agreement between the EU and Mercosur would boost Argentina's exports to the EU by 80 percent by 2030, relative to the baseline. An agreement between the EU and Mercosur would reduce bilateral tariffs by more than the other liberalization scenarios. As a result, Argentine exports would increase by at least 7 percent and imports by 6 percent over baseline projections by 2030, with slightly lower effects in an FTA with the EU, excluding the United Kingdom (table 1.7). Argentina's exports to the EU alone would grow by 80 percent and imports from the EU would expand by close to 50 percent, relative to baseline projections (figure 1.22). Similarly, trade between Argentina and the rest of Mercosur would expand, although to a lesser extent, as the two economic blocks integrated by reducing nontariff barriers. The sizable expansion in trade with the EU would divert trade from other parts of the world. An FTA with the EU would expand real GDP by at least 0.4 percent above baseline projections to 2030 (table 1.7).

Reforms within Mercosur would have a smaller effect on total trade but a larger permanent impact on overall economic activity. When compared with the EU scenario, the scenario of "community reforms at Mercosur" would boost trade to a slightly lesser degree because tariff liberalization would only be partial in all sectors (table 1.7). This liberalization, however, would apply to all countries in the world, so allocative efficiencies would be expected to be larger. Except for slightly lower exports to other Mercosur countries, relative to baseline projections, exports to all other regions would be higher (figure 1.22). This most-favored nation liberalization, albeit partial, would increase real GDP by at least 1 percent over baseline projections to 2030 (table 1.7).

FIGURE 1.22

Argentine exports (by region), deviations from the baseline due to multilateral reforms, 2030

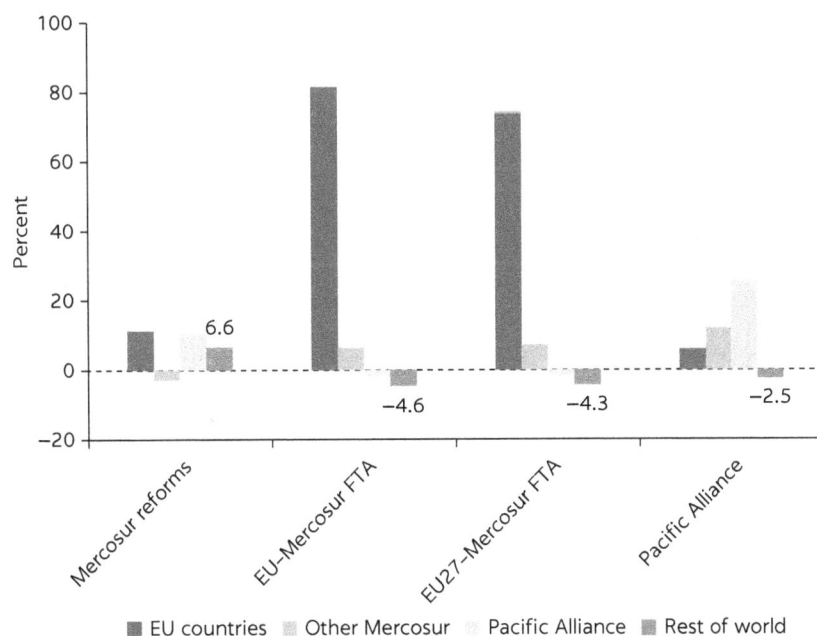

Source: Estimates from CGE analysis.

Integration with the Pacific Alliance would also contribute to the growth of the Argentine economy, mostly through exports to Pacific Alliance countries. Bilateral exports to Pacific Alliance countries would increase by 25 percent and imports by about 10 percent over baseline projections to 2030 (figure 1.22). In this scenario, where integration within Mercosur would also be enhanced, trade with other Mercosur countries would also expand. Real GDP in this scenario would be 0.2 percent higher than baseline projections to 2030 (table 1.7).

Different regional integration scenarios have distinct output effects across sectors. An FTA with the EU would boost real output relative to baseline projections in the agriculture and food sector (figure 1.23); this would be driven by expansion of soybean products and beef.[54] Real output in manufacturing, however, would be lower (−1.6 percent) relative to baseline projections to 2030, driven mainly by contractions in auto parts and pharmaceutical activities. On the other hand, output in the vehicle sector would expand relative to the baseline. The sectoral pattern is similar under a unilateral reform by Mercosur, with a larger contraction in manufacturing (−3.3 percent) relative to baseline projections to 2030. In this case, the vehicle sector would see lower real output (relative to the baseline), owing to increased import competition, and the same would occur in the auto parts, textiles and apparel, furniture, and footwear sectors. Real output in all other sectors would expand relative to baseline projections to 2030 as resources would shift to other activities. The sectoral impact of integration with the Pacific Alliance would be more modest and less heterogeneous relative to the baseline. Real output in the agricultural and food sector would expand above the baseline—driven, as in the other integration scenarios, by higher real output of soybean products and beef activities. In manufacturing, some sectors, such as auto parts, textiles and apparel, and footwear, would

FIGURE 1.23

Sectoral output deviations from the baseline due to multilateral reforms, 2030

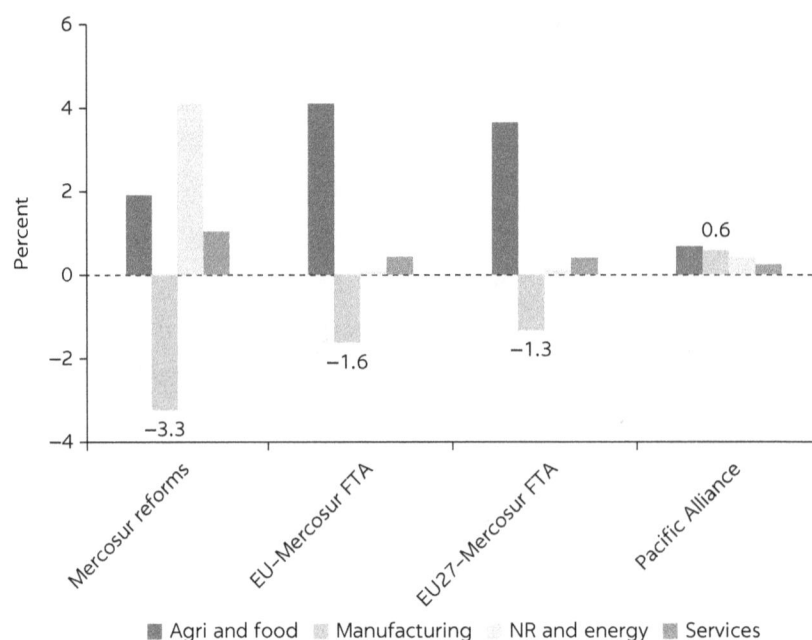

Source: Estimates from CGE analysis.

experience a decrease in real output, but the pharmaceutical and vehicle sectors would expand, and the real output for manufacturing overall would be 0.6 percent above baseline projections to 2030. Real output in overall services would expand, although by less than in other scenarios. Finally, output in natural resources and energy products would expand, driven by higher exports of fuel and fuel products.

Employment effects would vary by regional trade integration scenario, with certain sectors being more susceptible to losing jobs relative to the baseline scenario, which would need to be absorbed by expanding activities. By linking the CGE estimations of changes in the sectoral wage bill with formal employment numbers by sector (from the *Boletín Trimestral de Empleo Registrado*),[55] it is possible to identify sectors that would release formal employment relative to the baseline to 2030 under different trade negotiation scenarios.[56] Table 1.8 displays the results for each trade integration scenario using a "heat map," in which the varying colors indicate relatively small (light green), moderate (orange), or large

TABLE 1.8 Heat map of sectors in which employment would be lower than the baseline to 2030, by trade integration scenario

	"COMMUNITY REFORMS" AT MERCOSUR	EU–MERCOSUR FTA	PACIFIC ALLIANCE–MERCOSUR FTA
Dairy			
Sugar			
Fruits and vegetables			
Wine			
Meats			
Other agriculture and food			
Natural resources and fuel			
Agricultural machinery			
Computers			
Other machinery and equipment			
Metal products			
Footwear			
Textile and apparel			
Furniture			
Home appliances			
Pharmaceuticals			
Vehicles			
Auto parts			
Other manufacturing			
Communication, financial, and business services			
Other services			

Source: Estimates from CGE analysis.
Note: Light green indicates small losses in formal employment, orange indicates moderate losses, and red indicates large losses. Dark-green cells indicate sectors that would absorb labor, but the table makes no distinction with respect to the relative intensity at which labor is absorbed in those sectors.

(red) losses of formal employment; dark green sector cells indicate sectors that would absorb formal employment.[57] Key results are summarized below:

- Reforms within Mercosur would trigger moderate or largely negative impacts on formal employment in the following sectors: sugar, fruits and vegetables, metal products, footwear, textile and apparel, furniture, vehicles, auto parts, and other manufacturing.
- Under the EU-Mercosur scenario, sugar, natural resources and fuel, other machinery and equipment, metal products, footwear, pharmaceuticals, auto parts, and other manufacturing sectors would experience moderate to large losses in formal employment, relative to the baseline.
- Under the Pacific Alliance–Mercosur scenario, sugar, metal products, and footwear sectors would experience a moderately negative impact on formal employment, relative to the baseline.

Overall, this analysis suggests that, relative to the baseline, the sugar, metal products, footwear, auto parts, and other manufacturing sectors would be more susceptible to experiencing moderate or large losses in formal employment for most of the trade integration scenarios modeled. On the other hand, some sectors emerge as formal employment generators above the baseline, regardless of the trade integration scenario modeled; these include overall services, as well as meats and other agricultural and food products. Measures that can support the transition process and the affected labor force are discussed later in the chapter.

THE IMPORTANCE OF FDI, TRADE IN SERVICES, E-COMMERCE, AND COMPETITIVE DOMESTIC MARKETS: MAKING THE MOST OF THE NEW GLOBAL TRADE LANDSCAPE

The current trade scenario poses substantial challenges for outward economic growth strategies. Trade growth has been low since 2011; growth in total trade volumes has shrunk to an average of 3 percent since 2012, substantially lower than the average of 7.1 percent in 1987–2007, before the global financial crisis. Structural factors, rather than cyclical components, largely explain this slow growth. A decline in the ratio between world trade elasticity and GDP suggests that trade has been growing more slowly since the global crisis—not only because global GDP growth has been lower, but also because trade itself has become less responsive to GDP.[58] Opening the economy in this context is a challenge, especially in light of the renaissance in protectionist rhetoric.[59]

Changes in the characteristics of world trade also bring new opportunities, however. First, the unbundling of production of export goods has given rise to GVCs, and the signing of deep FTAs has been the main vehicle for bringing in new disciplines that allow factories to connect across borders in a seamless way. Second, trade in services has given rise to new export and diversification opportunities. Argentina can take advantage of both, and the attracting of strategic foreign investment can be a key to success. Investors that seek efficiencies in Argentina—as opposed to resources or market access—are in a position to connect to GVCs and to develop more competitive service exports, such as knowledge-based services. Third, growth in cross-border e-commerce opens opportunities for small and medium enterprises (SMEs) to participate in global markets.

FIGURE 1.24

Deep free trade agreements and GVC-related trade: Simple correlations

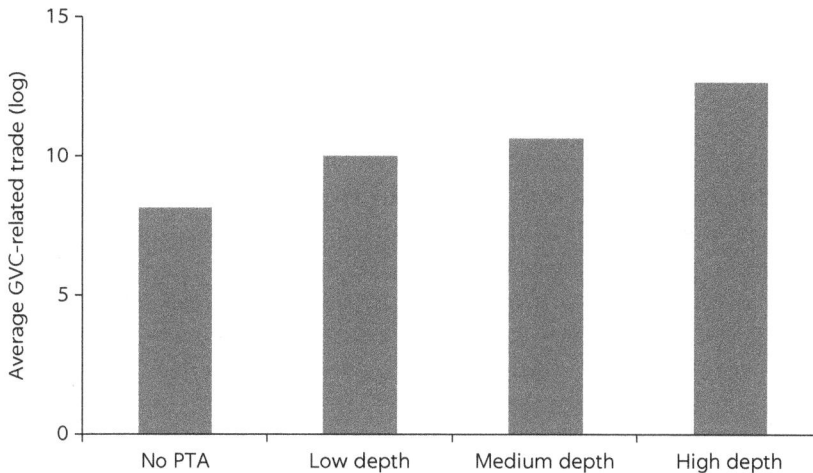

Source: Calculations based on World Bank PTA Content dataset (https://wits.worldbank.org /gptad/trade_database.html).
Note: Low depth = agreements with less than or equal to 15 provisions; medium depth = agreements with 15 or more provisions, but less than or equal to 30; and high depth = agreements with more than 30 provisions.

Integrating into GVCs requires deeper trade agreements, with provisions in areas such as investment and competition. The world has witnessed an acceleration of FTA deals while Argentina has sat on the sidelines. The depth of coverage of these FTAs has been increasing as well; agreements signed before 1991 included 9 policy areas, on average, whereas agreements signed between 2005 and 2015 included 15 policy areas, on average.[60] Mercosur, the only preferential trade agreement to which Argentina is a signatory,[61] includes provisions in 17 areas.[62] By contrast, the maximum depth of agreements signed by other Latin American countries ranges from 20 to 30 provisions.[63] Evidence suggests that GVC-related trade (proxied by trade in parts and components) is higher on average for countries that have signed deeper agreements (figure 1.24).

Signing deep FTAs would be a fruitful way for Argentina to connect to specific segments of RVCs and GVCs and attract foreign investment. Results of a gravity model show that deepening Mercosur would further increase Argentina's GVC-related exports to its FTA partners (box 1.7). If Mercosur had the same depth as the EU–Colombia and Peru agreement, Argentina would export between 1 percent and 9 percent more (US$54 million–$480 million) to Mercosur members.[64] Revising Mercosur would require introducing policy areas such as visa and asylum, data protection, health, and industrial cooperation. By the same token, if Mercosur and the Pacific Alliance were to sign an agreement as deep as the Pacific Alliance's deepest agreement with an economic bloc (EU–Colombia and Peru, with 20 policy areas), then Argentina's GVC-related exports to Pacific Alliance countries would increase between 6 percent and 13 percent. The agreement would need to include three policy areas that are not in Mercosur— investment, movement of capital, and innovation policies—to achieve this boost.

Building on existing capabilities, some segments of the automotive industry emerge as providing good opportunities to connect domestic firms to global markets. Half (50 percent) of local production in the automotive industry is

BOX 1.7

Methodology for estimating the impact of deep integration on GVC-related trade

Gravity equations are derived from models that seek to explain or predict the relationship between a (dependent) variable (in this case, bilateral trade in parts and components) and a set of other (independent or explanatory) variables whose values can be estimated (in this case, elements of deep integration).

An augmented gravity equation is estimated for 93 countries, using data from 1990 to 2014, to investigate the effect of deep integration on GVC-related trade. This methodology has been used extensively by economists to test empirically the determinants of trade flows and to estimate the effects of preferential trade opening on trade flows. Estimation of the effects of free trade agreements (FTAs) on bilateral trade flows using a gravity equation is susceptible, however, to an endogeneity problem.

Endogeneity arises when an explanatory variable in an equation is correlated with the error term of the equation, and the error term is the unexplained deviation of sample data from their unobservable "true" value. Studies such as Baier and Bergstrand (2007) show that omitted variables and, to a lesser extent, simultaneity are the two most important sources of endogeneity bias caused by FTAs. The omitted variables problem of FTAs arises because the error term may retain the effect of some unobservable country-specific policy variables, which at the same time affect both trade and the probability of forming an FTA. If, for example, the formation of an FTA also induces reforms in trade-restrictive domestic regulation, the likelihood of an FTA is higher (since the expected gains from the FTA are higher), and the omission of the domestic regulation variable will bias the FTA

coefficient downward. A simultaneity problem can arise, for instance, when the governments of two countries that trade more than their "natural" levels of trade may be induced to form a FTA, as there is less probability of trade diversion. In this case, the FTA coefficients will be biased upward.

To account for this potential bias, the approach used by Baier and Bergstrand (2007) is followed here.[a] Specifically, we estimate a fixed-effect gravity regression:[b]

$$GVC_{ijt} = \beta_1 Depth_{ijt} + \beta_2 Depth_{ijt} * ARG + \delta_{ij} + \delta_{it} + \delta_{jt} + \varepsilon_{ijt},$$

where GVC_{ijt} is a measure of GVC-related trade between countries i and j. GVC-related trade is proxied by trade in parts and components.[c] $Depth_{ijt}$ is a measure of the depth of FTAs. A statistically significant and positive coefficient β_1 implies that signing a deeper agreement is associated with greater GVC-related trade. This variable is calculated as the number of enforceable provisions that are included in a certain agreement (normalized between 0 and 1).[d] $Depth_{ijt} * ARG$ is an interaction term between depth and a dummy variable equal to one if the exporting or importing country is Argentina. This variable captures the heterogeneous effects of deep FTAs for Argentina. A positive (negative) and significant coefficient implies that for the same level of depth, Argentina exported or imported relatively more (less) than the average country in the sample. The δs are a series of fixed effects: i for importer, j for exporter, and t for five-year periods from 1980 to 2014. Finally, ε_{ijt} is the error term.

a. As an additional robustness check for endogeneity, the regressions are estimated using an instrumental variables approach. In particular, the variable of interest—depth between country i and country j—is instrumented with the (weighted) average depth of all the agreements signed by i and j with any other country, excluding the agreement(s) they have in common.
b. To account for the presence of zeroes in trade flows, equation (1) is estimated using the Poisson pseudo-maximum likelihood (PPML) estimator proposed by Silva and Tenreyro (2006).
c. Parts and components are defined as BEC 21, 22, 42, and 53.
d. Other indices based on principal component analysis are used to calculate the depth of FTAs. See Osnago, Rocha, and Ruta (2015).

BOX 1.8

Tax benefits for the use of local auto parts in the automotive industry

In July 2016, the new Regime for the Development and Strengthening of the Argentine Auto Parts Sector (Régimen de Desarrollo y Fortalecimiento del Autopartismo Argentino, Law No. 27263) was introduced. The law gives automotive companies and road and agricultural machinery manufacturers tax benefits when they give preference to the use of local components, with the overall objective of strengthening the auto parts sector and fostering greater national integration.

The law grants an electronic tax credit that may be used by motor vehicle and auto parts producers to pay domestic taxes. The tax credit ranges from 4 percent to 15 percent, depending on the product and the amount of domestic content used in the assembly of each vehicle or part. Automobiles incorporating at least 30 percent domestic auto parts can access this benefit. In addition, companies are expected to present new projects or substantially modify the units they are producing to ensure that they are using new and exclusive car platforms (that is, platforms that are developed only in Argentina within Mercosur) and to maintain their staffing levels.

By some accounts, this legislation is seen as a short-term palliative measure for the auto parts industry, which mainly comprises domestic companies, while longer-term strategic initiatives to address the sector's competitiveness are developed and implemented.

exported, with Brazil accounting for 80 percent of exports. While exports of car parts and accessories are oriented mostly toward Mercosur and other neighboring countries like Chile, foreign firms in Argentina also export final vehicles—trucks—to Australia, the EU, Mexico, and South Africa. Argentina could further attract FDI in these segments, while strengthening linkages with local suppliers to reorient the production structure and integrate into GVCs and RVCs.

The recent design of incentives in this sector has not been conducive to attracting strategic FDI and fostering global integration, however. Rather than allowing firms to source inputs from the most efficient producers and supporting local producers in increasing their productivity, the tax incentives distort the market by offering tax benefits for the preferential use of local components (box 1.8).

Supporting domestic linkages by tackling market failures and building capacities can help Argentina take better advantage of FDI and add more value to exports. Argentina's automotive industry, for example, has significant production capacity in the form of 11 international car manufacturers and over 600 auto parts firms. Most of the auto parts firms are small and produce standardized, less sophisticated auto parts, which may be destined for car manufacturers or for the aftermarket. Programs to support their linkages with larger firms would need to improve the timeliness, quality, and quantity of their production, given the industry's demanding standards and just-in-time system of production. Appropriate measures would include behavioral incentives for technical training, skill building, and attainment of international certifications. In addition, an online database of national suppliers could help overcome imperfections in information markets. If larger firms had online access to high-quality information on local auto parts companies, this would increase industry-wide efficiency by bringing down the costs associated with identifying adequate and reliable

BOX 1.9

Potential deeper linkages in the automotive industry

The strategic importance of the automotive industry in Argentina has motivated consecutive governments to pay special attention throughout its 60-year history in the country. Today's industry has significant production capacity, which was stimulated gradually by protectionist measures coupled with an attractive domestic market, public policies aimed at supporting the growth and development of local firms, early development of technical know-how, and availability of a large supply of skilled workers.

The auto parts sector comprises a number of companies that directly supply auto companies (Tier 1 companies), involving engineering processes and often global production. These are typically multinational subsidiaries or large companies that work closely with auto companies through confidentiality agreements and on the basis of detailed specifications and design. A second group of companies (Tier 2) supplies specialized auto parts and components to Tier 1 firms. A third group of companies (Tier 3) produces standardized, less sophisticated auto parts that may be destined for car manufacturers or for the aftermarket. There are around 200 Tier 1 and Tier 2 firms, and about 450 Tier 3 companies. Tier 3 companies are mostly SMEs.

While there are existing linkages between Tier 1 and automakers, and between Tier 1 and Tier 2 firms, there is room to promote adequate and stronger linkages between Tier 3 companies and larger firms. To do so, many Tier 3 companies will need to be brought up to higher standards—in terms of timeliness, quality, and quantity of production—given the industry's demanding standards and just-in-time system of production. The design of behavioral incentives aimed at promoting technical training, skill building, and attainment of international certifications could help bring Tier 3 companies up to the required standards.

In addition, an online database of national suppliers is an important tool for promoting linkages. Global experience has shown that imperfections in information markets often lead to suboptimal levels of linkages in an economy. Providing online access to high-quality information on local auto parts companies would not only help overcome this market failure, but it would also bring down the costs associated with identifying adequate and reliable local suppliers for automakers and Tier 1 firms. To be useful, the database would need to be designed carefully to ensure that it is easy to access and search, and that it includes prescreened, up-to-date information, including contact details, a description of the company's products, production capabilities, technical specifications, and quality standards and certifications. Importantly, the database would need to be updated periodically.

In addition, systematically organizing matchmaking events to bring together Tier 3 firms and local and foreign buyers—and following up on such events to obtain feedback and measure results—would help bridge information asymmetries. The biennial Automechanika Buenos Aires fair, which includes side events where local auto parts companies meet foreign buyers and local automakers, is a step in the right direction.

local suppliers. Matchmaking events, such as the biennial Automechanika Buenos Aires fair, can mitigate information asymmetries between Tier 3 firms and local and foreign buyers (box 1.9). A more detailed GVC analysis could provide further insights into strategic areas and segments in which to upgrade.

The second significant change in the global trade landscape is in trade in services. Over the last two decades, the four modes of trade services have expanded rapidly: shipping services, such as software, from one country to another; consumers purchasing services abroad (tourists); service providers establishing a commercial presence in the consumer's country; and service providers (a mining engineer, for example) traveling to the consumer's country. Today, the service trade accounts for over a quarter of global trade flows. Developing countries' share of world service exports has grown from 3 percent in 1970 to 20 percent in 2014.[65]

While opening the economy could be detrimental to certain protected sectors in Argentina, it would also provide opportunities to expand other activities, such as services. The CGE simulations show that easing barriers to trade in Argentina would improve the overall economy, with positive impacts on trade and GDP in the medium and long terms. Different activities would face different effects, however. As illustrated in figure 1.23, manufacturing as a whole would suffer the largest contraction in real output, relative to baseline projections, in almost all integration scenarios modeled (despite the heterogeneity across sectors within manufacturing). Real output of overall service activities, on the other hand, would grow, relative to baseline projections, in all regional integration scenarios.

Trade in services is determined by a country's connectivity, capacity, and regulatory framework; in Argentina, therefore, investment, trade, and competition reforms are essential. First, high-quality and efficient electronics and information and communications technology (ICT) infrastructure (telecommunications networks, for example) are critical for effective communication, dissemination, and processing of information. Second, the availability of skilled labor is particularly essential for knowledge-based service (KBS) exports, which require education and skills development. Finally, the quality of a country's institutions has been shown to have a strong influence on trade in services. Corruption and complex export procedures can stifle trade in services. Case studies of developing countries that have succeeded in exporting services shows that reducing barriers to trade and fostering investment contribute to the importance of the service sector and enhance a country's export potential.[66]

The KBS sector represents a fruitful opportunity for Argentina, not only as a source of export revenues but also as an input to manufacturing exports and competitiveness.[67] Despite a decline in overall trade in services as a proportion of GDP since 2007 (figure 1.6), Argentina maintained a positive trade balance in central KBS activities. These included "other business services" (sectors such as legal services, accounting and tax consulting services, business consultancy, advertising, and technical services) and "telecommunications, computer, and information services" (table 1.9). KBS activities have also contributed to the

TABLE 1.9 **Service trade balance in value, Argentina**

SERVICE LABEL	2012 (US$, THOUSANDS)	2016 (US$, THOUSANDS)
Other business services	2,348,000	1,370,070
Telecommunications, computer, and information services	864,080	547,502
Construction	(11,090)	(2,117)
Government goods and services n.i.e.	(223,580)	(36,103)
Financial services	(72,181)	(267,078)
Personal, cultural, and recreational services	(141,355)	(283,161)
Insurance and pension services	(340,733)	(317,443)
Charges for the use of intellectual property n.i.e.	(1,970,532)	(1,950,244)
Transport	(2,415,990)	(2,446,178)
Travel	(1,015,080)	(3,597,592)
All services	(2,978,500)	(6,982,344)

Source: Data from International Trade Centre's Trade in Services Statistics database (http://www
.intracen.org/itc/market-info-tools/trade-statistics/).
Note: Figures in parentheses are negative values. n.i.e. = not included elsewhere.

FIGURE 1.25

Services' share of value added in total gross exports, Argentina, 2011

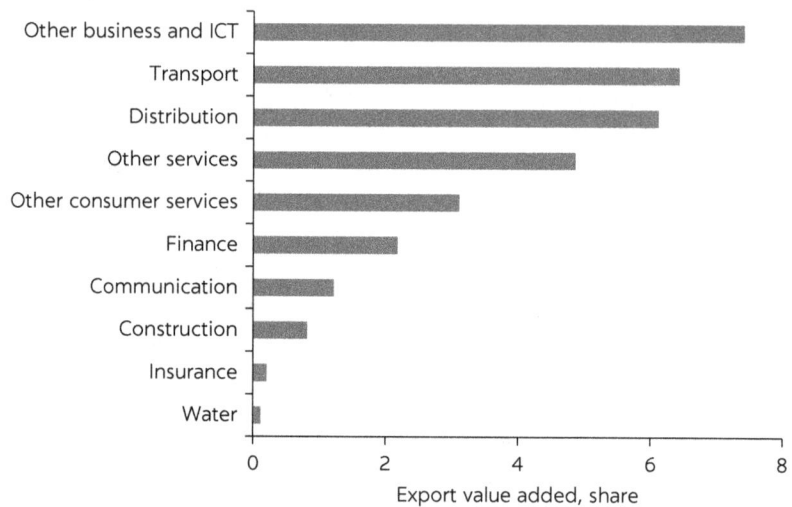

Source: Data from World Bank's Export Value Added database (https://wits.worldbank.org/analyticaldata/evad/Country/ARG /Year/2011/Summary).

value added embodied in total gross exports from Argentina.[68] The "other business services and ICT" sector generates the most export value added. It is responsible for 7.4 percent of total export value added (figure 1.25), more than services that have traditionally been considered major catalysts for economic activity (such as transport and distribution).

The positive performance of KBS to date in Argentina reflects a combination of comparative advantages and investment incentives. The widespread use of investment incentives (both nationally and locally), combined with major comparative advantages (such as human capital and relatively widespread English proficiency) has promoted the development of several clusters across the country.[69] Argentina ranks higher on the United Nations Development Programme's Human Development Index than competitors such as Brazil, Costa Rica, and Mexico (figure 1.26). Based on the Knowledge Economy Index, Argentina can compete with Brazil and Mexico in the knowledge economy (figure 1.27). In fact, because KBS activities typically do not require high capital investments, several smaller cities and towns have been promoting the development of KBS to create jobs and diversify exports.[70] As a result of these widespread policies, there are more than 28 KBS clusters or poles in Argentina, mostly in software and information technology (IT) services, with over 1,000 companies employing over 37,000 workers. Many of the world's leading IT companies (IBM, HP, Accenture, Intel, Motorola, SAP, Google, and Tata, to name a few) are established in Argentina. Many local companies (for example, Fuego and Core Security Technologies) export highly innovative software globally. Moreover, a variety of companies (Globant, ASSA, and Prominente, among others) provide services to the global market.[71]

To continue attracting FDI into the sector, however, it is crucial that Argentina exploit potential synergies among the main institutional actors. When it comes to how well a country uses ICT to boost competitiveness and well-being, Argentina falls behind its competitors, despite having improved in the

FIGURE 1.26

Human Development Index, 2015

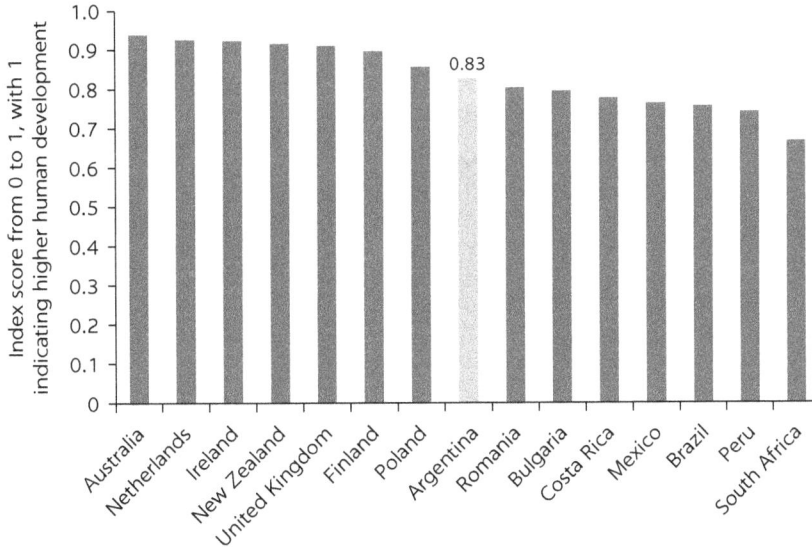

Source: Data from UNDP Human Development Indicator dataset (http://hdr.undp.org /en/composite/HDI).

FIGURE 1.27

Knowledge Economy Index, 2012

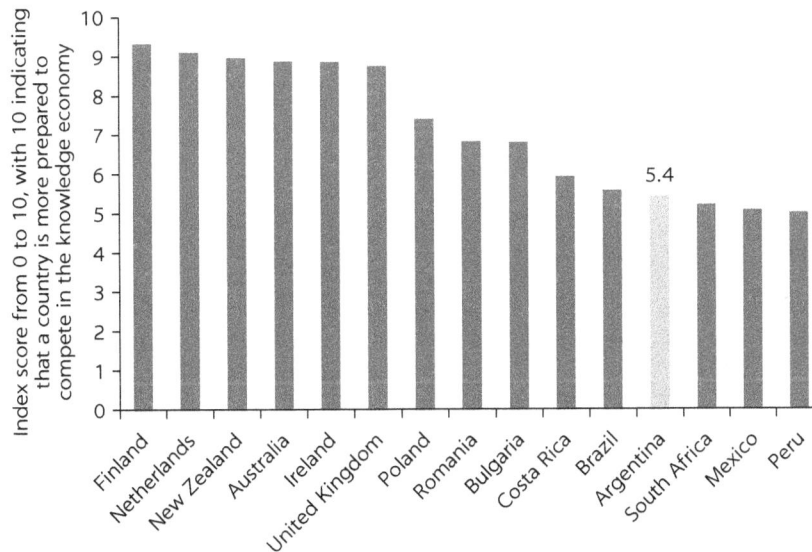

Source: Data from World Bank's Knowledge Economy Index dataset (https://knoema .com/WBKEI2013/knowledge-economy-index-world-bank-2012).

networked readiness index ranking from 100th to 91st out of 143 countries between 2014 and 2015 (figure 1.28). Argentina could enhance its institutional environment to facilitate innovation, given existing weaknesses in the business and regulatory environment (figure 1.29). Strengthening the positive performance of the KBS sector will, therefore, require further coordination among the main institutional actors. They include the AAICI, the Undersecretariat for Technological and Productive Services (which hosts an Observatory of the Knowledge Economy), Argencon (an association of companies exporting KBS),

FIGURE 1.28

Networked Readiness Index, 2015

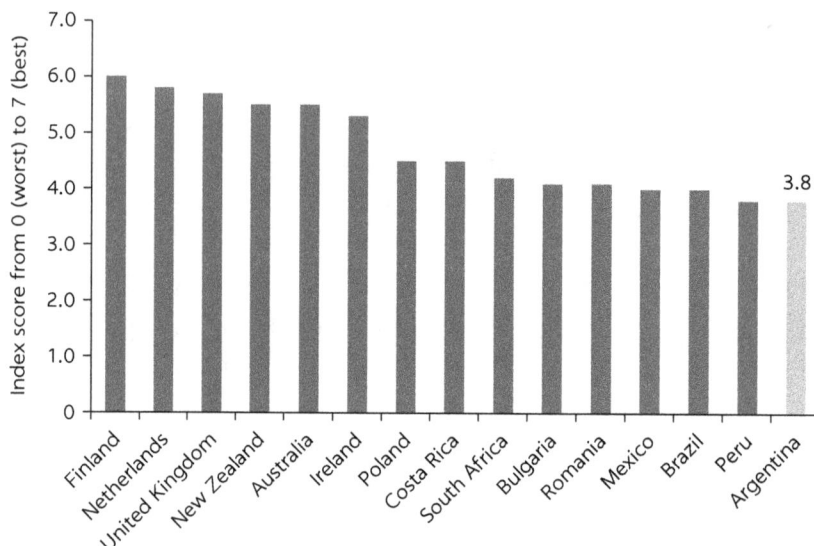

Source: Data from World Economic Forum's Networked Readiness Index dataset (http://reports.weforum.org/global-information-technology-report-2016/networked-readiness-index/dataset).

FIGURE 1.29

Global Innovation Index, 2017

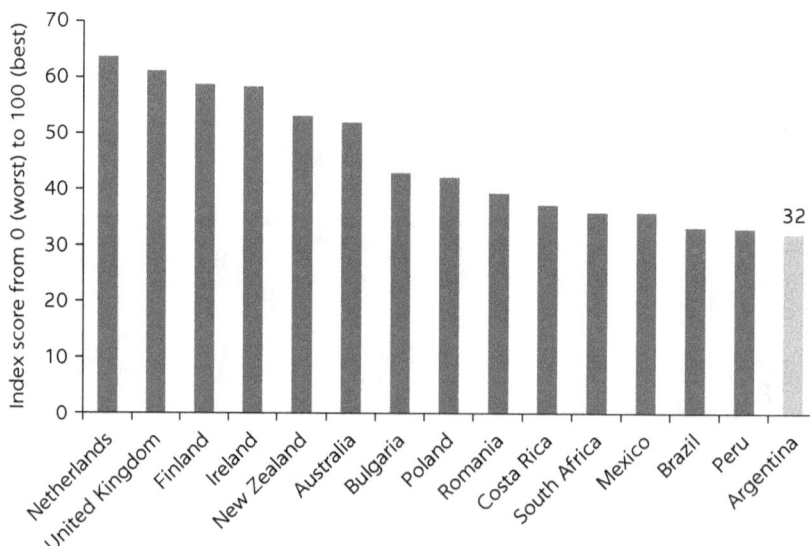

Source: Data from Global Innovation Index dataset (https://www.globalinnovationindex.org/analysis-indicator).

and other strong industry chambers, such as the Chamber of the Argentine Software Industry. The recently created "Red Federal"[72] might be a useful platform for attracting more FDI into the sectors while ensuring that investment incentives provided to KBS activities across the country are well coordinated, balanced, and properly monitored to avoid tax wars across provinces.

Third, strengthening e-commerce can provide an opportunity to spread the benefits of trade integration to SMEs. In principle, the advent of new ICT tools can facilitate cross-border e-commerce and participation in global markets for smaller and new entrants by lowering barriers to entrepreneurship and boosting their ability to reach a sufficient scale. The growth of retail e-commerce in

FIGURE 1.30

Retail e-commerce sales, Argentina vs. selected peers, 2010–15

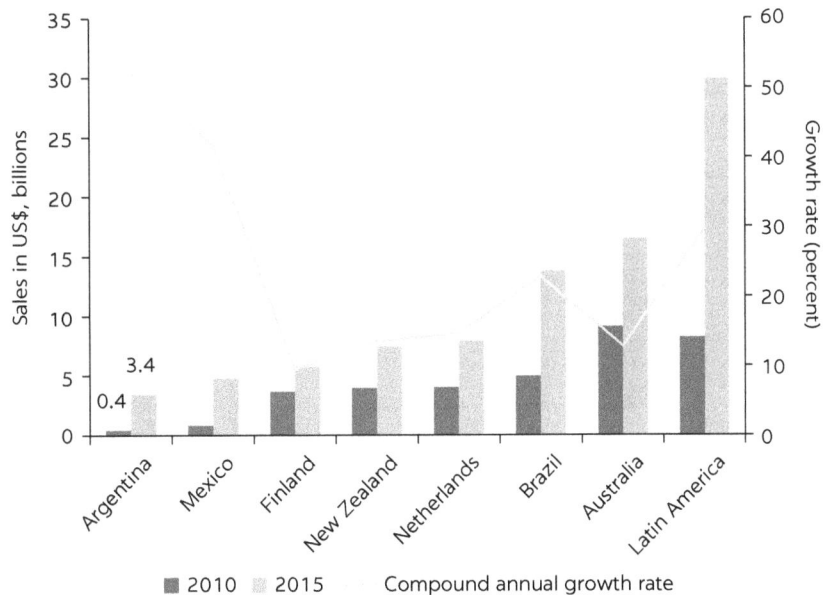

Source: Data from eMarketer dataset.

Argentina has been impressive over the past decade; the 2010–15 compound average growth rate of retail e-commerce sales was 52 percent, well above selected LAC peers and even the LAC average (figure 1.30). However, Argentina's share of worldwide retail e-commerce was well below that of its peers in 2015, at 0.2 percent as compared to 1 percent for Brazil, 0.3 percent for Mexico, 1.9 percent for the LAC region, and 1.1 percent for Australia.[73] This discrepancy suggests that Argentina has untapped potential in e-commerce.

Reinforcing procompetition regulation in the telecommunications sector, enhancing trade facilitation, and streamlining specific e-trade laws and regulations could provide a substantial boost. In practice, Argentina could lose many potential gains if the right conditions for SMEs are not in place. In this regard, Argentina lags behind its peers in infrastructure and the quality of Internet services. As discussed in chapter 4, this lag results, in great part, from gaps in the telecommunications sector regulatory regime. In addition, Argentina lags in e-commerce skills development, measured using a qualitative indicator of business-to-business use of ICT as a proxy (figure 1.31). On the other hand, Argentina has laws and regulations to promote e-commerce, particularly regarding electronic transactions and signatures, privacy and data protection, consumer protection for online purchases, and cybercrime prevention. Moreover, certain provisions in Argentina's rules on e-signatures and e-documents (including mandatory licensing of commerce service providers and mandatory e-government with free certification service) are exemplary.[74] Room for improvement remains, however. For example, Argentina still needs to update the legislation in several ways to reflect the evolution of e-commerce. One is granting validity to all types of e-signatures while recognizing digital signatures as the enhanced alternative. Another is removing the exemptions from coverage, allowing the use of e-signatures and e-documents in all cases. Still, Argentina also has consumer protection and intermediary liability laws and regulations. Argentina's Civil and Commercial Code of 2014 calls for contracts to be interpreted in the sense that is most favorable to the consumer, while online transactions are

FIGURE 1.31

Extent of business-to-business ICT use, Argentina vs. selected peers, 2015

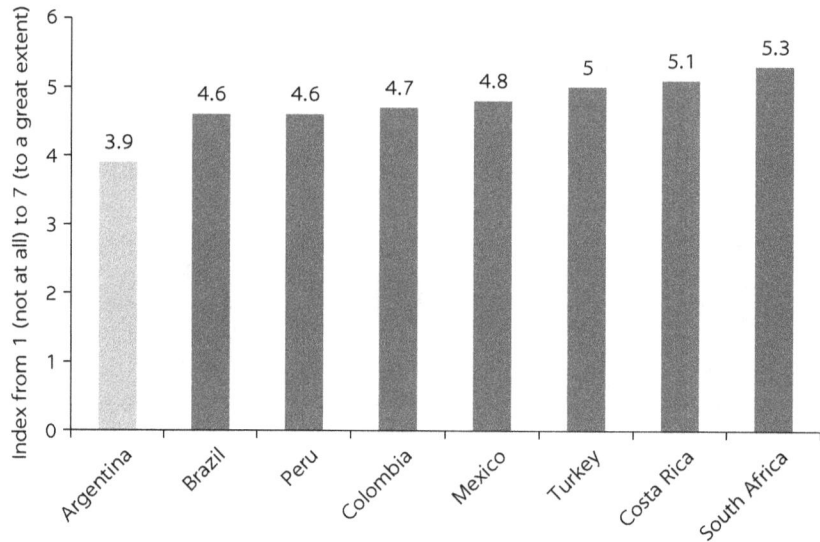

Source: Data from World Economic Forum's Networked Readiness Index dataset (http://reports.weforum.org/global-information-technology-report-2016/networked-readiness-index/dataset).

subject to the Consumer Protection Law, which requires fair and dignified treatment of consumers. Updates to this legislation could help strengthen the protection of Argentine electronic consumers, facilitating the growth of international e-commerce. One recommendation would be to enact legislation for consumer protection that is specific to electronic consumers; the law could include provisions for e-payments, dispute resolution mechanisms, and redress. In addition, trade facilitation—particularly cross-border procedures—need to be enhanced to facilitate e-commerce and trade more broadly.

WHAT MITIGATION MEASURES CAN ARGENTINA IMPLEMENT TO COUNTERVAIL THE TRANSITION EFFECTS OF MICROECONOMIC REFORMS IN SENSITIVE SECTORS?

Microeconomic reforms and the associated changes in relative prices trigger a reallocation of production factors (within and between firms and sectors) that entails efficiency gains, but also adjustment costs. Underlying the process of integration into global markets is a reallocation and churning movement, through which productive resources are expected to move to more productive uses, also within and between firms and sectors, which is then expected to bring productivity growth. As part of this process, both firms and workers bear adjustment charges that are asymmetrical across sectors, regions, and worker types. Typically, low-skilled workers and firms in sensitive sectors, along with regions where the latter operate (especially if an industry is regionally concentrated), tend to bear the brunt of the adjustment costs.

Some segments of Argentina's manufacturing sector are susceptible to adjustment costs, as industries producing electronics, household appliances, automobiles, and textiles will have to compete with production coming from countries that enjoy comparative advantages. As discussed above, the analysis in this report suggests that employment losses are most likely to occur in sugar, metal products, footwear, auto parts, and other manufacturing sectors, while employment gains can be expected in meat, other agriculture and food, and services. Factors such as wage levels and logistics costs play a role in how susceptible industries will be international competition. In the textile industry, for example, low-income countries like Cambodia and Haiti pay monthly wages of US$115, on average, whereas an Argentine worker receives US$1,300 for the same job.[75] This wage differential may not be explained fully by productivity differences; Argentina's infrastructure currently lags in the region, and logistics costs are high (see chapter 4). According to data from the Argentine Chamber of Commerce and Services, the total number of occupied workers in the private sector in sensitive sectors such as automobiles, home appliances, and textiles is close to 350,000, or 1.7 percent of Argentina's total labor force. These industries are concentrated mainly in Buenos Aires and the central region, particularly in Córdoba and Santa Fe.

Policymakers in Argentina can take early and comprehensive action to ensure that policy shocks lead to more widespread gains for the country. International experience shows that most countries that have gone through a structural reform process have resorted to adjustment or compensatory programs, along with a welfare system that served as a safety net. The design and implementation of each mitigation measure is specific to each country and depends on different variables, such as the country's fiscal situation and political pressures. Countries listed in table 1.10 used various types of adjustment or compensatory programs, such as retraining to facilitate reallocation in the labor market, early retirement and entrepreneurial programs, compensatory measures for affected firms, and incentives for lagging regions.

Australia designed structural adjustment programs for each industry, especially the sensitive ones. Analysis of government policy documents found 135 structural adjustment programs between 2000 and 2012.[76] The nature of these programs is diverse: industry restructuring (especially in primary industries), enterprise assistance, labor market reforms, and investment attraction strategies. Australia determined the programs' objectives, specific restructuring

TABLE 1.10 Compensatory measures applied in selected country experiences

GENERAL MECHANISM	BENEFICIARIES	AUSTRALIA (1983)	POLAND (1989)	SWEDEN (1991)	MEXICO (1993)
Unemployment compensation	The unemployed	✓	✓	✓	✓
Subsidies		✓	✓	✓	✓
Technical assistance/training		✓	✓	✓	✓
Social initiatives		✓			
Support for entrepreneurship		✓	✓	✓	
Quotas on number of dismissals			✓		
SPECIAL MECHANISMS	**BENEFICIARIES**				
Direct compensation	Firms and workers affected by structural adjustment measures	✓	✓	✓	✓
PROCAMPO (cash transfers)	Farmers affected by NAFTA				✓
Regional support programs	Disadvantaged regions	✓	✓	✓	✓

Deregulation of the dairy industry and compensation measures in Australia, 2001

Australia established the Dairy Adjustment Authority to manage the implementation of adjustment programs. The authority offered three types of assistance:

- The Dairy Structural Adjustment Program provided financial support to all herders who were in the industry on September 28, 1999. This was the largest of the aid programs, granting US$1.6 billion in assistance over eight years.
- As an alternative to the Dairy Structural Adjustment Program, the Dairy Exit Program granted up to US$45,000, tax-free (subject to an asset assessment), to farmers who were leaving the industry. (Australia designed this program for farmers who believed that this alternative would better compensate their decision to exit the market.)
- Dairy Regional Assistance provided funding for diversification to communities previously dependent on the dairy industry.

incentives, duration, and government budget according to the industry (box 1.10). These programs have not targeted a single policy objective but have instead sought to secure employment for displaced workers or business owners, support industries in their transformations, compensate property owners for the loss of rights or other economic opportunities, and generate new economic opportunities in communities affected by change. A primary goal of industry restructuring programs has been—and remains—to help industries adjust to new economic conditions to ensure their long-term viability. Many programs introduced since 2000 have sought to do this by helping nonviable enterprises exit the industry.

There is mixed evidence regarding the effectiveness of adjustment programs directed toward firms and regions, which highlights the importance of ensuring well-tailored policy design if one of these approaches is to be implemented. In the case of firms, individual support measures could distort the level playing field or violate competitive neutrality principles that prevent firms from attaining undue competitive advantages vis-à-vis their competitors so that the most efficient firms succeed in the market. In the case of support for regions, there is a risk of misdirecting public policy efforts and resources in trying to promote industries in places where the location or resource endowments may not yield competitive production or services, rather than letting each region find its vocation.

The recent literature suggests focusing on protecting workers, not jobs. Programs to assist workers can take the form of active labor market adjustment policies, such as training and acquisition of new skills, job search assistance, and subsidized employment through short-term contracts for displaced workers. Such programs can also take the form of passive labor market policies, such as direct compensation to workers, unemployment benefits, or insurance.[77] It is important to strike the right balance between active and passive labor market programs, since they are complementary to each other and each has its drawbacks. Passive programs support the economic well-being of laid-off workers and help reduce political pressures, but they generate fiscal pressures. Active programs boost incentives to seek new jobs, but a moral hazard problem remains if these training and job search programs are not temporally limited. As stated by IMF, WBG, and WTO (2017), the balance between the use of active and passive labor market programs will ultimately depend on a country's labor market institutions and rigidities. Social protection policies serve as complementary measures to curtail adjustment costs. These typically comprise health insurance, severance payments, and general income support. Among the comparator countries, and according to OECD data, Finland has the most expansive coverage of labor market policies; in 2015, the Finnish government spent 2.94 percent of GDP on (active and passive) labor market policies (figure 1.32).[78] Mexico lies at

FIGURE 1.32

Public expenditure on labor programs in OECD countries, 2015

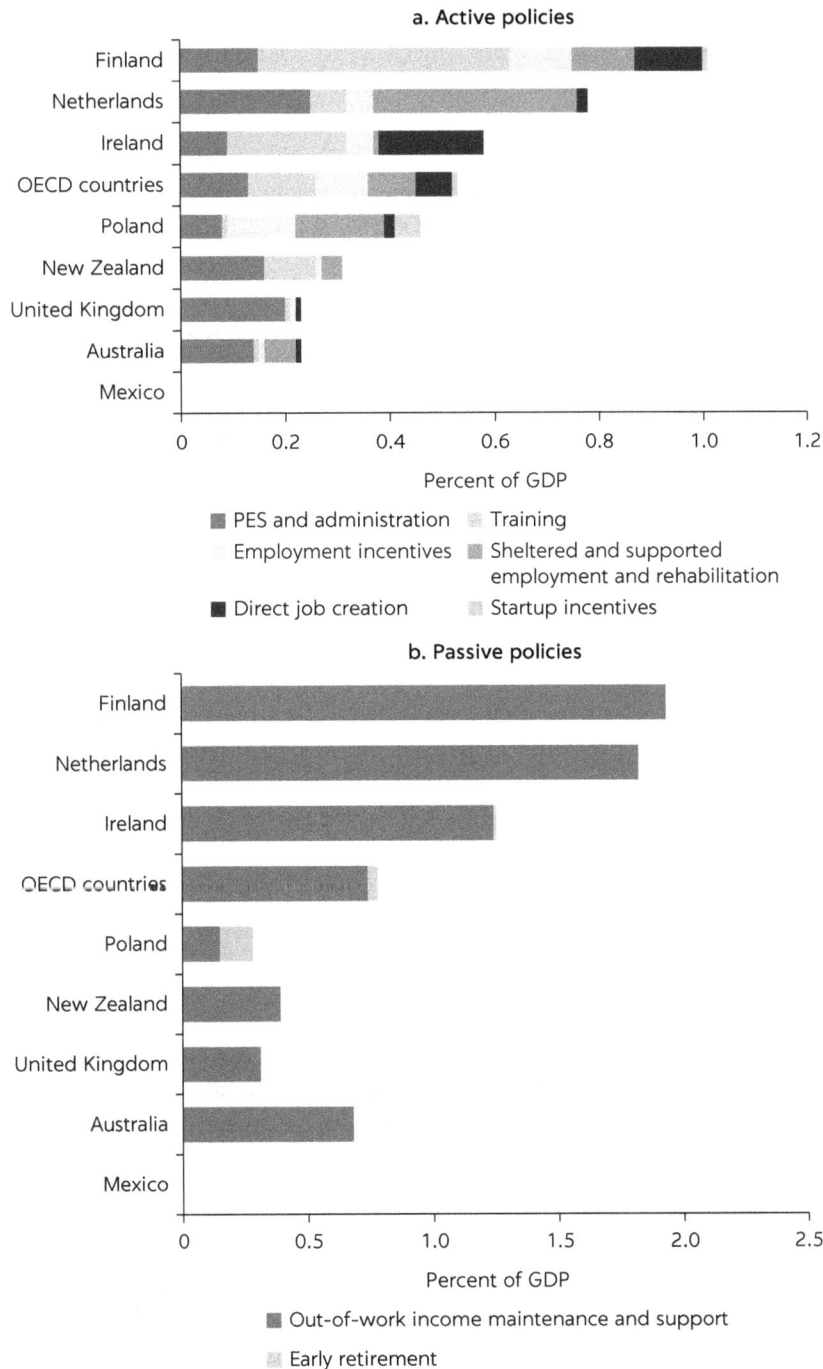

a. Active policies

b. Passive policies

Source: Data from OECD Labor Market Policies and Institutions database (http://www.oecd.org/els/emp/employmentdatabase-labourmarketpoliciesandinstitutions.htm).
Note: Figures for the United Kingdom are for 2011.

the opposite end of the spectrum, having spent only 0.01 percent of GDP for the same purpose during the same period.

Well-targeted and well-designed labor adjustment assistance programs can achieve results even with limited resources. Despite reduced spending on labor market programs overall, Mexico has one of the most successful programs. Mexico established its Farmers Direct Support Program (Programa de Apoyos Directos al Campo, or PROCAMPO) in 1993–94 to compensate crop producers who were expected to see prices decline after the initiation of the North American Free Trade Agreement (NAFTA) with the United States and Canada. The program provided per-hectare cash transfers to farmers who had land dedicated to staple production before NAFTA. PROCAMPO has been in place for over 15 years and is now the largest agricultural program in Mexico. Although it has changed over time, it continues to provide a subsidy per hectare of land cultivated to all farmers who subscribed initially. Cord and Wodon (2001) found that PROCAMPO had a positive effect on poverty reduction and a multiplier effect on household income: one peso in PROCAMPO cash transfers resulted in a two-peso increase in household income.[79]

Argentina has recently put in place adjustment programs to help domestic workers and companies become more competitive. The programs encompass incentives to both workers and companies. Argentina launched the Programa de Transformación Productiva (Productive Transformation Program) at the end of 2016. This adjustment program is designed to help companies enhance their competitiveness through mechanisms that facilitate improving productive processes; implementing jumps in scale or technology; developing new products; and reorienting production toward more competitive and dynamic activities that demand long-term, high-quality employment. Within three months of the launch of this program, about 20 firms had presented expansion or conversion projects, with the potential to add up to 1,000 more workers (box 1.11). The government has also launched the Programa "111 mil, aprende a programar," an initiative that seeks to train "100,000 programmers, 10,000 professionals, and 1,000 technological entrepreneurs" to meet the demand of companies in the KBS sector.

Argentina's Programa de Transformación Productiva

Objective

Business growth in existing and new markets, along with job creation.

Benefits

For workers: capacity building for employed workers who want to perform new tasks and for unemployed workers who want to re-enter the labor market. The latter receive extended unemployment insurance (up to six months at up to 50 percent of their most recent salaries, guaranteeing at least the minimum living wage), integral family assistance, and state facilitation of their reintegration into companies that are part of the program.

- For firms that identify opportunities for productive transformation: financial and technical assistance, including a guarantee fund with the aim of promoting innovation to

continued

Box 1.11, *continued*

improve production processes and business models. Specifically, companies can receive loans of up to US$140 million, with rate bonuses up to 6 percentage points, or access to guarantees.

- For "dynamic" firms with feasible, sustainable investment projects and job demand: employment subsidies for hiring workers seeking to re-enter the labor market through the program and assistance with expanding their productive capacity. Specifically, for each worker hired under the program, the company can receive credits of US$500,000 to US$140 million, with a bonus of up to 5 percentage points or access to

guarantee funds. The company also benefits from lower labor costs.

Eligibility

- Companies of any size, located in Argentina, that are part of any activity or productive sector, except public services, mining, fishing, and agriculture. Mutual associations and cooperatives are not eligible.

Requirement

- Presenting a project for productive transformation or a project to implement short-, medium- or long-term investment that proves to be feasible and sustainable and demands labor.

Targeted trade-specific programs can complement labor adjustment assistance programs and help reduce opposition to trade openness, but the effectiveness of these programs has been mixed, and their coverage and size tend to be small. The most prominent examples of such programs are the United States' Trade Adjustment Assistance (TAA) program[80] and the EU European Globalization Adjustment Fund. The TAA and the EU fund had budgets of US$800 million (2015) and €115 million (2014), respectively. So far, the effectiveness of the TAA program has been limited. On the one hand, as stated by the IMF, WBG, and WTO (2017), a comprehensive evaluation of the TAA found that the training obtained by workers did not improve their earning and employment outcomes (D'Amico, et al. 2007). On the other hand, others found evidence that the training component did have a positive effect (Park 2012) (Rosen, 2008), although smaller in terms of wage insurance, since take-up rates for the insurance were low. Additional findings suggest that low take-up rates could partially be linked to lack of knowledge about the program (D'Amico, et al. 2007). Other relevant adjustment programs include the EU's Common Agricultural Policy and the Austrian Steel Foundation programs. They include direct compensation (such as direct payments to EU farmers) and unemployment insurance and wage subsidies (as in the TAA).

As a complement to implementing programs, understanding frictions (coming from different sectors, markets, and society) and tailoring policies to tackle them is essential to accelerating adjustment and maximizing the gains from trade. Many obstacles can impede workers from switching firms, sectors, or regions. These frictions can vary, from skill mismatches to job search and travel costs, social barriers, housing policies, job protection regulations, and lack of capital mobility. In the case of Argentina, possible frictions include the fact that it is a federal country, since this implies that each region can have different policies, which could potentially deter interstate mobility; the geographical extension of the country, which increases travel costs; and rigid labor systems that complicate the reallocation of resources. Artuc et al. (2013) and

Dix-Carneiro (2014) found that adjustment frictions in advanced economies can reduce the gains from trade by up to 30 percent (IMF, WBG, and WTO 2017). Evidence from Mexico and Brazil support these findings. Kambourov (2009) finds that a lack of flexibility in Mexico's labor market slowed the reallocation of labor in response to trade reform, such that the benefits of the reform were as much as 30 percent less than what could have been achieved under a more flexible labor market. Likewise, Dix-Carneiro (2014) finds that the reallocation in the labor market following trade liberalization in Brazil would accelerate from 14 years to 4 years if capital were completely mobile. Credit policies can facilitate the overall adjustment process. For workers, a well-functioning mortgage market and easy access to credit to help finance education, self-employment, or startups could ease adjustment.[81]

Finally, macroeconomic stabilization policies can help ease the adjustment process. Macroeconomic stabilization policies should complement active labor market policies, since displacement costs are known to be higher during periods of growth slowdown (Davis and von Watcher 2011).

NOTES

1. The bill was already approved in the Chamber of Deputies in November 2017 and, as of this writing, was under discussion in the Senate.
2. World Bank (2015) showed that total factor productivity growth in Argentina averaged 0.4 percent per year from 1961 to 2014, below the average experienced by comparator countries in Latin America and the Caribbean (LAC), such as Brazil (0.42 percent) and Chile (0.86 percent), as well as Asian economies, such as Hong Kong (1.73 percent), Malaysia (1.10 percent), Singapore (1.99 percent), and South Korea (2.38 percent).
3. Economy-wide, productivity increases as resources move from lower-productivity sectors to higher-productivity sectors (the so-called structural transformation process). Within a sector, productivity increases when (a) firms become more efficient at using resources (within-firm efficiency gains), (b) firms that are more efficient gain market share at the expense of laggards (between-firm efficiency gains), and (c) new and more productive firms enter the market while obsolete ones cease their activities (entry and exit gains).
4. See Altomonte et al. (2013) for an analysis of the patterns of interaction among firm-level internationalization, innovation, and productivity across seven European countries (Austria, France, Germany, Hungary, Italy, Spain, and the United Kingdom).
5. Argentina's import and export values may be underestimated, because reportedly, some of the trade flows became informal during the Kirchner era.
6. Trade in intermediate goods contributed more than trade in final goods did to the growth of total manufacturing trade in 2001–2008 and 2009–14 (World Bank et al. 2017).
7. More recent data points (after 2011) are not available from the OECD TiVA dataset.
8. It is likely that the good performance of Bulgaria, Poland, and Romania is linked to their proximity to a large GVC market, namely the European Union. Similarly, Mexico is relatively close to the United States, a market for automotive GVCs.
9. From the 1950s on, the number of active FTAs increased continuously to almost 70 in 1990. Thereafter, FTA activity accelerated noticeably, with the number of FTAs more than doubling over the next five years and more than quadrupling until 2010 to reach close to 300 FTAs in force as of this writing.
10. This is based on a World Bank dataset on the content of preferential trade agreements (https://data.worldbank.org/data-catalog/deep-trade-agreements), which includes the set of agreements that have been notified to the WTO. In addition to Mercosur, Argentina has in place an agreement with Israel, in force since 2010, that has not been notified to the WTO. Also not counted are partial scope and Economic Complementation Agreements (ACEs). Argentina is a member of five partial scope agreements: Global System of Trade Preferences among Developing Countries, Latin American Integration Association (LAIA), Protocol on Trade Negotiations, MERCOSUR–India, and Mercosur–SACU. A partial scope agreement is not defined or referred to in the WTO agreement, such that the agreement

covers only certain products. Partial scope agreements are notified under paragraph 4(a) of the Enabling Clause (WTO 2017). Argentina has also signed a series of bilateral ACEs with countries such as Chile, Colombia, and Peru. These agreements fall within the legal framework of LAIA and point to a greater opening compared to partial scope agreements.

11. The ECI was originally elaborated in Hidalgo and Hausmann (2009) and assesses the overall complexity of the export basket. The ECI is based on export data and, in part, captures export complexity.

12. In 2016, Argentina's ECI was −0.882 (68th in the ranking)

13. The FDI complexity index is a weighted average of the product complexity index associated with industries where there is FDI activity, with the weights being the share of FDI in the sector over total FDI in tradable industries received in Argentina. Just as with ECI, the FDI complexity index is standardized, so that a value of 0 corresponds with the global average for the index.

14. The OECD-WBG PMR data are part of the WBG's Markets and Competition Policy Database. Each area addressed within the PMR methodology sheds light on specific restrictions of the regulatory framework, both economy-wide and in key sectors of the economy, on 12 topics: electricity; gas; telecommunications; post; transport; water; retail distribution; professional services; other sectors; administrative requirements for business startups; treatment of foreign parties; and other, such as governance of publicly controlled enterprises or antitrust exclusions and exemptions.

15. The program was extended to 151 products in addition to the 325 already in the program. See https://www.elsol.com.ar/extendieron-el-programa-precios-cuidados.html. In January 2018, 50 more products were included under this program. https://www.clarin.com/economia/precios-cuidados-productos-incluidos-mayo_0_Sky6i0xEM.html.

16. See Argent and Begazo Gomez (2015) and Licetti et al. (2017) for a comprehensive discussion.

17. This figure includes the summary categories of fruits and vegetables, while only some of those products have been included in the regressions. Discounting those two aggregate categories, the analysis still covers 66 percent of the food consumption basket.

18. Countries outside Latin America, especially those in the OECD, are appropriate comparator countries in that they exhibit, arguably, a less distorted regulatory environment, on average, than developing economies.

19. "Numbeo" is an online database of user-contributed data on cost of living.

20. The Latin American comparator countries with available data include Belize, Bolivia, Brazil, Chile, Colombia, Costa Rica, Ecuador, Guatemala, Mexico, Panama, Peru, Uruguay, and Venezuela.

21. In this model, the cost to import does not have the expected effect on the level of prices, which may be due to the fact that the caveats in the methodology for this indicator are more accentuated for these four countries. However, the cost of import does not explain a significant share of the variance in prices, nor does it change the difference in price levels significantly.

22. In countries where the population is concentrated, most of the price information reported to Numbeo is likely to refer to the capital.

23. First, the previous regressions already control for differences in the average income level, measured in PPP. Second, the original unit prices in local currencies were converted into U.S. dollar values using the market exchange rate (which falls between the parallel market rate and the official rate), and therefore account for the exchange rate fluctuations affecting prices of traded goods. The parallel exchange rate (blue chip swap rate) was used in around 20 percent of the transactions.

24. The R-squared is less than half in some of the specifications, compared to the ones in table 1.3.

25. The values for the PPP conversion factor, GDP (local currency units per international $), are extrapolated from the 2011 International Comparison Program (ICP) benchmark estimates or imputed using a statistical model based on the 2011 ICP. This means that if food prices are higher in Argentina due to lack of competition along the value chain, then the ICP benchmark estimate itself would have been affected by this distortion.

26. See Rabinovich (2013) for more details.

27. See http://www.pregonagropecuario.com/cat.php?txt=8619.

28. The economic characteristics of the production process, the functioning of the supply chain, and the strategic behavior of firms can affect the relationship between market

concentration and price levels. Furthermore, prices are only one of the variables that firms decide on; they can also compete on price, quality, intangible value, customer service, and other features. When market rigidities impede a firm's ability to vary prices, the firm may compete by adjusting these nonprice variables. As a result, the level and behavior of prices do not necessarily indicate the intensity of competition, and it becomes necessary to look at market behavior.

29. See, for instance, Aghion et al. (2005) and Aghion, Braun, and Fedderke (2008).

30. See, for instance, World Bank (2013), World Bank (2014), and Iootty and Dauda (2018).

31. See Nickell (1966) for further details.

32. PCMs are measured as the difference between value added and salaries, as a proportion of sales. Results hold for various robustness checks: (1) using sectoral data from national accounts; (2) employing a different proxy for competition intensity; (3) using distinct estimation techniques, such as robust regression and quantile regression; and (4) employing different price deflators. Even in the case of an alternative specification that is less conservative and does not explain as much of the variance in PCMs, the same change would yield an additional 1.7 percent in annual productivity growth (specifications (3) and (4)). See Goodwin, Dauda, and Gramegna (2017) for further methodological discussion.

33. See Kitzmuller and Licetti (2012) for further discussion.

34. This relation has been demonstrated by Barone and Cingano (2011).

35. This is based on an ex ante simulation of potential impact on value added and associated GDP growth of service sector reforms that would reduce restrictive PMRs, using a sensitivity analysis with four alternative simulation methods (appendix E).

36. The tariffs for the 10 most protected sectors in 2015 were footwear (23 percent), furniture (20 percent), textiles and apparel (19 percent), wine (17 percent), sugar (14 percent), biofuels (14 percent), metal products (13 percent), computers (13 percent), machinery and equipment (11 percent), and home appliances (11 percent). Import tariffs for certain computer items were brought down to zero in March 2017.

37. This is done given current commitments in the context of Mercosur and the restrictions imposed by the use of national exceptions to CET.

38. In this scenario, a sector with a small number of lines with nonzero tariffs, such as footwear, could be fully liberalized (from an average tariff of 23 percent to 0 percent). For a large sector, such as textiles and apparel, however, the average tariff could be reduced from 19 percent to 7 percent at the most. Two other sectors are assumed to open only partially: metal products (from an average tariff of 13 percent to 2 percent) and machinery and equipment (from an average tariff of 11 percent to 5 percent). Overall, the following tariff reductions are assumed for each sector: footwear (from 23 percent to zero), furniture (20 percent to 0 percent), textiles and apparel (19 percent to 7 percent), wine (17 percent to 0 percent), sugar (14 percent to 0 percent), biofuels (14 percent to 0 percent), metal products (13 percent to 1.5 percent), computers (13 percent to 0 percent), machinery and equipment (11 percent to 5.1 percent), and home appliances (11 percent to 0 percent).

39. It is worth stressing that the hypothetical scenario of simultaneous tariff liberalization (of all high-tariff sectors) goes beyond what can be done while keeping the CET. In other words, this scenario would involve expanding the national exceptions or "leaving" the CET.

40. As highlighted in the executive summary, the elimination of DJAI and introduction of SIMI at the end of 2015 is considered to be a partial reform scenario, since nonautomatic import licenses still cover a share of trade in certain sectors. As of October 2016, about 1,600 tariff lines remained with import licenses not subject to automatic approval.

41. About 27 percent of tariff lines were above the international peak of 15 percent, and about 5 percent of lines were at the WTO bound of 35 percent.

42. The 10 most protected sectors in 2015 were footwear (23 percent), furniture (20 percent), textiles and apparel (19 percent), wine (17 percent), sugar (14 percent), biofuels (14 percent), metal products (13 percent), computers (13 percent), machinery and equipment (11 percent), and home appliances (11 percent).

43. As explained in box 1.6, the long-term baseline reflects a projection of the Argentine and global economies with current policies in place. Starting from 2015 as the base year, the baseline provides "business-as-usual" scenarios for every year through 2030. The impact of a counterfactual policy is assessed by looking at deviations from the baseline.

44. Simultaneous liberalization is not feasible due to CET commitments, suggesting the importance of a Mercosur-wide initiative.

45. As highlighted above, the introduction of the new regime (SIMI), to replace the DJAI, maintained about 1,400 tariff lines subject to nonautomatic licenses, with the remaining 8,600 tariff lines with automatic licenses subject to preregistration for monitoring purposes.

46. Export taxes remained for certain products, including soybeans, soybean products (soybean meals and oil), biodiesel, and scrap metals. This reform reduced to zero nearly 98 percent of tariff lines that had export taxes above zero. The vast majority were products facing an export tax of up to 5 percent. Indeed, a "blanket" export tax rate of 5 percent applied to about 93 percent of lines not subject to a different rate. For soybeans and soybean products, a gradual elimination of their export taxes is expected to take place, starting in 2018.

47. Removal of import tariffs and/or export taxes would have fiscal implications in terms of declining trade tax revenue relative to GDP. Cage and Gadenne (2016) analyze episodes of trade liberalization across 130 countries from 1792 to 2006 and find evidence that trade taxes have fallen by more than 3 percentage points of GDP, on average, and half of the countries that have experienced an episode of trade liberalization have not recovered the lost tax revenues five years after the start of the episode. In this regard, maintaining constant fiscal expenditure levels will depend on specific efforts to safeguard total tax revenue, particularly through a domestic tax reform that could broaden tax bases by purging exemptions, simplifying rate structures, and improving revenue administration.

48. The expansion of the soy sectors in this scenario is so large that output of wheat and corn would now be lower relative to the baseline projections to 2020. The rapid expansion of agriculture would, indeed, shift resources from other sectors of the economy, to the extent that most model sectors would produce at lower levels relative to the baseline; however, services—the largest sector in the model—would also expand.

49. The specific scenarios used here are hypothetical because negotiations as of this writing were ongoing and private.

50. In addition, NTMs are streamlined among Mercosur parties—resulting in a 15 percent reduction in the tariff equivalents for goods and services—and export taxes are eliminated among the parties.

51. Also, NTM tariff equivalents are reduced by 15 percent and export taxes are eliminated among Mercosur and EU countries.

52. With "Brexit" underway at this writing, a completed agreement may apply to a EU27 membership. The results with and without the United Kingdom are qualitatively similar, and both are presented for comparison.

53. Under the Mercosur–Pacific Alliance scenario, NTM tariff equivalents are reduced by 15 percent and export taxes are eliminated among the parties. Moreover, bilateral market access is assumed so that existing liberalization among partners remains. Existing tariff barriers with Pacific Alliance countries were lowered by previous bilateral or Mercosur agreements under the framework of the *Asociación Latinoamericana de Integración*, especially with respect to Chile and Peru. Most tariff liberalization under this scenario would be with respect to Mexico and, to a lesser extent, Colombia. Liberalization with the Pacific Alliance is assumed to take place both more quickly and more comprehensively than with the EU. No products are excluded from liberalization, and all tariffs are either removed or partially reduced for the most sensitive products.

54. This reflects a reduction in import barriers for beef in the EU and the elimination of export restraints in Argentina, which include export taxes on soybean products.

55. *Boletin Trimestral de Empleo Registrado* is a publication from Ministerio de Trabajo, Empleo y Seguridad Social, available at http://www.trabajo.gob.ar/left/estadisticas/oede/estadisticas_nacionales.asp.

56. The model does not keep track of the number of jobs by sector. To translate proportional changes in labor payments into employment changes, the model's results are combined with administrative data on formal employment in the private sector (based on the *Sistema Integrado Previsional Argentino*). This dataset provides detailed data by industry classification, but it represents only a partial sample of total employment, reflecting 6.5 million jobs in 2015. Nonetheless, these data permit us to obtain a relative scale of employment across sectors. The employment effects are thus best seen as relative, as they take into account the relative labor intensity in the sector, while the levels represent partial numbers only. With this caveat in mind, the notional gradation in the heat map reflects employment losses below 1,000 as relatively small, between 1,000 and 2,000 as relatively moderate, and above 2,000 as relatively large. These bands were defined to keep roughly one-third of cases in each category.

57. While all the sectors in the CGE model are included in the heat map, the different aggregations in the model and the employment statistics do not allow us to identify all the sectors separately. Several model sectors related to agriculture and food were combined. To the extent that there are different effects, say, between wheat and soybeans, the aggregation "other agriculture and food" in the table shows the net effect, which is an expansion and absorption of employment.

58. See Constantinescu, Mattoo, and Ruta (2015) for an analysis of the determinants of the decline of trade elasticity in the 2000s.

59. See Evenett and Fritz (2015) for further discussion on this topic.

60. More than 50 percent of agreements include deeper provisions in areas such as antidumping and countervailing measures, rules on competition, movement of capital, intellectual property rights (IPRs), and trade-related aspects of intellectual property rights (TRIPs). Moreover, technical barriers to trade, investment disciplines, and sanitary and phytosanitary measures are often included in FTAs.

61. According to the World Bank dataset on the content of preferential trade agreements (https://data.worldbank.org/data-catalog/deep-trade-agreements), which includes the set of agreements that have been notified to the WTO. In addition to Mercosur, Argentina has in place an agreement with Israel that has not been notified to the WTO and five partial scope agreements that are not defined or referred to in the WTO Agreement, as the WTO Agreement covers only certain products.

62. Mercosur covers all 14 WTO+ areas, which include disciplines related to market access, customs, standards, state trading enterprises, antidumping and countervailing measures, and trade-related investment and intellectual property, among others. In addition, it covers three WTO-X provisions: competition policy, movement of capital, and intellectual property rights.

63. For instance, the maximum depth of FTAs is 20 in Chile, 21 in Colombia and Mexico, and 30 in Peru. See Signoret, Rocha, and Molinuevo (2017) for further discussion and results.

64. GVC-related exports to Brazil and Paraguay would increase by US$43 million–$477 million and US$4 million–$46 million, respectively. Figures vary according to the shallowness of current enforceable provisions within Mercosur; the 1 percent effect (with a US$54 million variation) reflects an increase in depth from 17 to 20 provisions, while the 9 percent effect (with a US$480 million variation) reflects an increase in depth from 6 to 20 provisions.

65. The share of service exports increased from around 9 percent in 1970 to around 20 percent in 2014 (Choi et al. 2016).

66. See Gosawmi, Mattoo, and Saez (2012) for further discussion.

67. As defined by OECD (2017), KBS includes activities that make intensive use of high technology or require highly skilled labor to take advantage of technological innovations. KBS encompasses many activities, including accounting and legal services, audiovisual services, design, advertising, software and IT services, research and development, health care, and education. For analytical purposes, it comprises four sectors: (1) software and services; (2) business, professional, and technical services (which includes business process outsources, as well as engineering, architecture, design, research and development, and so on); (3) services related to intellectual property rights (licenses and royalties); and (4) audiovisual, media, and advertising services.

68. Both in direct value added (value added within the same sector—that is, not involving sectoral linkages) and inputs to other sectors.

69. Nationally, two main laws provide fiscal benefits to IT companies. First, Law No. 25.856 (2003), allows software development companies to receive tax reductions, loans, and other benefits available to other industrial activities. Second, the Software Promotion Law No. 25.922 (2004) created a 10-year special fiscal regime for the software and IT service sector and was extended until 2019 through Law 26.692 (2011). Under the Promotional Regime, companies that develop software or provide information technology services as their core activity can enjoy the following benefits: (1) tax stability for taxpayers registered with the system; (2) tax credits amounting to 70 percent of social security contributions paid for staff working on software development activities, which can be used to offset national tax liabilities (such as the value-added tax, or VAT); (3) a 60 percent reduction in the income tax burden for each fiscal year; and (4) exemption from VAT withholding or reverse withholding.

70. For example, Córdoba's Technology Cluster supports the development of clusters within the province to help young entrepreneurs grow their businesses without having to move to the capital city.

71. Please see Nahirñak (2016) for further details.
72. The AAICI recently created an initiative, the "Red Federal," to guarantee coordination in investment promotion and export promotion with subnational entities. The Red Federal aims to partner with the provinces, guarantee standardized services to investors and exporters, and collaborate with provinces in the promotion and facilitation of investment and exports. To date, memoranda of understanding have been signed with 15 provinces: Buenos Aires, Chaco, Ciudad de Buenos Aires, Córdoba, Corrientes, Jujuy, La Rioja, Mendoza, Misiones, Neuquén, Salta, San Juan, Santa Fe, Tierra del Fuego, and Tucumán.
73. According to data from eMarketer.
74. See Blythe (2011) for further discussion.
75. Cámara Argentina de Comercio y Servicios (2017).
76. See Beer (2014) for further discussion.
77. Empirical evidence provided by Hollweg et al.(2014) suggests that, when a trade shock hits a developing country, the costs associated with worker decisions are notably higher than those associated with employer decisions. That is, the mobility costs borne by workers far outweigh the adjustment costs borne by firms. This would, in principle, justify stronger protection of workers, but not necessarily of jobs or employers.
78. See OECD data on public spending on labor markets at https://data.oecd.org/socialexp/public-spending-on-labour-markets.htm.
79. Household income is defined here as the combined gross income of all the members of a household.
80. The TAA's current structure features four components of trade adjustment assistance, targeting workers, firms, farmers, and communities. Each cabinet-level department is tasked with a different sector of the overall TAA program. The program for workers is the largest and administered by the United States Department of Labor. The program for farmers is administered by the Department of Agriculture, and the firms and communities programs are administered by the Department of Commerce.
81. Credit to firms facing greater foreign competition could also help those firms reorient their business models and invest in new or different technology. Credit to potential exporter firms could facilitate entry and help harness the benefits from trade (Manova 2013). It is important to keep in mind, however, that policies for credit to firms must be designed and implemented in line with competitive neutrality principles in order to ensure a level playing field for firms competing in the market.

REFERENCES

Aghion, P., N. Bloom, R. Blundell, R. Griffith, and P. Howitt. 2005. "Competition and Innovation: An Inverted-U Relationship." *Quarterly Journal of Economics* 120 (2): 701–28.

Aghion, P., M. Braun, and J. Fedderke. 2008. "Competition and Productivity Growth in South Africa." *Economics of Transition* 16 (4), 741–68.

Altomonte, C., T. Aquilante, G. Békés, and G. Ottaviano. 2013. "Internationalization and Innovation of Firms: Evidence and Policy." *Economic Policy* 28 (76): 663–700.

Argent, J. T., and T. P. Begazo Gomez. 2015. "International Benchmarking of Merger Notification Thresholds." Unpublished memo.

Artuc, E., G. Bet, I. Brambilla, and G. Porto. 2013. "Trade Shocks and Factor Adjustment Frictions: Implications for Investment and Labor." Working paper no. 101. Department of Economics, Faculty of Economics and Sciences, Universidad Nacional de La Plata, Argentina.

Barone, G., and F. Cingano. 2011. "Service Regulation and Growth: Evidence from OECD Countries." *The Economic Journal* 121 (555), 931–57.

Beer, A. 2014. "Structural Adjustment Programmes and Regional Development in Australia." *Local Economy: The Journal of the Local Economy Policy Unit* 30 (1): 21–40.

Bernard, A., and B. Jensen. 1999. "Exceptional Exporter Performance: Cause, Effect or Both?" *Journal of International Economics* 47: 1–25.

Blythe, S. E. 2011. *E-Commerce Law Around the World: A Concise Handbook.* Bloomington, IN: Xlibris Corporation.

Brambilla, I., N. Depetris Chauvin, and G. Porto. 2016. "Examining the Export Wage Premium in Developing Countries." *Review of International Economics* 25: 447–75.

Cagé, J., and L. Gadenne. 2016. "Tax Revenues, Development, and the Fiscal Cost of Trade Liberalization, 1792–2006." Warwick Economics Research Paper Series (TWERPS) 1132, University of Warwick, Department of Economics.

Camara Argentina de Comercio y Servicios. 2017. "Informe CAC: Costo Argetnino Agosto de 2017." http://www.cac.com.ar/data/documentos/11_CAC%20-%20Informe%20Costo%20 Argentino%20-%20Agosto%202017.pdf.

Choi, S., D. Furceri, Y. Huang, and P. Loungani. 2016. "Aggregate Uncertainty and Sectoral Productivity Growth: The Role of Credit Constraints." IMF (International Monetary Fund) Working Paper 16/74. https://www.imf.org/en/Publications/WP/Issues/2016/12/31 /Aggregate-Uncertainty-and-Sectoral-Productivity-Growth-The-Role-of-Credit -Constraints-44189.

Constantinescu, C., A. Mattoo, and M. Ruta. 2015. "The Global Trade Slowdown: Cyclical or Structural?" International Monetary Fund, IMF Working Paper 15-6 (15/6). https://www .imf.org/external/pubs/ft/wp/2015/wp1506.pdf.

Cord, L., and Q. Wodon. 2001. "Do Agricultural Programs in Mexico Alleviate Poverty? Evidence from the Ejido Sector." *Cuadernos de Economía* 38 (114): 239–56.

D'Amico, R., K. Dunham, A. Goger, M. Mack, R. Kebede, J. Lacoe, and J. Salzman. 2007. *Initial Implementation of the 2002 TAA Reform Act: A Report Prepared as Part of the Evaluation of the Trade Adjustment Assistance Program.* Washington, DC: U.S. Department of Labor, Social Policy Research Associates.

Davis, S., and T. von Watcher. 2011. "Recessions and the Costs of Job Loss." National Bureau of Economic Research. NBER Working Paper 17638. https://www.nber.org/papers/w17638.

Dix-Carneiro, R. 2014. "Trade Liberalization and Labor Market Dynamics." *Econometrica* 82 (3): 825–85.

Evenett, S. J., and J. Fritz. 2015. "The Tide Turns? Trade, Protectionism, and Slowing Global Growth." In *The 18th Global Trade Alert Report.* Geneva: Centre for Economic Policy Research.

Felbermayr, G., J. Prat, and H. Schmerer. 2011. "Trade and Unemployment: What Do the Data Say?" *European Economic Review* 55 (6), 741–58.

Goodwin, T., S. Dauda, and S. Gramegna. 2017. "Unlocking Competition in Argentina's Domestic Markets." Background paper prepared for this report.

Gosawmi, A. G., A. Mattoo, and S. Saez. 2012. *Service Exports: Are the Drivers Different for Developing Countries?* Washington, DC: World Bank.

Hidalgo, C. A., and R. Hausmann. 2009. "The Building Blocks of Economic Complexity." *Proceedings of the National Academy of Sciences* 106 (26): 10570–75.

Hollweg, C. H., D. Lederman, and D. Mitra. 2014. *Structural Reforms and Labor Market Outcomes: International Panel Data Evidence.* Washington, DC: World Bank Group.

Hollweg, C. H., D. Lederman, D. Rojas, and E. R. Bulmer. 2014. *Sticky Feet: How Labor Market Frictions Shape the Impact of International Trade on Jobs and Wages.* Washington, DC: World Bank Group.

IMF (International Monetary Fund), WBG (World Bank Group), and WTO (World Trade Organization). 2017. *Making Trade an Engine of Growth for All: The Case for Trade and for Policies to Facilitate Adjustment.* https://www.wto.org/english/news_e/news17_e/wto_imf _report_07042017.pdf.

INDEC (2016) "Valorización mensual de la Canasta Básica Alimentaria y de la Canasta Básica Total - Gran Buenos Aires - Abril a Agosto de 2016," available at https://www.indec.gov.ar /uploads/informesdeprensa/canastas_09_16.pdf.

INDEC. 2017. *Mercado de trabajo: Principales indicadores.* Buenos Aires, Argentina: Instituto Nacional de Estadística y Censos. http://www.indec.gov.ar/uploads/informesdeprensa /EPH_cont_2trim16.pdf.

Iootty, M., and S. Dauda. 2018. "Assessing Firm Competitive Behavior in China: First Insights into the Manufacturing Industry." Unpublished memo.

Kambourov, G. 2009. "Labour Market Regulations and the Sectoral Reallocation of Workers: The Case of Trade Reforms." *Review of Economic Studies* 76 (4): 1321–58.

Kitzmuller, M., and M. Martinez Licetti. 2012. *Competition Policy: Encouraging Thriving Markets for Development.* Public Policy for the Private Sector; note no. 331. Washington, DC: World Bank. http://documents.worldbank.org/curated/en/778181468328582034/Competition-policy-encouraging-thriving-markets-for-development.

Licetti, M., G. Pop, S. Nyman, and T. Begazo Gomez. 2017. *A Step Ahead: Competition Policy for Shared Prosperity and Inclusive Growth.* Washington, DC: World Bank.

Manova, K. 2013. "Credit Constraints, Heterogeneous Firms and International Trade." *Review of Economic Studies* 80 (2): 711–44.

Melitz, M. 2003. "The Impact of Trade on Intra-Industry Reallocations and Aggregate Industry Productivity." *Econometrica* 71: 1695–1725.

Nahirñak, P. 2016. *Informes de cadenas de valor: Software y servicios informáticos* (10.13140/RG.2.2.21708.82567 ed.). Buenos Aires, Argentina: Ministerio de Hacienda y Finanzas Públicas.

Nickell, S. J. 1996. "Competition and Corporate Performance." *Journal of Political Economy* 104 (4): 724–46.

OECD (Organisation for Economic Co-operation and Development). 2017. *OECD Science, Technology and Industry Scoreboard 2017: The Digital Transformation.* Paris: OECD Publishing. "http://dx.doi.org/10.1787/9789264268821-en" \t "_blank" \o "http://dx.doi.org/10.1787/9789264268821-en" http://dx.doi.org/10.1787/9789264268821-en http://dx.doi.org/10.1787/9789264268821-en.

Osnago, A., N. Rocha, and M. Ruta. 2015. "Deep Trade Agreements and Vertical FDI: The Devil Is in the Details." The World Bank. World Bank Policy Research Working Paper WPS 7464. http://documents.worldbank.org/curated/en/739621468001166726/Deep-trade-agreements-and-vertical-FDI-the-devil-is-in-the-details.

Park, J. 2012. "Does Occupational Training by the Trade Adjustment Assistance Program Really Help Reemployment? Success Measured as Occupation Matching." *Review of International Economics* 20 (5): 999–1016.

Rabinovich, J. 2013. *Significación y consecuencias de la concentración y extranjerización económica, casos sectoriales: Acero, aluminio y cemento.* Buenos Aires: Centro de Investigación y Gestión de la Economía Solidaria.

Rosen, H. 2008. "Strengthening Trade Adjustment Assistance." Peterson Institute for International Economics, policy brief 08-2. https://www.researchgate.net/publication/241760390_Strengthening_Trade_Adjustment_Assistance.

Schiantarelli, F. 2016. "Do Product Market Reforms Stimulate Employment, Investment, and Innovation?" IZA World of Labor, no. 266. https://wol.iza.org/uploads/articles/266/pdfs/do-product-market-reforms-stimulate-employment-investment-and-innovation.pdf.

Signoret, J., N. Rocha, and M. Molinuevo. 2017. "Trade Policy Reform in Argentina." Background paper prepared for this report.

Silva, J. S., and S. Tenreyro. 2006. "The Log of Gravity." *Review of Economics and Statistics* 88 (4): 641–58.

World Bank. 2013. *Turkey—Reform for Competitiveness Technical Assistance: Fostering Open and Efficient Markets through Effective Competition Policies.* Washington, DC: World Bank.

World Bank. 2014. *The Unfinished Revolution: Bringing Opportunity, Good Jobs and Greater Wealth to All Tunisians.* Washington, DC: World Bank.

World Bank. 2015. *Argentina: Notas de políticas públicas para el desarrollo.* Report no. 106122. http://documents.worldbank.org/curated/en/899411467995396294/Argentina-Notas-de-pol%C3%ADticas-p%C3%BAblicas-para-el-desarrollo.

World Bank, IDE-JETRO (Institute of Developing Economies–Japan External Trade Organization), OECD (Organisation for Economic Co-operation and Development, and WTO (World Trade Organization). 2017. *Global Value Chain Development Report: Measuring and Analyzing the Impact of GVCs on Economic Development.* Washington, DC: World Bank.

WTO (World Trade Organization). 2017. *Regional Trade Agreements Information System: User Guide.* https://rtais.wto.org/UserGuide/RTAIS_USER_GUIDE_EN.html (accessed August 23, 2017).

2 International Experience with Structural Microeconomic Reforms

When integrating into the global economy, governments often face challenges—in particular, the need to stimulate a rapid export response and the need to manage strategically the timing, sequencing, and costs of reform. Experience with comprehensive reforms to open the economy and integrate into global markets suggests that, in the course of opening, countries often face a short-term increase in imports, while responses in exports tend to be slow (figure 2.1). This asymmetry can trigger a variety of problems, such as growing trade imbalances, less resilience to external shocks, a short- (to medium-) term increase in unemployment, and difficulties in maintaining political support for reforms. Notably, in such cases, growth of trade has accelerated rapidly after the reform period, although this cannot necessarily imply a causal relationship.

Reform experiences in Australia, Mexico, Poland, and Sweden are relevant to Argentina for various reasons. All of the selected countries' economies already had a large and developed manufacturing and service sector. In all cases, the state still participated directly in important sectors. Australia and Sweden both had strong social safety nets that were used to cushion adjustment costs, as discussed in chapter 1. Mexico's and Poland's structural reforms were triggered by regional integration efforts, which could be informative for Argentina in terms of the potential gains of enhancing Mercosur and signing further free trade agreements (FTAs). Furthermore, three of the four countries (with Poland being the exception) had strong subnational governments that were part of their reforms' political economy, as well as competition laws that started being enforced during the reform process (table 2.1).

International experience with the design and implementation of microeconomic trade, investment, and competition reforms undertaken by these countries offers valuable lessons. Australia, a country rich in resources with a high standard of living, lost productivity during the 1960s and 1970s when its economy was closed and highly protected, and state-owned enterprises (SOEs) were the leading network and public utility service providers. The resulting economic instability led to structural reforms starting in 1982, based on opening

FIGURE 2.1

Trends in import and export levels among countries that have experienced structural reforms

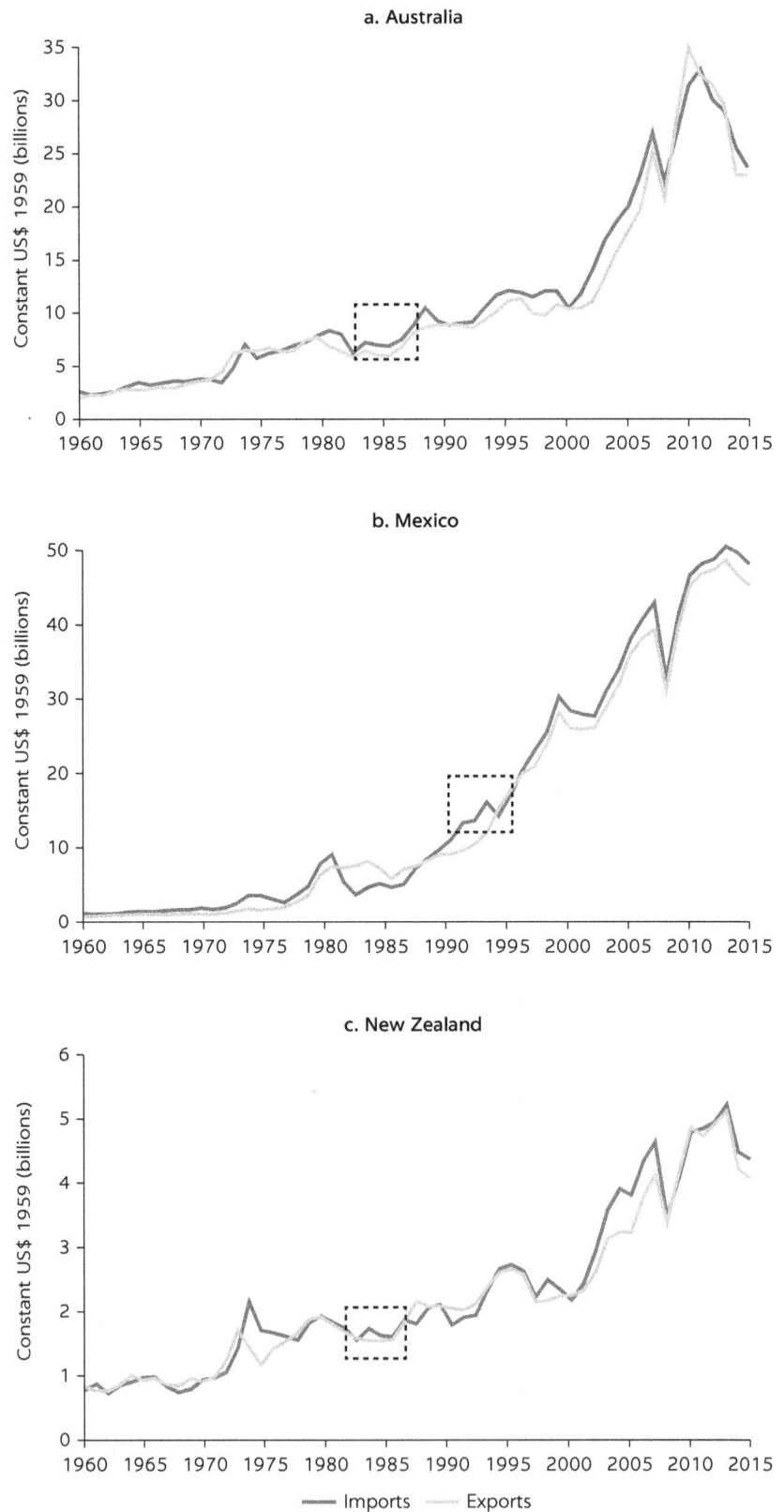

a. Australia

b. Mexico

c. New Zealand

Imports — Exports

continued

FIGURE 2.1, *continued*

d. Poland

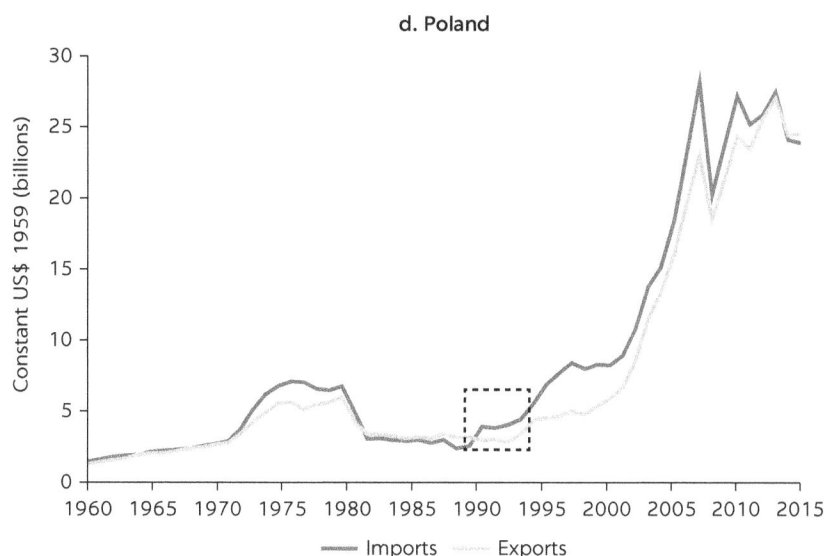

Source: Data from World Development Indicators (WDI) dataset (http://wdi.worldbank.org/tables).

TABLE 2.1 Country indicators

CHARACTERISTICS	AUSTRALIA (1982)	POLAND (1989)	SWEDEN (1990)	MEXICO (1994)	ARGENTINA (2016)
GDP (% change)	0.1	3.8	0.8	4.7	(2.3)
GDP per capita (constant US$, 1979 = 100)	9,213	1,035	16,550	2,776	3,782
GDP's main component	Manufacturing and services[a]	Manufacturing, mining, and agriculture	Manufacturing and services	Manufcturing and services	Manufacturing and services
General government revenue (% of GDP)	n/a	n/a	54.7	n/a	33.7
Role of subnational governments	✓	X	✓	✓	✓
Competition law	Trade Practices Act (1974)	Monopolistic Practices Law (1987)	Competition Act (1983)	Federal Law of Economic Competition (1993)	Competition Law (1999)

Source: Data from IMF World Economic Outlook database, April 2017 (https://www.imf.org/external/pubs/ft/weo/2017/01/weodata/index.aspx).
Note: GDP percentage change with respect to the previous year. For Australia, the GDP percentage change refers to 1982 as compared to 1981.
a. Distribution services and public utility services. In the indicator "role of subnational governments" the check mark indicates countries that have a federal system where subnational governments can decide on policies and regulations, whereas the X means that the government is centralized.

the economy to trade and investment, as well as implementing competition policy principles at the national level. In 2017, Australia reached 25 years without recession, despite recent global economic crises, which is at least partly attributable to its strong post-reform economic foundations. In the 1990s, Mexico negotiated and signed the North American Free Trade Agreement (NAFTA), which first triggered domestic economic reforms, and Mexico's 2013 constitutional reform later opened network sectors (such as energy and telecommunications) to competition and improved the competition law. Sweden, a country with high state participation and a strong welfare system, lost productivity during the 1980s. However, the country managed to recover in the 1990s following a gradual process of privatization and deregulation in the context of regional integration with the European Union (EU). Poland's transition to a market economy in 1989–91 resulted in abrupt changes that led rapidly to high unemployment. Poland compensated for this trend with a series of active and passive labor market policies implemented in close coordination with unions in industries where the unions were strong. Furthermore, the liberalization of professional services in Poland in 2013 serves as a reference for a targeted implementation strategy.

The reform processes in these countries have common features, the first of which is that reform measures were anchored in broader national policies. Australia began some reforms in the 1970s, accelerated them sharply in the early 1980s with the reduction of import barriers, and consolidated them over the following decades. In 1995, all governments in Australia's federal system agreed on a national competition policy that exposed previously sheltered activities to competition and promoted the long-term interests of consumers.[1] Mexico's first wave of reforms took place throughout the 1980s and, especially, in the first half of the 1990s. In this period, the overarching objective was to join the General Agreement on Tariffs and Trade, sending an unambiguous signal that an export-led economy would be the foundation for the new growth strategy. The subsequent goal was to ratify and implement NAFTA. More recently, Mexico embarked on a bold package of structural reforms. These reforms were organized initially around the 2013 "Pacto por México," which brought together the three largest parties to agree on a single, multifaceted package of specific reforms. The parties agreed to improve competition, education, energy, the financial sector, labor, infrastructure, telecommunications, and the tax system, among many other aspects of the economy (box 2.1).

Second, new and existing institutions worked coherently to lead different segments of the overall microeconomic reform program. In Australia, important political institutions (such as the office of the prime minister, the treasury, and the Ministry of Finance) supported the reform.[2] Moreover, Australia built independent institutions (including the National Competition Policy and Productivity Commission) to provide additional support. The Productivity Commission still serves as the Australian government's principal review and advisory body on microeconomic policy, regulation, and a range of other social and environmental issues. Sweden achieved coherence across institutions and over time by implementing a rotation scheme for public employees. This system helped avoid policy capture and spread technical expertise about reform implementation.

Third, efforts to assess the impact of reforms, maintain consistent and corrective monitoring and evaluation regimes, and communicate positive results were critical to sustaining the reform process. In Australia, for example, the Productivity Commission developed the "Impact Project" with Monash University. The team assessed the impact of reforms in different sectors and at different levels of the economy (national and regional). These assessments were useful in communicating the successful results achieved by reform, reaching or promoting consensus, and adapting measures that were not contributing as expected.[3]

Fourth, the sequencing and timing of reforms were as important as their content. For all countries under review here, the trade liberalization process combined "shock" reforms (such as the early elimination of nontariff measures (NTMs) to reduce severe distortions in pricing and supply, as well as tariff reductions) with a more gradual approach in some sensitive sectors. The sensitive sectors usually included manufacturing, particularly labor-intensive

Australia's National Competition Policy and Pacto por México

The objective of Australia's National Competition Policy was to promote competitive markets, because they best serve the interests of consumers and the wider community, and to "achieve and maintain consistent and complementary competition laws and policies which [would] apply to all businesses in Australia regardless of ownership."

The following were its principal components:

- Extension of anticompetitive conduct legislation to cover previously exempt government and unincorporated enterprises
- Review of some 1,800 items of anticompetitive regulation
- Reforms to public monopolies, including "competitive neutrality" enforcement mechanisms, certain structural reform requirements, and price regulation where public monopolies persisted
- An open-access regime for network infrastructure

The objective of Mexico's Pacto por México was to complete the democratic transition, boost economic growth, and generate good-quality jobs to reduce poverty and social inequality.

The following were its principal economic components:

- Labor reform that increased the flexibility of hiring substantially
- Reform of "Amparos," which made the legal system more efficient and fair
- Introduction of a national code of criminal procedure
- Wide-ranging educational reform that introduced clearer standards for teachers and schools
- Fiscal reform that improved the efficiency of the tax system
- Economy-wide competition reform
- Reforms to the financial, telecommunications, and energy sectors that opened long-closed sectors to competition and strengthened the powers of regulators
- Reforms allowing politicians to be reelected, giving them a longer-term perspective on policy

sectors (such as textiles, clothing, and footwear), steel, and automobiles. In Australia's first automotive export facilitation scheme, launched in 1985, the country first turned quantity quotas into tariff quotas, then abolished them and gradually reduced the tariff from 57.5 percent in 1985 to 35 percent in 1992. Subsequent plans included gradual and previously announced reductions, reaching a tariff of 10 percent in 2004 and programmed to fall to 5 percent in 2010. This gradualism contrasted with the unilateral tariff reduction programs applied to nonsensitive sectors, in which the tariff reached 5 percent or less by 1996. It is important to highlight that the Australian economy was opened to trade first, which created the need to reduce input costs in labor markets and (nontraded) public utility services. In turn, pressure mounted for the reform of government policies and institutions that were impeding these changes, and an increasingly broad-ranging program of domestic microeconomic reform was hatched (Banks 2005). There is no consensus in the economic literature on whether "shock therapy" or gradualism is a better strategy for trade openness and investment liberalization reforms. Countries that have followed a gradualist approach (such as Australia, Mexico, and Sweden) have usually had political incentives to do so, including avoiding excessive costs, especially for the government budget; avoiding excessive downgrades in living standards at the start of the reform; allowing trial-and-error and mid-course adjustments; and helping the government gain credibility over time (Roland 2012). While trade reforms typically have combined shock measures with gradualism in sensitive sectors, investment and competition reforms have usually followed a steadier path.

NOTES

1. See Banks (2005) for further discussion.
2. See Kelly (2000) for further discussion.
3. See Banks (2005) for a detailed discussion on the Australian experience.

REFERENCES

Banks, G. 2005. *Structural Reform Australian-Style: Lessons for Others?* Productivity Commission. Based on presentations to the International Monetary Fund (IMF) and World Bank (Washington, DC, May 26–27, 2005) and the Organisation for Economic Co-operation and Development (OECD) (Paris, May 31, 2005). https://www.oecd.org/australia/39218531.pdf.

Kelly, P. 2000. "The Politics of Economic Change in Australia in the 1980s and 1990s." In *The Australian Economy in the 1990s: Proceedings of a Conference held at the H.C. Coombs Centre for Financial Studies, Kirribillion, 24–25 July 2000,* ed. D. Gruen and S. Shrestha, 222–34. http://www.rba.gov.au/publications/confs/2000/pdf/conf-vol-2000.pdf.

Roland, G. 2002. "The Political Economy of Transition." *Journal of Economic Perspectives* 16 (1): 29–50.

3 Strengthening Institutions for Effective Integration into the Global Economy

International experience provides examples of institutional setups that have helped countries implement broad national policies of integration into the global economy. As described in chapter 2, countries such as Australia have set up new commissions and councils to design, monitor, and/or implement medium- and long-term policy programs to reform domestic markets. Such institutions require funding, accountability mechanisms, and high-level endorsement to be effective. A strong, high-level endorsement of a strategic objective, action plan, or road-map can give institutions the space they need to coordinate effectively around an overarching goal and to implement changes on a day-to-day basis.

Institutions in charge of trade, investment, and competition policy are key to implementing these reforms and should thus be structured efficiently with a view to allowing complementarity and coordination among them.

INVESTMENT: BEST GOVERNMENT PRACTICES FOR JUMP-SHIFTING INVESTMENT PROMOTION POLICY

According to international experience, successful institutions in charge of promoting foreign direct investment (FDI) have certain best practices in common, regardless of their institutional structure. In March 2016, Argentina set up its investment promotion agency (IPA) through the transformation of Fundación Exportar, a private entity dedicated exclusively to export promotion. The new Agencia Argentina de Inversiones y Comercio Internacional (AAICI) is now also dedicated to investment promotion and facilitation. The AAICI benefited from the record of Fundación Exportar and from its established governance and overall structure. The internal organizational structure was adjusted, with trade promotion and investment promotion operating as independent business units, with distinct performance indicators but sharing a series of administrative "back office" services. Activities related to trade promotion and investment promotion have, by nature, different needs in terms of staff expertise, skills, target audiences, clients, and stakeholders.[1] Best practices point, in general, to the split of trade promotion and investment promotion, although some IPAs with joint mandates have been successful in attracting FDI. Table 3.1 displays the pros and cons of joint promotion. Successful IPAs with joint mandates have some commonalities: they tend to follow an umbrella structure, pool together administration and overseas office infrastructure, invest in market intelligence and image building, and operate a separate technical team for each promotion stream, leading to greater efficiency.[2]

Another best practice is to separate regulatory and promotional functions. The most effective investment promotion agencies focus on promoting specific locations (table 3.2). They do not have regulatory roles to allow or deny applications for registration or grant incentives (box 3.1). Functions such as granting

TABLE 3.1 **Pros and cons of joint export and FDI promotion**

PROS	CONS
One umbrella for investment and trade promotion policy	Different functions and objectives. Loss of accountability and loss of focus in the agency
Shared support services: information technology (IT), human resources, accounting, legal services, public relations, research and analysis, shared office accommodation	Possible problems in coordinating investment and trade promotion activities and managing staff with different skills and perspectives
Knowledge sharing to benefit strategy development	Different time frames, with generally a longer time perspective in investment promotion
Potentially more continuity in service delivery. A single point of contact in government—for example, for export-oriented investors	Often different clients and contact points in companies

TABLE 3.2 **IPA best practices**

		MUST DO (CORE MANDATES)	MAY DO (AS ADDITIONAL FUNCTIONS, BUT REQUIRING INDEPENDENT SETUP AND RESOURCES)	SHOULDN'T DO (INCOMPATIBLE WITH INVESTMENT PROMOTION)
Investment promotion	Marketing	X		
	Information provision	X		
	Facilitation of meetings, site visits, and government procedures	X		
	Advocacy	X		
General promotion	Exports		X	
	Outward investment		X	
	SME linkages to FDI		X	
	SME development			X
Administration/ Regulation	Administration of government procedures (such as one-stop shops, licenses, incentives)			X
	Management of state land or assets			X
	Administration/negotiation of government concessions (for example, infrastructure or extractive industries)			X
	Administration of public–private partnerships			X

BOX 3.1

Separation of promotion and regulation functions: The case of Canada

- The origins of Canada's IPA, Invest in Canada, go back to the Foreign Investment Review Agency. The Foreign Investment Review Agency was established in 1973 as a purely regulatory agency, prompted by a surge of acquisitions of Canadian firms by corporations in the United States.

- Investment Canada, a promoter-regulator, replaced the Foreign Investment Review Agency in 1985. It continued to screen investments

and began promotional functions as part of the Ministry of Industry.

- In 2003, the government split promotion and regulation functions by establishing a new unit with a stronger FDI mandate, Invest in Canada, under the Ministry of Foreign Affairs and International Trade. It left investment review under the Ministry of Industry.

- Today, Invest in Canada is devoted to investment promotion, ranking among the top national IPAs.[a]

a. See World Bank (2011) for further details.

permits, issuing licenses, or administering and negotiating government concessions or public–private partnerships can create conflicts of interest and send confusing signals to investors. They can denaturalize the IPA, diverting resources from its core function of promoting and attracting investment.

An IPA's institutional mandate and organization should allow for effective interaction with investors. In conducive investment climates, IPAs can interact effectively with investors at all stages of the investment life cycle: (1) vision and strategy; (2) investment attraction; (3) investment entry and establishment; (4) investment protection, expansion, and retention; and (5) linkages and spillovers. It is crucial to ensure that the IPA has a clear mandate, an efficient organizational structure, and sufficient resources (box 3.2). The mandate to serve investors should be precise and focus not only on domestic investors, but in particular on foreign investors. The mandate should define the range, depth, and quality of services that will be provided to different types of FDI and investors along the investment life cycle, a time-phased approach to delivering marketing, information, facilitation, and policy advocacy services.

Among investment promotion efforts, policy advocacy is a vital activity with high returns. Although the particularities and strengths of each country should be taken into account, best practices and empirical results[3] highlight that, among other key functions such as image building and investor services, advocacy is the function most closely associated with higher levels of investment. IPAs' budget allocations do not often reflect this prioritization. IPAs might benefit from investing more resources in advocacy activities, such as surveys of the private sector, participation in task forces, policy and legal proposals, and lobbying activities.

Empirical analysis suggests that Argentina may achieve greater gains from directing investment promotion activities at foreign investment and the specific characteristics of a few sectors. When IPAs target foreign investment (as opposed to domestic investment), the likelihood increases of attracting the type of foreign investment that can yield substantial benefits for the local economy. Using a sample of 105 countries, Harding and Javorcik (2012) found that FDI

BOX 3.2

Highlights of some best-practice IPAs

The following examples highlight some best practices of IDA Ireland, EDB Singapore, Korea's KOTRA, and UKTI United Kingdom, which are considered successful IPAs.

IDA Ireland: Incorporated as an autonomous state-sponsored body in 1969, the Irish government's Industrial Development Agency, also known as IDA Ireland, has a track record of consistent achievement. Founded at a time when Ireland was not regarded as an attractive investment destination (due to economic stagnation, limited natural resources, one of the lowest per-capita incomes in Europe, and a small population), IDA Ireland changed global perceptions and helped transform Ireland into a powerhouse of FDI attraction. Some highlights:

- *Clear mandate and sector strategy.* With the single mandate of attracting FDI, IDA Ireland has developed a focused strategy to promote industrial development by targeting industries in which Ireland could achieve a competitive advantage. Today, these are life sciences; information and communications technology; and international and financial services.
- *Collaboration with other entities at the national/ subnational levels.* Ireland created a combination of well-funded state agencies and advisory councils that work together and collaborate with IDA Ireland and have specialized functions. These include Forfas (focused on strategic planning); Enterprise Ireland (promoting small and medium enterprises [SMEs], domestic industry, and export development); and the Science Foundation Ireland (focusing on innovation). In addition to their own synergies, these agencies have good working relationships with key regulatory agencies at national and local levels, as well as with private sector organizations. They all employ professional and permanent staff who do not change when the government changes.
- *Adequate institutional and financial autonomy.* IDA Ireland has a separate legal mandate that grants it a substantial degree of institutional and financial autonomy and a sufficient and sustained

budget. Its board of directors builds on private sector representation, but board members are clearly appointed to represent public interests instead of private ones.

EDB Singapore: EDB Singapore was established in 1961 as a centralized agency for investment promotion and has since been the agency responsible for Singapore's success in attracting FDI and promoting the country's economic development. Since 1993, it has also supported the regionalization initiatives of companies in Singapore, administered the FDI incentives regime, administered grants/loans to promote the internationalization of local companies, and supported inward and outward investment. Some highlights:

- *High-level support:* EDB enjoys support from the highest level of government, with credibility and visibility.
- *Four key strategic areas:* (1) investment attraction: a "single window" promotes, attracts, facilitates, and supports investors in the manufacturing and service sector; (2) support for the retention, expansion, and vertical integration of existing industries; (3) improvement of the investment climate: policy advocacy to improve the investment climate; and (4) toward the future: serving as a "guiding compass" in preparing Singapore for the future.

Korea's KOTRA: Korea transformed from one of the poorest agrarian economies into an industrialized country, mainly through an export-based industrialization strategy. In the early 1960s, it abandoned the import-substitution strategy and adopted the "Export First" policy. KOTRA was founded in 1962 to assist businesses in exploring foreign markets, basically as a trade promotion organization. FDI promotion was included as one of KOTRA's functions in 1997. KOTRA currently carries out trade promotion and investment promotion under one roof. Regarding investment promotion, it facilitates the entry and successful establishment of foreign businesses in Korea and provides aftercare services designed to retain and expand foreign investment in Korea.

continued

Box 3.2, *continued*

UKTI United Kingdom: Named British Trade International until 2003, United Kingdom Trade and Investment (UKTI) is a joint government agency of the Department for Business, Innovation, and Skills and the Foreign and Commonwealth Office. Although UKTI has its own objectives, it also contributes to the objectives of both parent ministries. Some highlights:

- *Great flexibility:* The model allows for great flexibility in terms of how UKTI presents business offers and targets clients. The common factor for

all UKTI clients, both local exporters and potential investors, is the UKTI brand.

- *A strong brand:* The brand has global reach and impact. It is recognizable, and the addition of a crest identifies it as a body of the government of the United Kingdom—in other words, as trustworthy. It also clearly brands the United Kingdom and is positioned to be the natural choice for companies interested in either trading with or investing in the country.

TABLE 3.3 IPAs and their focus in strategic sectors

IPA	NO. OF STRATEGIC SECTORS	SOME STRATEGIC SECTOR EXAMPLES
Invest in France	9	Aerospace, IT, health, agribusiness
Invest HK (Hong Kong)	9	Financial services, IT corporate services
CINDE (Costa Rica)	4	Life sciences (medical devices manufacturing), IT, advanced manufacturing

Note: IT = information technology.

TABLE 3.4 Strategic focus of Argentina's IPA

1.	Oil and gas
2.	Telecommunications
3.	Machinery and equipment
4.	Agroindustry
5.	Renewable energies
6.	Knowledge-based services

Source: AAICI's website: http://www.inversionycomercio.org.ar/en/invest_argentina.php.

---

targeting by investment promotion agencies can be key in attracting efficiency-seeking FDI. It can also raise the quality of exports from the host economy. The cross-country analysis found an increase in the unit values of exports from sectors that are considered priorities in efforts to attract FDI. The top 33 IPAs (25 national, 8 subnational) have targeted specific priority sectors and prominently display them on their websites (table 3.3).[4] In the case of AAICI and its website, six sectors are listed as core to the agency (table 3.4). Keeping a restricted list of sectors for investment promotion is expected to yield gains to Argentina. Because not all foreign investment is homogeneous, and in some sectors efforts to attract investors are less relevant since the main drivers of investments are available natural resources or the size of the market, focusing marketing services on a few sectors seem to be a more efficient way to use the

Main institutional recommendations for fostering IPAs

Most successful IPAs have focused mandates and functions. Giving IPAs responsibilities for several other economic mandates different from those of investment promotion can lead to investment promotion officials' lacking the resources, policy support, or strategic freedom necessary to achieve these substantial goals:

- Ensure clarity on the tasks to be carried out as part of investment promotion (including promotional but not regulatory functions, independent from export promotion).
- Focus investment promotion strategies on a few sectors, including knowledge-based services (KBS).
- Achieve the appropriate balance in promoting domestic versus foreign investment.
- Redefine the range, depth, and quality of services provided along the investment life cycle, from marketing information to investment facilitation and policy advocacy.

An autonomous organization with freedom to allocate resources according to a results-oriented strategy helps to preserve a private sector-like clarity of mission and means:

- Provide an institutional outlet for addressing investment problems before they escalate into investor–state disputes.
- Foster a private-sector-minded culture by hiring staff with private sector experience, offering performance bonuses, and prioritizing competency in English and other foreign languages.
- Reallocate and prioritize tasks with a view to maximizing efficiency.
- Develop deep business knowledge through research capacity, account managers, and knowledge and relationship management systems.
- Establish a stronger network with provinces and at subnational levels of investment and trade promotion units to guarantee investors an adequate level of service that is homogeneous across subnational entities.
- Prioritize investment facilitation through internal systems and improved accessibility.[a]

a. See World Bank (2009) for further details.

agency's limited promotional efforts and resources. Top-performing agencies have some good practices in common that can be adapted and implemented by agencies seeking to increase their share of the market for foreign investment (box 3.3).

COMPETITION: ENABLING IMPACTFUL AND INDEPENDENT COMPETITION POLICY IMPLEMENTATION

The institution in charge of promoting competition could benefit from additional resources and more functional autonomy. To implement the proposed substantial procompetition reforms, Argentina's competition authority, the Comisión Nacional de Defensa de la Competencia (CNDC) would benefit from more technical and functional autonomy, which would help shield it from potential political pressure. On the operational side, the CNDC will require more resources and will need to dedicate these resources toward more impactful competition policy instruments. Currently, Argentina has fewer public officials than countries of comparable size, and this aggravates the procedural workload generated by an ineffective legal framework, especially regarding merger control.

A bill already approved in the Chamber of Deputies for a new competition law addresses some of these challenges effectively.

A new and more autonomous competition authority could increase the likelihood of overcoming potential pressure by interest groups when opening markets to competition and breaking up cartels. National regulatory authorities are generally considered independent when they are able to implement regulations and policies without intrusion from the executive, but they are still obliged to follow general government policy.[5] In Argentina, the CNDC's decisions on sanctions for cartels or remedies for proposed merger transactions are reviewed and signed by officials outside the agency and within the Ministry of Production. While some established competition authorities are part of ministries or governmental departments and still exhibit a high level of autonomy—in Chile, the European Union (EU), and the United States, for example—it is more common to find an administratively independent competition agency in charge of investigating and adjudicating restrictions on competition. More than half of the 120 competition agencies in the world are institutionally independent from ministerial control. Of these, 22 are in developing and transition economies.[6] The bill for a new competition law, approved in the Camara de Diputados in November 2017,[7] proposes the establishment of a new authority with technical and functional autonomy.[8] This would be an important step toward ensuring that political pressures by interest groups do not interfere with technical decisions by the agency.

The competition authority should be well resourced to conduct sophisticated and procedurally consistent investigations and to implement advocacy initiatives proactively. The CNDC employs fewer public officials than agencies in comparator countries (figure 3.1). While agency size differs substantially across

FIGURE 3.1

Number of public officials in competition authorities

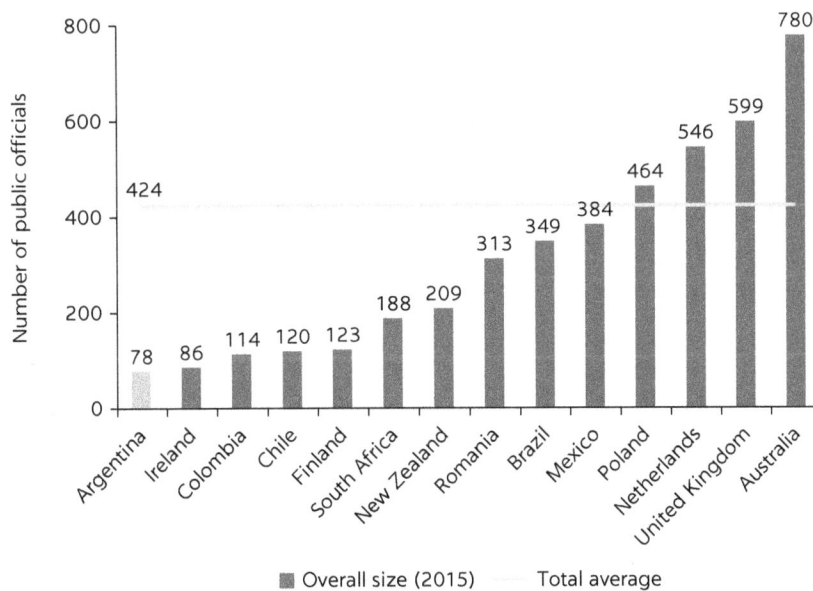

Source: Data from Global Competition Review's (GCR) Rating Enforcement dataset. (https://globalcompetitionreview.com/series/rating-enforcement).
Note: The data reflect overall staff, not necessarily those involved directly in competition enforcement. Agencies such as Australia's have other mandates, but even if only half the staff worked on competition enforcement, Argentina would have a comparatively small staff group. Data for Colombia correspond only to competition enforcement staff, given that the institution is the Superintendence of Industry and Commerce, with 1,200 staff in total.

countries, larger economies tend to have more staff. To undertake enforcement actions (which can involve, for example, simultaneous onsite inspections of alleged cartel members on multiple premises), the agency needs a minimum cadre of well-trained, full-time officials who are knowledgeable in cartel investigation techniques and procedural matters, such as confidentiality guarantees. The ability to procure modern investigation equipment, such as special IT forensics equipment, is critical to tackling sophisticated cartel agreements. For Argentina to boost its anticartel enforcement, tackle government interventions that limit competition through proactive advocacy initiatives, and effectively review merger notifications, the agency requires significantly more staff.

Merger notification thresholds in Argentina should be adjusted to currency fluctuations and to ensure effective use of ex ante merger review.[9] Thresholds for merger transactions that trigger a review by the CNDC need to be set low enough that they do not exclude a large volume of transactions that may have negative effects on competition, but high enough that they do not unduly burden the competition authority and hamper the progress of (efficient) mergers. International benchmarking suggests that these thresholds are relatively higher in countries with larger economies (figure 3.2). Strong currency devaluations are typically followed by an adjustment of the notification thresholds, as seen in recent reforms in Norway and Turkey. In Argentina, owing to currency devaluation, the threshold is now low relative to the size of its economy. As a result, the procedural workload that is generated aggravates the scarcity in staff and resources. A much-needed reform of merger review provisions would introduce further improvements (such as individual thresholds[10] and a fast-track procedure for mergers that are unlikely to reduce competition).

An increase in staff and a reform to streamline the merger control system would allow the agency to strengthen anticartel enforcement. Cartels can raise the prices of affected goods and services by 49 percent on average (Connor 2014).

FIGURE 3.2

Merger notification thresholds and size of the economy

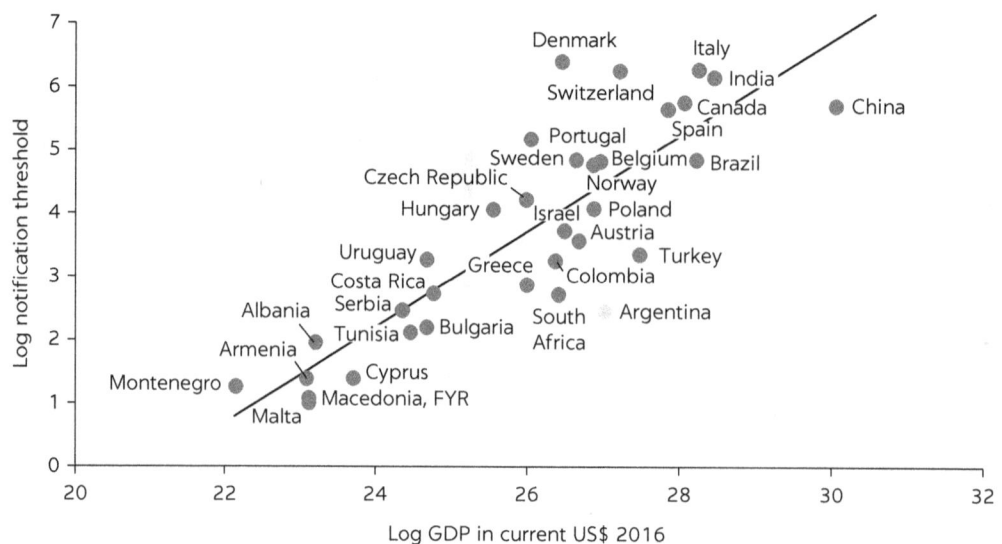

Source: Data from International Merger Law Database and updates by World Bank Group based on methodology from Argent and Begazo Gomez (2015).
Note: The values of the notification threshold reflect the status as of 2013, except for Norway and Turkey, which have raised their thresholds since 2013. All values are expressed in US dollars using the exchange rate in 2016. Any threshold increase not captured here would take Argentina farther away from international practice.

FIGURE 3.3

Number of cartel investigations started and concluded before and after 2007

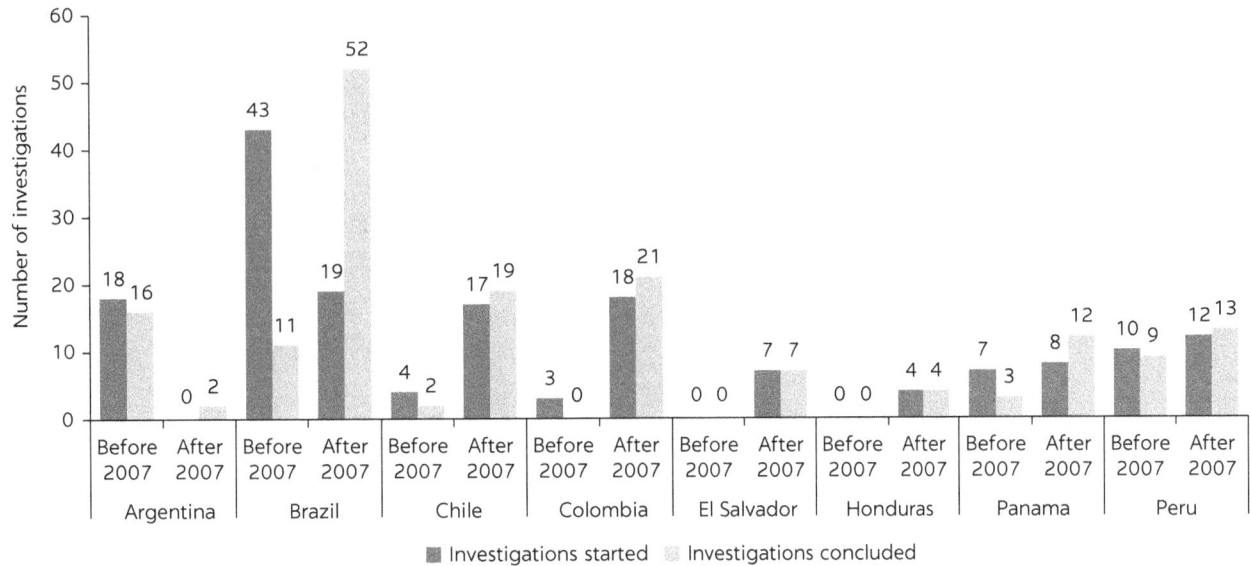

Source: Data from World Bank Anti-Cartel Enforcement database, as of April 2017.

Given their harmful effects, agencies are focusing their resources increasingly on anticartel enforcement. Among Latin American agencies, detection of cartels has increased threefold over the last decade in comparison to the decade before (figure 3.3). Agencies in Latin America now detect two cartel cases per year, on average, while the most mature agencies can detect five or more cases each year. Argentina sanctioned only two cases between 2007 and 2016. The CNDC's new leadership has already organized capacity-building sessions for staff and quickly upgraded investigation techniques. In September 2017, it successfully detected and fined a number of health clinics in the Province of Salta for price fixing. Building an effective anticartel program that deters collusive agreements will require continued efforts to strengthen capacities and implementation.

In addition to detecting and deterring anticompetitive business practices, the CNDC should devote a substantial portion of its resources to tackling government restrictions that facilitate anticompetitive business practices in the first place. The Argentine legal framework does not provide for exemptions of any sector or type of firm, and regulatory protection of incumbents is driven instead by legal barriers to market entry by domestic or foreign firms, as well as barriers to network sectors (figure 3.4). These restrictions can be addressed by the competition advocacy unit in the CNDC, which could increasingly influence policy decisions and regulatory design. This change would not necessarily require a change in the legal framework; international evidence suggests that the compulsiveness of opinions issued in advocacy initiatives is not a necessary condition for successful advocacy (figure 3.5), and that the specific strategy in advocating for procompetition solutions is more important.

The competition authority and sector regulators can collaborate more effectively to strengthen competition principles in network regulation. While comparator countries such as Mexico and South Africa exhibit even

FIGURE 3.4

Contribution of "legal barriers" to restrictiveness of product market regulation subindicator "regulatory protection of incumbents"

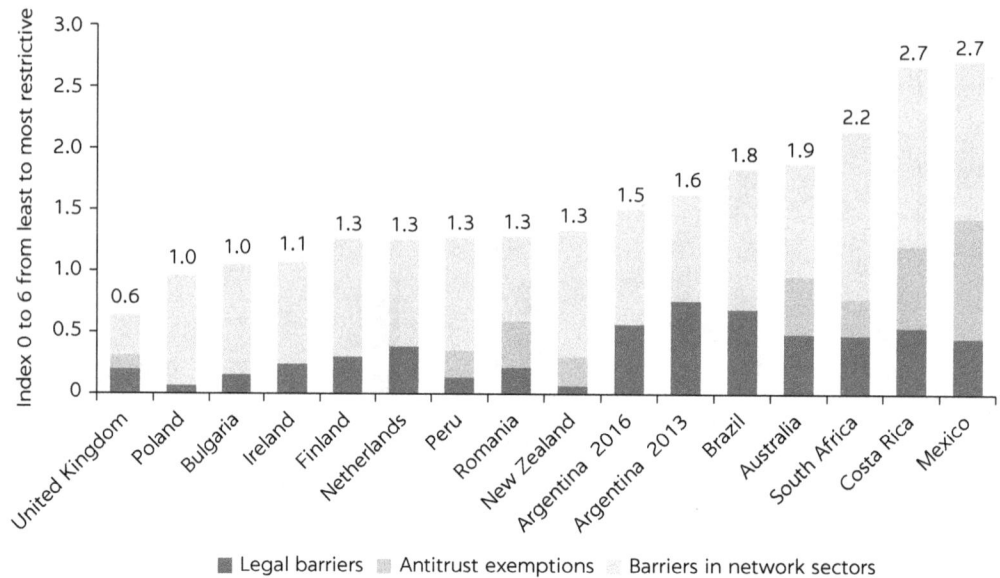

Source: OECD Product Market Regulation database, and OECD-World Bank Group Product Market Regulation database for non-OECD countries 2013, 2016, as of March 2018. (http://www.oecd.org/eco/growth /indicatorsofproductmarketregulationhomepage.htm). The OECD-WBG PMR data are part of the WBG's Markets and Competition Policy Database.

FIGURE 3.5

Compulsiveness of opinions issued in advocacy initiatives

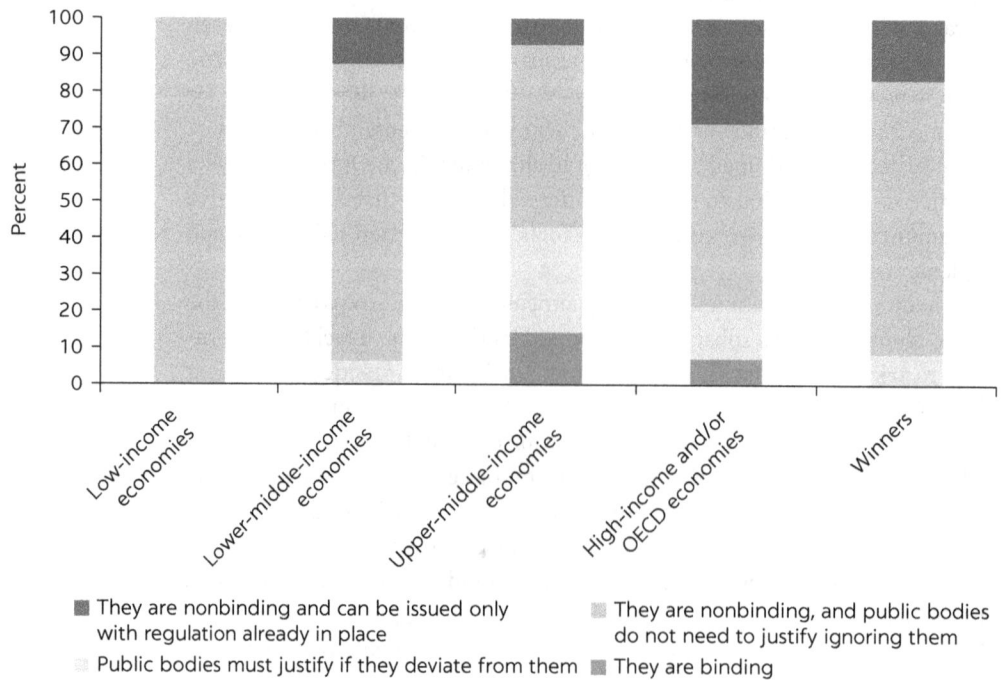

Source: Goodwin and Licetti (2016).
Note: Based on review of all winners of the annual WBG-ICN (World Bank Group–International Competition Network) International Advocacy Contest.

FIGURE 3.6

Restrictiveness of network sector regulation in telecommunications, electricity, gas, post, and rail, air, and road transport, 2013

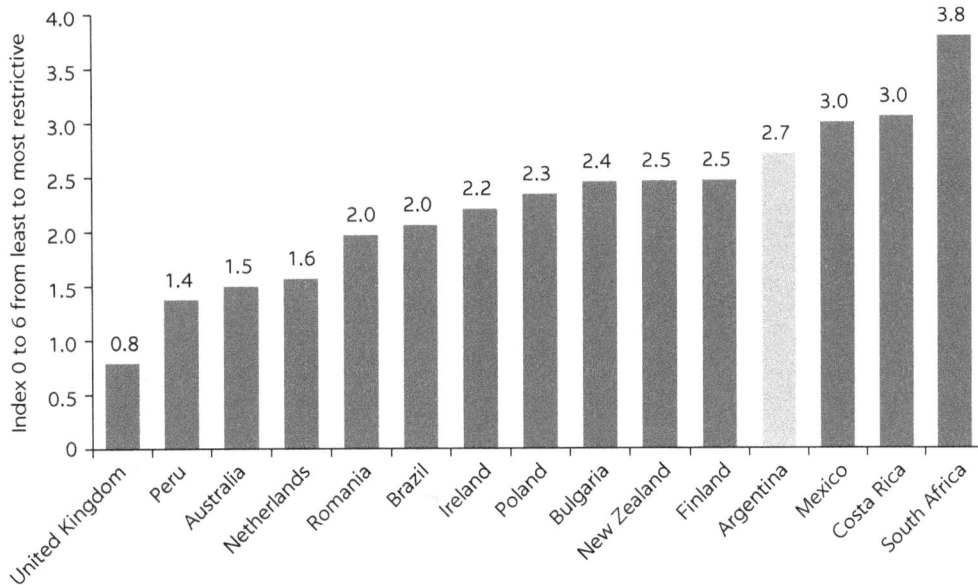

Source: OECD Product Market Regulation database, and OECD–World Bank Group Product Market Regulation database for non-OECD countries 2013, 2016, as of March 2018. (http://www.oecd.org/eco/growth /indicatorsofproductmarketregulationhomepage.htm).

BOX 3.4

Main institutional recommendations to foster competition in Argentina

Competition law enforcement and advocacy can become more effective if the Argentine Competition Authority is granted greater autonomy, especially in the decision-making process. The government of Argentina can further enhance institutional effectiveness by taking the following measures with respect to organization and resources:

- Continue expanding staff capabilities in volume and technical profile.
- Reorient staff and resources according to priorities for competition policy in Argentina (for example, cartel enforcement).
- Strengthen advocacy program and resources to engage with sector regulators.

greater restrictiveness in the regulation of network sectors (figure 3.6), Argentina's restrictiveness score in the road and air transport sectors is the highest among comparators. In the case of railway networks, and given the vertical connections between majority shareholders and cargo rail transport end-users, regulators and the competition authority could, for example, collaborate to ensure effective third-party access regulations are in place where appropriate (figure 3.7). The competition authority and sector regulators could sign a memorandum of understanding to ensure coherent regulatory implementation. In the telecommunications sector, this could increase procedural predictability in merger reviews, where both the telecommunications regulator and the competition authority would have specific regulatory functions.

FIGURE 3.7

Extension of rail networks in Argentina, majority shareholders of each network, and their main product market, 2017

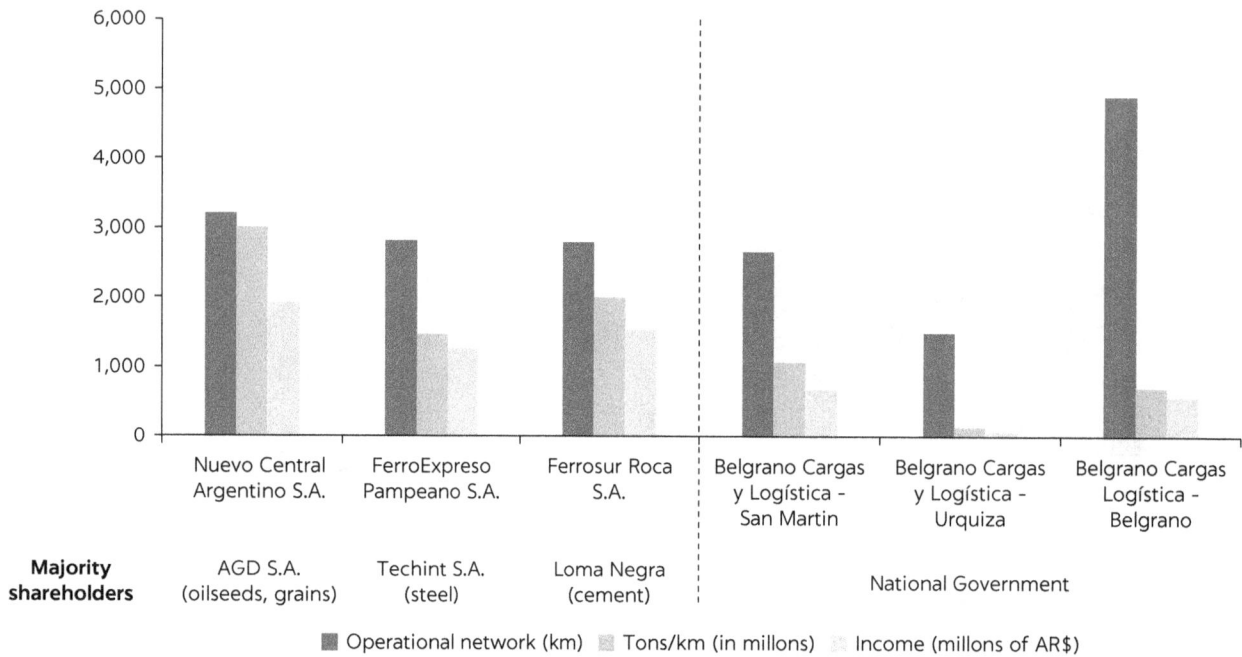

Source: Data from Comisión Nacional de Regulación de Transporte, 2017 (https://www.cnrt.gob.ar/estad%C3%ADsticas-del -transporte-ferroviario).

TRADE: BEST INSTITUTIONAL PROCESSES FOR TRADE POLICY FORMULATION AND IMPLEMENTATION

The preparation and conduct of negotiations, together with the implementation of trade policy, are the core responsibilities of trade institutions.[11] Mandates and institutional arrangements for trade policy vary from one country to another. In some countries, a single entity is in charge of trade (for example, the Ministry of Trade). In other countries, trade policy is the purview of an institution housed within another institution (such as a ministry of foreign affairs, economy, or treasury). In still others, a special trade policymaking body brings together representatives from different ministries. Regardless of the institutional setup, three tasks need to be performed to ensure effective participation in the trade system: analysis, communication and coordination, and representation (box 3.5).

Interagency coordination is an especially important feature in trade policy, which involves several government agencies. Coordination might entail resistance to the transfer of authority from governmental bodies with trade-related issues to the responsible ministry of trade or equivalent; hence, the establishment of mechanisms of information sharing is paramount. The United States model, while not easily replicable in other countries because of the idiosyncrasy of its constitutional arrangement and the amount of resources it requires, offers some good examples of interagency coordination through the Trade Policy Review Group and the Trade Policy Staff Committee (box 3.6). Secondment of personnel to the Office of the United States Trade Representative from other departments, such as state, agriculture, and the treasury, for instance, are another way of fostering cooperation. In the case of the European Union, coordination takes place among its different institutions and those of its member states,

---

BOX 3.5

Main responsibilities for effective trade negotiation

Effective efforts in negotiating and implementing trade agreements involve several key activities, including those related to analysis, communication and coordination, and representation.

Activities on analysis include to:

- Build institutional capacity to collect, analyze, utilize, and disseminate trade-related information, including statistical data on the domestic and international economy, tariff and nontariff barriers, treaties and other legal instruments, national laws and regulations, and academic and own analyses to support negotiations
- Conduct independent assessment of negotiated agreements to allow public scrutiny and ensure legitimacy

Communication and coordination responsibilities include those to:

- Implement mechanisms that facilitate communication among the ministry in charge of trade (or equivalent), other government agencies, and civil society—before, during, and after negotiations

- Foster high level of interagency coordination to manage the complexity of trade matters nowadays
- Promote stakeholder consultations and outreach efforts on trade agreements to maximize opportunities for all involved stakeholders, including SMEs and civil society

Responsibilities related to representation should:

- Represent the interests and positions of the country to foreign counterparts and international organizations and include permanent presence in foreign missions, participation in ministerial meetings, hosting of international gatherings, and so on
- Be carried out by someone with a formal diplomatic title or an official government official. Trade representatives should be fully trained in trade policy and negotiation techniques, active, informed, and involved (at home and abroad), and able to cover "a wide range of issues in a shifting array of bilateral, regional, and multilateral negotiations."[a]

a. See Van Grasstek (2008) for further discussion.

BOX 3.6

Interagency coordination in the United States

This box describes the mechanisms for coordination and consensus building among government agencies of the United States on matters of trade policy. This interagency process in the United States is often held up as an example of best practices. The United States Trade Representative (USTR) develops its responsibilities in consultation with an interagency policy organization established under the Trade Expansion Act of 1962. The National Economic Council, a cabinet-level committee chaired by the president, deals only with issues of high importance.

Two subcabinet committees, each chaired by the USTR and made up of 20 agencies, complement the interagency coordination system. One, the Trade Policy Staff Committee (TPSC), is composed of more than 80 subcommittees. The USTR solicits inputs from the appropriate subcommittees, which in turn provide recommendations to the full TPSC as the basis for reaching interagency consensus. The Trade Policy Review Group is composed of representatives at the undersecretary level and is advised by the Trade Policy Staff Committee.

The United States International Trade Commission is a nonvoting member of these communities.

adding a layer of coordination at the supranational level. International trade agreements are negotiated through the Council of the European Union and the European Commission, and member states participate independently where the agreement involves mixed responsibilities. The Directorate General for Trade of the European Commission develops specific trade policies. Domestic trade falls under the competency of each member state.

Specialized trade units are the best places to conduct consultations and legitimize internal negotiations with the private sector during trade negotiations. Countries like Mexico have established a recognized consultation process through which to channel the participation of the private sector and strategic social groups. The Coordinating Body of Foreign Trade Business Associations (Coordinadora de Organismos Empresariales de Comercio Exterior, in Spanish) is the private sector coordinating body for North American Free Trade Agreement (NAFTA) negotiations and an advisory body to the government. It comprises business organizations that are involved in foreign trade and international matters. Another consultation body is the Advisory Council, which integrates representatives of the private sector (which constitutes the majority), the government, academia, labor, and the agricultural sector. Consultations take place throughout the trade policymaking process, including the ratification and implementation of trade agreements.

Many countries in Latin America have opted for trade negotiation institutions with functions that are separate from international diplomatic matters, while others have chosen to concentrate these functions under one ministry. While institutional setups vary, countries like Colombia, Costa Rica, and Peru have arguably benefited from dividing economic and political advisory roles across different ministries—the Ministry of Trade (or equivalent) and the Ministry of Foreign Affairs, respectively. Costa Rica created its Ministry of Foreign Trade in 1996 and to date has signed 14 regional trade agreements. On the other hand, Chile, which participates in 30 regional trade agreements, is an example of how trade responsibilities can also be handled under the Ministry of Foreign Affairs. Well-defined functions and close interagency coordination seem to be more important than the specific institutional location of responsibilities. Chile's Directorate General for International Economic Relations (Dirección General de Relaciones Económicas Internacionales in Spanish), under the Ministry of Foreign Affairs, is the public entity in charge of executing and coordinating international economic relations. The directorate coordinates all government agencies that are involved in foreign trade. In this sense, trade negotiations are coordinated with other ministries through the Interministerial Commission for International Economic Relations, chaired by the Ministry of Foreign Affairs and integrating the ministries of finance, economy, and agriculture, as well as the secretary general of the presidency.

Several recommendations can be advanced on the institutional aspects of trade policy (see also box 3.7). Assessing the technical capacity and skills needed to prepare, conduct, and implement trade policy, in light of recent international experience, can help streamline roles, support effective coordination, and ultimately contribute to boosting trade. Trade policy is technical, and trade agreements must guarantee predictability. It is important, therefore, to assess which resources and skills are necessary for implementing and negotiating trade policies—and coordinating with stakeholders, including the private sector—among other matters.

BOX 3.7

Main recommendations for effective trade policy making and implementation

Main recommendations on trade policy institutional aspects center on improving interagency processes and stakeholder participation, as well as on building technical capacity on trade agreements. These include to:

- Reassess the trade policy formulation process and compare it with practices in other countries. This should consider, in particular, the coordination and consensus-building mechanisms among government agencies and processes to maintain active consultations with private sector and social groups, as well as other stakeholders, before and after negotiations

- Reassess resource gaps regarding the specific expertise needed to prepare, negotiate, and implement trade agreements effectively. Key capabilities to consider include expertise in technical areas of deep agreements, such as competition, service trade, intellectual property, e-commerce, and so on; region-specific expertise, such as analytical units focused on regional areas (for example, Asia or China); and resources to conduct independent assessments of negotiated agreements.

NOTES

1. See Llobet et al. (2017) for a detailed discussion of common elements of the governance structures of best-in-class IPAs.
2. See UNCTAD (2013) for further discussion.
3. See Morisset and Andrews-Johnson (2004) for further details.
4. See World Bank (2009).
5. See Lavrijssen and Ottow (2012) for further discussion.
6. See UNCTAD (2011).
7. The bill ("Ley de Defensa de la Competencia") was pending approval by Argentina's Senate at the time of this writing.
8. The bill could be strengthened further by clarifying the rules for designation and removal of board members to avoid undue discretion and political pressure or even the risk of judicial prosecution for the due exercise of their functions.
9. For a full discussion, see Argent and Begazo Gomez (2015).
10. This means that a notification would be needed only if the combined volume of sales (or assets) *and* the individual volume of sales (or assets) of each company, or at least one of the companies (in some cases, for example, the company being acquired), exceeded the thresholds.
11. See Van Grasstek (2008) for further details.

REFERENCES

Argent, J. T., and T. P. Begazo Gomez. 2015. International Benchmarking of Merger Notification Thresholds. Unpublished memo.

Connor, J. M. 2014. Price-Fixing Overcharges: Revised 3rd Edition. https://ssrn.com/abstract=2400780 or http://dx.doi.org/10.2139/ssrn.2400780.

Goodwin, T., and M. Licetti. 2016. *Transforming Markets through Competition*. Washington, DC: World Bank Group. http://documents.worldbank.org/curated/en/640191467990945906/pdf/104806-REPF-Transforming-Markets-Through-Competition.pdf.

Harding, T., and B. Javorcik. 2012. "Foreign Direct Investment and Export Upgrading." *Review of Economics and Statistics* 94 (4): 964–80.

Llobet, G., V. di Fiori, E. von Uexkull, J. Ramon Perea, D. Gomez Altamirano, and R. Echandi. 2017. "Leveraging Foreign Direct Investment to Transform Argentina's Export to the World: Considerations for the Modernization of Argentina's Investment Policies and Promotion Efforts." Background paper prepared for this report.

Morisset, J., and K. Andrews-Johnson. 2004. "The Effectiveness of Promotion Agencies at Attracting Foreign Direct Investment." Foreign Investment Advisory Services, Occasional Paper 16. World Bank, Washington, DC.

Lavrijssen, S., and A. Ottow. 2012. "Independent Supervisory Authorities: A Fragile Concept" *Legal Issues of Economic Integration* 39 (4): 419–31.

UNCTAD (United Nations Conference on Trade and Development). 2011. *Foundations of an Effective Competition Agency.* Geneva: UNCTAD.

UNCTAD (United Nations Conference on Trade and Development). 2013. "Optimizing Government Services: A Case for Joint Investment and Trade Promotion?" *The IPA Observer*, no. 1. http://unctad.org/en/PublicationsLibrary/webdiaepcb2013d1_en.pdf.

Van Grasstek, C. 2008. "The Challenges of Trade Policymaking: Analysis, Communication and Representation." Policy Issues in International Trade and Commodity Series, no. 36. https://www.peacepalacelibrary.nl/ebooks/files/UNCTAD_VanGrasstek_Challenges-Trade-Policymaking_e.pdf.

World Bank. 2009. "Investment Promotion Essentials: What Sets the World's Best Investment Facilitators Apart from the Rest." Investment Climate in Practice, no. 6. https://openknowledge.worldbank.org/bitstream/handle/10986/10526/503560BRI0Box31acticelGIPB01PUBLIC1.pdf?sequence=1&isAllowed=y.

World Bank. 2011. "Investment Regulation and Promotion: Can They Coexist in One Body?" Investment Climate in Practice, no. 16. http://documents.worldbank.org/curated/en/832851474483734837/pdf/802530BRI0Inpr00Box0379802B00OUO-90.pdf.

4 A Step-by-Step Reform Agenda That Will Allow Companies to Integrate into the Global Economy

Trade, investment, and competition policies are closely interlinked. In an open economy, trade and investment policies are complementary, not interchangeable. Enhancing trade openness spurs foreign investment. Foreign direct investment (FDI), in turn, increases trade flows, as multinational corporations can help host countries overcome fixed costs and barriers to entry into international markets by importing new inputs, expanding networks of suppliers in the host economy, and exporting inputs or final goods.[1] Easing output tariffs and entry of foreign companies tighten competition in the domestic market, while competitive national markets create opportunities for investment and trade.[2]

These three policies also determine the conditions that firms face as they attempt to integrate into the global economy. Successful integration into the global economy relies on the following conditions faced by firms: (1) the opportunity to enter and invest in the domestic market—either as domestic firms or foreign firms; (2) access to efficient input markets (beyond labor and finance) through competitively priced inputs and services of adequate quality and variety; (3) the ability to compete on a level playing field through nondiscriminatory access to essential facilities and undistorted market conditions; and (4) the capacity to thrive in global markets (figure 4.1). All of these factors are influenced directly by trade, investment, and competition policies and are elaborated below.

1. **Opportunities to enter and invest.** Firms (domestic or foreign) can enter and invest in one market through various means: setting up a production plant, importing their products that have been produced elsewhere and developing retail and distribution activities for those products, or acquiring/merging with a local firm that is already established in the domestic market. Trade, investment, and competition policies directly influence these individual entry steps. For instance, the entry process may require licenses (which might be general or sector-specific), approval from a competition authority to acquire or merge with a local company, potentially an incentive from investment promotion agencies to

FIGURE 4.1

Essential conditions for successful integration into global markets

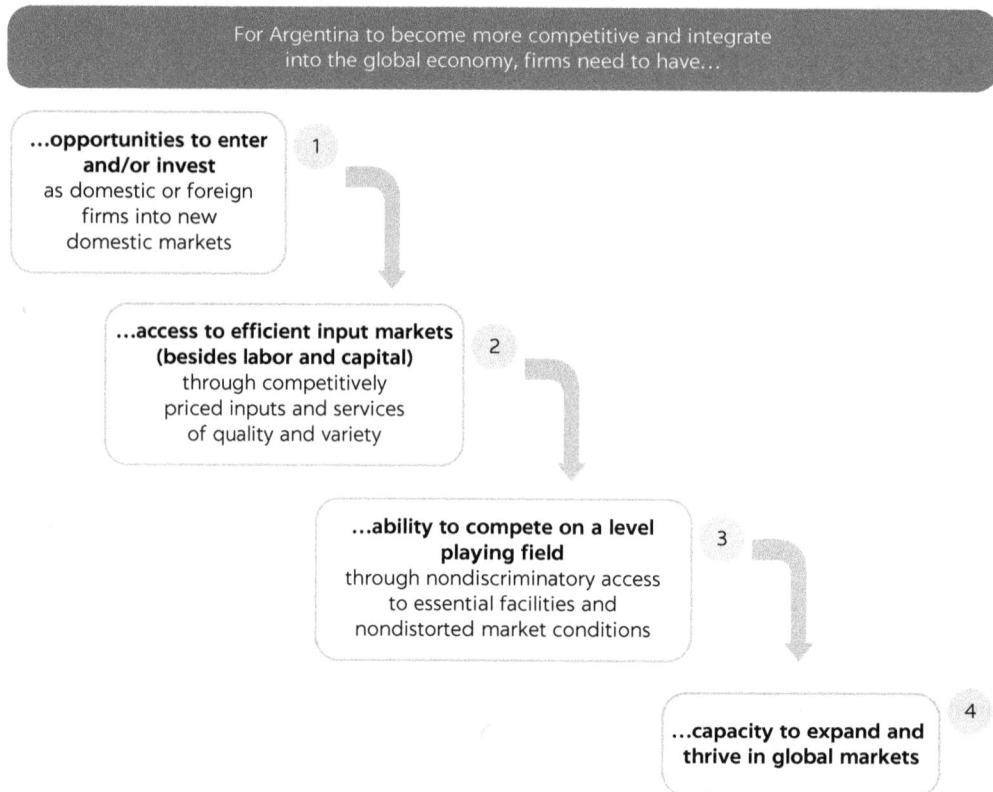

For Argentina to become more competitive and integrate
into the global economy, firms need to have...

**...opportunities to enter
and/or invest**
as domestic or foreign
firms into new
domestic markets

1

**...access to efficient input markets
(besides labor and capital)**
through competitively
priced inputs and services
of quality and variety

2

**...ability to compete on a level
playing field**
through nondiscriminatory access
to essential facilities and
nondistorted market conditions

3

**...capacity to expand and
thrive in global markets**

4

cover the risk and cost of investment (especially for foreign companies), approval
to import inputs (import licenses and tariffs), and so on.

2. **Access to efficient input markets**. Once settled in, firms must implement their
production strategies. It is then essential to access competitively priced inputs
and services (besides labor and capital) of adequate quality and variety. Trade,
competition, and investment policies directly affect the conditions under which
inputs and services are offered in the economy. For instance, the existence of tariff
barriers or nontariff measures (NTMs) influences the cost and availability of
intermediate inputs. Similarly, the price, availability, and quality of infrastructure
services (such as energy, telecommunications, transport, and logistics) are influenced by market regulation, while specific government policies might impose
certain requirements regarding the use of domestic inputs and services in allowing firms to operate in the economy.

3. **Ability to compete on a level playing field.** Firms cannot implement their production strategies efficiently if they cannot compete on a level playing field.
Having nondiscriminatory access to essential facilities and undistorted market
conditions is necessary to ensure that firms thrive based on merit. Trade, competition, and investment policies can protect—but also distort—the level playing
field. For instance, regulations that discriminate or allow for discretionary application distort the level playing field and therefore reduce incentives for firms to
invest, compete, and become more productive. Similarly, the lack of nondiscriminatory access conditions in infrastructure for all players can affect service
standards and ultimately influence the ability of firms to compete in the market.
Moreover, the absence of proper rules that guarantee competitive neutrality in

markets with state-owned enterprises (SOEs) can prevent firms from expanding their activities based on merit.

4. **Capacity to expand and thrive in global markets.** The capacity of firms to expand their activities, first domestically and then abroad, as (domestic or foreign) exporters of goods and services or by opening production plants abroad, is influenced by government interventions. Here again, trade, competition, and investment policies play a critical role. For instance, expansion and growth of firms in the domestic market can be impaired if merger control policies are lengthy and costly. In addition, high costs of export inspection and inefficient border management can ultimately influence the ability of firms to sell their products abroad. Similarly, export taxes and export bans influence the actual and potential volumes of exports sold by any firm. Moreover, the absence of investment protection and grievance policies can negatively affect FDI retention, which then reduces the propensity of foreign-owned companies both to expand their activities in domestic markets and to sell their products abroad.

When taken together and implemented in a coherent way, trade, investment, and competition policies can bring large, long-term payoffs. Figure 4.2 illustrates how specific measures designed under these three policy areas are associated with each of the conditions and highlight the positive effects on productivity dynamics and shared prosperity that would stem from coherent policy implementation in these three areas. A recent strand of the empirical literature finds that structural reforms combining trade, investment, and competition reforms (among others) bring positive impacts on economic growth and other outcome variables, such as productivity, capital intensity, and employment.[3]

Coherent design and implementation of these three policies relies on institutional coordination and interaction. Although, in Argentina, different institutions hold the primary mandate in each of these three policy domains, they can inform each other to ensure consistent policies that achieve the objectives of integrating Argentina into the world economy. Trade policy is under the auspices of the Undersecretariat for Foreign Trade (Subsecretaría de Comercio Exterior) and the Cancillería, which are under the Ministry of Production (Secretariat of Trade) and the Ministry of Foreign Affairs and Worship, respectively. Competition policy is managed by the Comisión Nacional de Defensa de la Competencia (CNDC) and sector regulators, and investment policy by the Agencia Argentina de Inversiones y Comercio Internacional (AAICI). These institutions define the objectives of each policy area independently; but implementing their respective policy programs can sometimes obstruct policy objectives defined under the other two areas, which can ultimately hamper the overall objective of integrating Argentina into global markets. For instance, the AAICI's objective of promoting FDI in global value chains (GVCs) can be impeded if trade policy institutions issue nonautomatic import licenses for intermediate products along those GVCs. By the same token, the CNDC's objective of keeping a level playing field among domestic and foreign competitors can be truncated by discretionary and selective investment incentives employed by the AAICI. Similarly, the Undersecretariat for Foreign Trade's objective of accessing new markets for exports can be impaired by distortionary regulation of input services (such as logistics, telecommunications, and energy) that hampers efficiency. In this context, institutional cooperation and interaction are essential to achieving the overall objective of integrating Argentina into the world economy. Box 4.1 shows some successful examples of interinstitutional cooperation.

FIGURE 4.2

Associations between trade, investment, and competition policy areas and conditions for successful integration into global markets

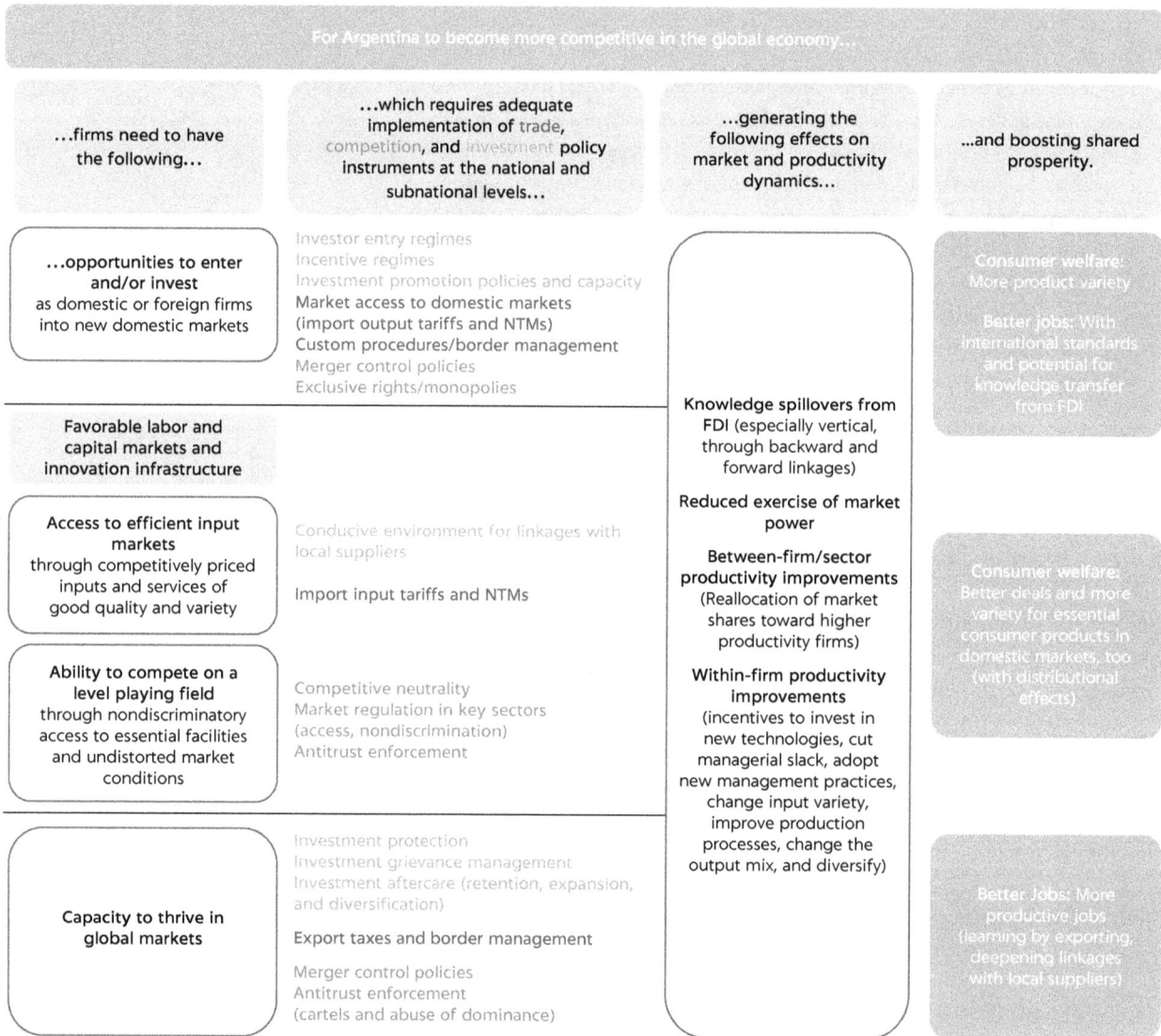

For Argentina to become more competitive in the global economy...

...firms need to have the following...	...which requires adequate implementation of trade, competition, and investment policy instruments at the national and subnational levels...	...generating the following effects on market and productivity dynamics...	...and boosting shared prosperity.
...opportunities to enter and/or invest as domestic or foreign firms into new domestic markets	Investor entry regimes Incentive regimes Investment promotion policies and capacity Market access to domestic markets (import output tariffs and NTMs) Custom procedures/border management Merger control policies Exclusive rights/monopolies	Knowledge spillovers from FDI (especially vertical, through backward and forward linkages) Reduced exercise of market power Between-firm/sector productivity improvements (Reallocation of market shares toward higher productivity firms) Within-firm productivity improvements (incentives to invest in new technologies, cut managerial slack, adopt new management practices, change input variety, improve production processes, change the output mix, and diversify)	Consumer welfare: More product variety Better jobs: With international standards and potential for knowledge transfer from FDI
Favorable labor and capital markets and innovation infrastructure			
Access to efficient input markets through competitively priced inputs and services of good quality and variety	Conducive environment for linkages with local suppliers Import input tariffs and NTMs		Consumer welfare: Better deals and more variety for essential consumer products in domestic markets, too (with distributional effects)
Ability to compete on a level playing field through nondiscriminatory access to essential facilities and undistorted market conditions	Competitive neutrality Market regulation in key sectors (access, nondiscrimination) Antitrust enforcement		
Capacity to thrive in global markets	Investment protection Investment grievance management Investment aftercare (retention, expansion, and diversification) Export taxes and border management Merger control policies Antitrust enforcement (cartels and abuse of dominance)		Better Jobs: More productive jobs (learning by exporting, deepening linkages with local suppliers)

Note: Purple-colored policy instruments refer to trade instruments, blue to competition policy instruments, and green to investment policy instruments.

BOX 4.1

Successful examples of interinstitutional cooperation

The current administration in Argentina has been working to strengthen cooperation among key policy institutions. As a successful example, the AAICI—through its Facilitation Unit (Gerencia de Facilitacion)—has been coordinating with other government institutions to ease the investment process in two main ways.

First, the AAICI has been facilitating and addressing specific bureaucratic hurdles faced by investors in key areas, including:

- Production (encompassing coordination with the Ministry of Production, particularly the Trade Secretariat)

continued

Box 4.1, *continued*

- Customs and fiscal duties (which includes coordination with the Federal Administration of Public Revenues, including the customs department, and the Secretariat of Public Revenue under the Treasury)
- Subnational government (including coordination with provincial authorities for investment and export promotion)

Second, the AAICI has been presenting proposals to streamline laws and regulations that affect the business environment, including key interventions such as these, so far managed by the AAICI :

- Land Law (Ley de Tierras): The AAICI has coordinated efforts with the national land registry to draft a decree aimed at making the framework under the Rural Lands Law (Ley de Tierras Rurales) more flexible to promote foreign investment. Decree No. 820 was approved in June 2016.
- Personal Data Law (Ley de Datos Personales): The National Directorate for the Protection of Personal Data (Dirección Nacional de Protección de Datos Personales, or DNPDP) has recently elaborated a proposal to modify Law No. 25326, which is perceived to obstruct innovation and investment in the sector. The AAICI conducted working groups with key players in the sector (including Cabase, Google, Facebook, Amazon, BT, Microsoft, and Nosis) to collect suggestions for potential changes to the proposal. A technical note was then elaborated and sent to the DNPDP, among other authorities, with proposed modifications to the law.

OPPORTUNITIES TO ENTER AND INVEST

Entrepreneurs in Argentina generally have difficulties in starting a business, registering property, and paying taxes. The country's overall investment climate is not conducive to the entry and establishment of new firms, whether they are domestic or foreign-owned. As reported in *Doing Business 2018* (World Bank Group 2018), Argentina ranks in the bottom third of countries on ease of doing business, at 117th out of 190 countries.[4] Overall, Argentina underperforms in areas related to entering the market, such as the ease of starting a business, dealing with construction permits, registering property, and paying taxes (figure 4.3; figure 4.4). According to *Doing Business 2018*, starting a business requires 13 procedures, takes 24 days, and costs 10.4 percent of per-capita income for men and women. Dealing with construction permits requires 22 procedures, takes 347 days, and costs 3.1 percent of the warehouse value.

In addition to the general obstacles that exist to opening a business, some firms cannot enter or invest in specific markets, which affects market competition. Barriers to entry in certain markets are so high that they can effectively prevent entry of new players. For example, professional bodies license lawyers, accountants, engineers, and architects. Membership in the association is mandatory for lawyers and accountants to practice, and the number of tasks that can be offered only by licensed professionals is higher than in other countries (figure 4.5). As discussed above, legal barriers to entry in Argentina are higher than in comparator countries and a main driver of overall regulatory protection of incumbents. Entry regulation in the air transport sector, for example, increases the sector's overall regulatory restrictiveness (figure 4.6). Only national carriers may serve the domestic air transportation market, and before new air carrier

FIGURE 4.3

Distance to frontier scores on *Doing Business* topics, Argentina, 2018

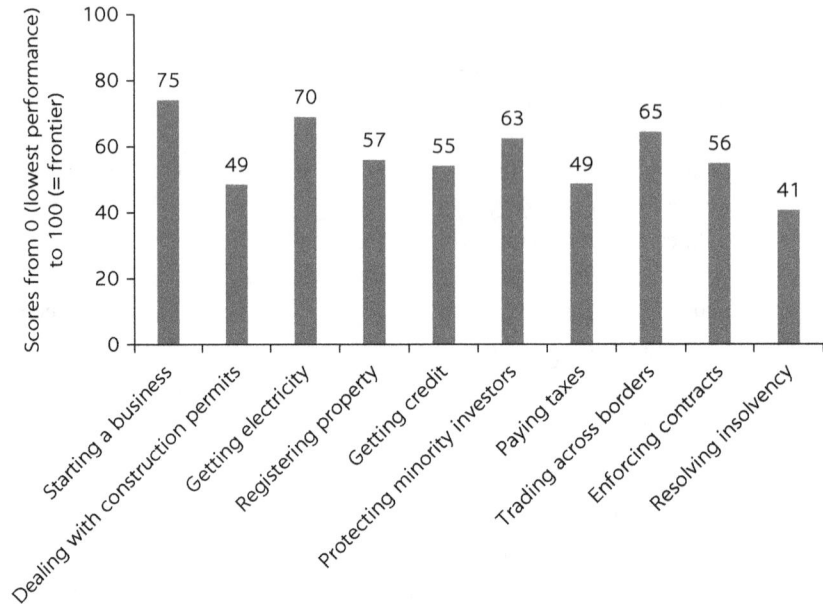

Source: Data from World Bank Group *Doing Business 2018* dataset (http://www.doingbusiness.org/data).

FIGURE 4.4

Argentina's ranking on *Doing Business* topics, 2018

Ranks range from 1st at center to 190th at outer edge

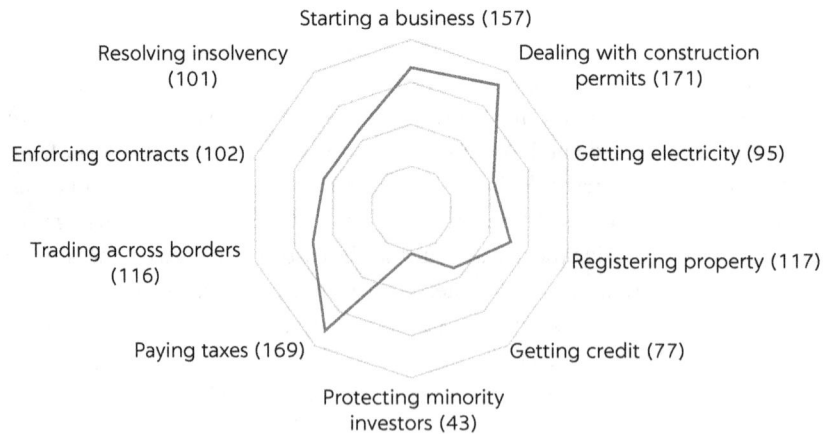

Source: Data from World Bank Group *Doing Business 2018* dataset (http://www.doingbusiness.org/data).

licenses can be granted, the executive government conducts a public hearing to determine whether granting the license would be convenient and serve the "public purpose" of airlines' services. In the media sector, Law No. 25750 establishes a limit on foreign ownership of newspapers, magazines, publishing companies, and television and radio companies. Article 2 allows foreign companies to hold up to a 30 percent stake in the capital and voting rights of such companies.

Where firms consider entering and investing, the incentives to do so are ineffectively designed and discretionary. As part of a complex fiscal regime,

FIGURE 4.5

Number of professional tasks with exclusive or shared exclusive rights, 2013

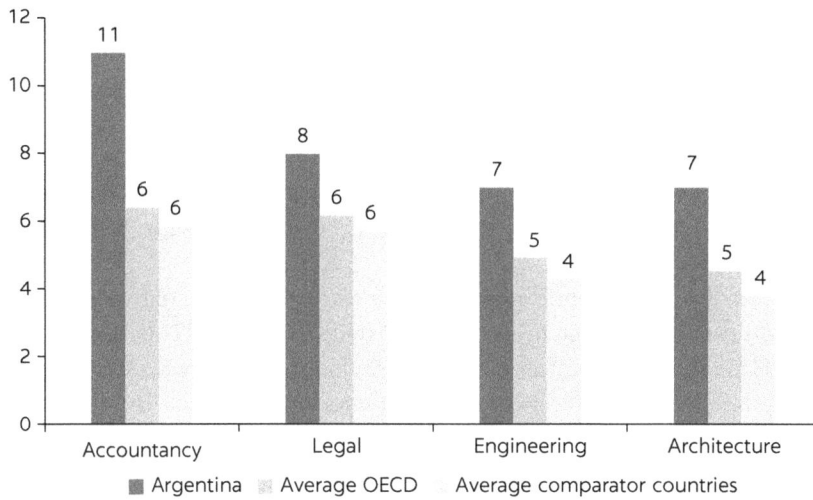

Source: OECD Product Market Regulation database, and OECD-World Bank Group Product Market Regulation database for non-OECD countries 2013, 2016, as of March 2018. (http://www .oecd.org/eco/growth/indicatorsofproductmarketregulationhomepage.htm)
Note: Comparator countries include Australia, Brazil, Bulgaria, Costa Rica, Finland, Ireland, Mexico, the Netherlands, New Zealand, Peru, Poland, Romania, South Africa, and the United Kingdom.

FIGURE 4.6

Contribution of "entry barriers" to restrictiveness of nonmanufacturing regulation subindicator "air transport," 2013

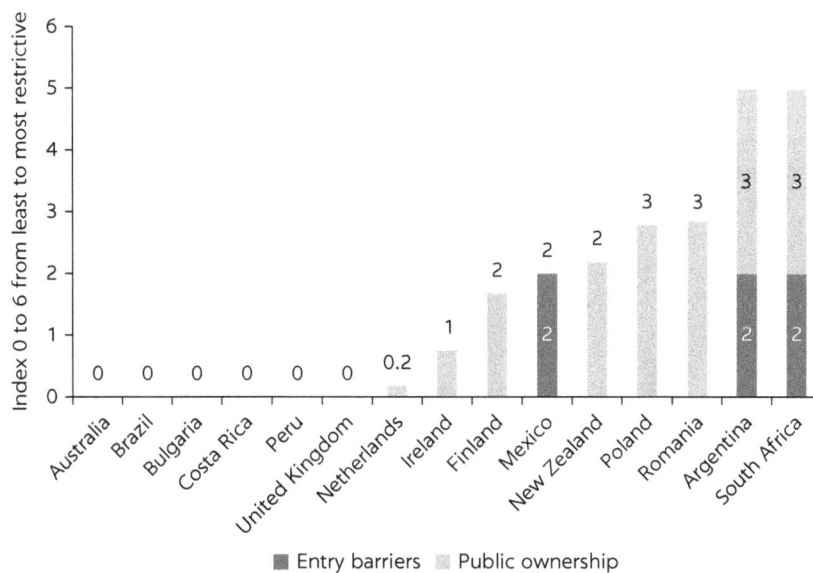

Source: OECD Product Market Regulation database, and OECD-World Bank Group Product Market Regulation database for non-OECD countries 2013, 2016, as of March 2018. (http:// www.oecd.org/eco/growth/indicatorsofproductmarketregulationhomepage.htm).

Argentina's federal, provincial, and municipal governments offer incentives to promote investment in certain sectors and localities. While this intervention can advance public objectives and correct market failures caused by informa-tion asymmetries, externalities, economies of scale, and other circumstances, it can also impose costs and create distortions that might outweigh their benefits.

Investment incentives offered by the federal and local levels of Argentina's government promote specific business decisions, such as expansion or hiring, rather than a firm's establishment in the respective territory (that is, behavioral rather than locational incentives) and are not targeted precisely. This lack of precise targeting entails significant costs for the country and results that are not necessarily effective. Moreover, there is neither an assessment of the effectiveness of incentives nor an inventory of incentives or mapping of procedures to adjudicate incentives. This can result in discretionary application of those incentives. Provincial governors often negotiate incentive packages bilaterally with large companies, in some instances to cover office rent costs and subsidize salaries and other benefits.

A firm that aims to enter a domestic market through trade (imports) rather than investment faces significant barriers to trade, especially NTMs. Beyond tariffs, NTMs and procedural obstacles in Argentina are widespread. According to NTM data by the United Nations Conference on Trade and Development (UNCTAD), over 600 measures affected essentially all tariff lines in Argentina in 2015.[5] Coverage ratios—the percentage of imports subject to at least one NTM—were close to 100 percent.[6] Prior to 2016, import licenses were the main NTMs. Even after excluding these horizontal measures, a large percentage of imports is subject to standards (such as sanitary and phytosanitary measures and technical barriers to trade) and quantity controls.[7] Quantity control measures reflected in the database, aside from import licenses that are not subject to automatic approval, include import restrictions for used machinery, equipment, instruments, and devices and their parts (figure 4.7).[8] The coverage ratio for these NTMs is higher than for other countries.[9] The restrictiveness of NTMs is also high, as measured by the ad valorem equivalents (AVEs) of NTMs.[10] According to estimated AVEs, NTMs during the years 2012–14 were, on average, at least twice as restrictive as tariff barriers; the estimated average NTM AVE for

FIGURE 4.7

Coverage ratios of NTMs in Argentina and other countries, 2015

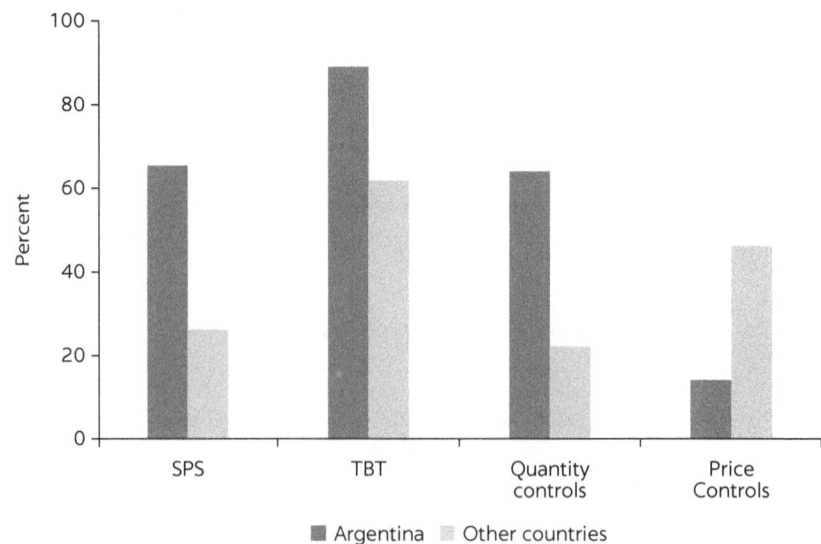

Source: Data from UNCTAD TRAINS dataset (http://unctad.org/en/Pages/DITC/Trade-Analysis/Non-Tariff-Measures/NTMs-trains.aspx) and UN COMTRADE dataset (https://comtrade.un.org/data).
Note: Coverage ratios capture how much trade is subject to an NTM measure. They do not reflect the restrictiveness of the NTM, only the incidence. They do not include local content requirements. SPS = Sanitary and Phytosanitary; TBT = Technical barriers to trade.

FIGURE 4.8

Estimated AVEs of goods NTMs in Argentina, 2012–14

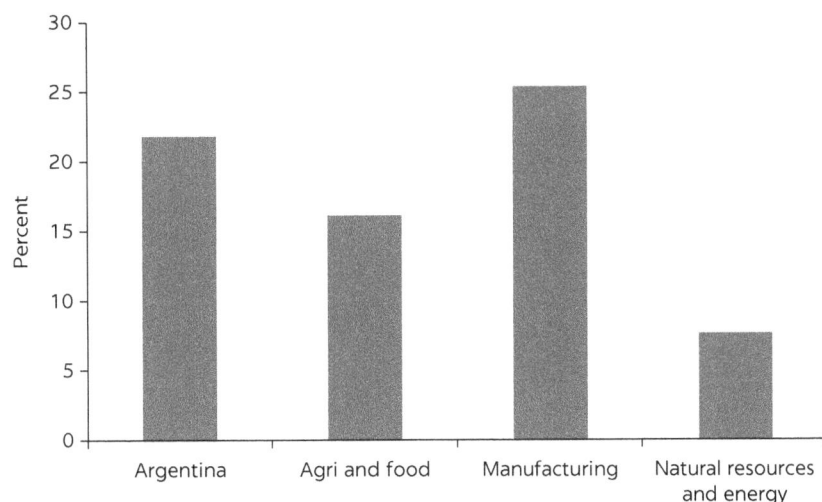

Source: Data from UNCTAD TRAINS dataset (http://unctad.org/en/Pages/DITC /Trade-Analysis/Non-Tariff-Measures/NTMs-trains.aspx) and UN COMTRADE dataset (https://comtrade.un.org/data).

Argentina was 22 percent, as compared to a (simple) average tariff of 12 percent in 2015. The largest restrictions were for manufacturing, where the AVE is about 26 percent, followed by agriculture and food (16 percent) and natural resources and energy products (less than 8 percent) (figure 4.8).

Foreign firms struggle with various procedures when they seek to enter the Argentine economy, either by investing or importing. In 2016, the AAICI managed 305 inquiries to facilitate investment; 195 cases were successfully resolved. Of these resolved cases, 64 percent were related to foreign trade issues (mainly import and export procedures and import duties), while 4 percent dealt with the Industry Secretariat and the tax authorities. Most of the facilitation cases (79 percent) related to facilitating procedures before governmental authorities, which suggests that the AAICI has acted as intermediary with different authorities to remove red tape that hampers business operations.

The government is already improving opportunities for foreign and domestic firms to enter and invest. Argentina introduced Sistema Integral de Monitoreo de Importaciones (SIMI), a new licensing system for importing, reducing the time required for documentary compliance. Paying taxes is now less costly due to the increase in the threshold for the 5 percent turnover tax, and easier due to improvements in the online portal for filing taxes. The CNDC has conducted 12 market studies to identify barriers to entry and competition in specific markets. It has supported the opening of the payment services sector to competition. The AAICI has already resolved at least 195 cases in which investors have encountered obstacles to entry and investment, while the Undersecretariat for Foreign Trade has advanced with multiple bilateral trade negotiations to open markets.

There is room for further improvement to help firms enter and invest. There are four main areas of potential reform (box 4.2). The first would be to address red tape and bureaucratic hurdles that affect the ease of doing business, particularly in the entry phase and in trading across borders. The second would be to open major sectors for investment and eliminate barriers that limit market entry. The third would be to improve the incentive framework so that it is effective in attracting FDI. The fourth would be to lower tariffs and NTMs in priority sectors. To ensure effective implementation of these suggested reforms, and to

BOX 4.2

Main policy recommendations for opening up opportunities to enter and invest

Potential reforms to boost opportunities for firms to enter and invest in Argentina would include the following:

Address red tape and bureaucratic hurdles that affect the ease of doing business, particularly in the entry phase and in trading across borders. For example:

- Create "one-stop shops" to provide all necessary information on the notifications and licenses required to open a business.
- Broadly apply the "silence is consent" rule.
- Introduce a general procedure for regulatory simplification.

Open key sectors for investment and eliminate barriers that limit market entry. For example:

- In the air transport sector, eliminate the "public hearing" requirement for granting new licenses, and open the domestic air transport market to foreign carriers.

Improve the incentive framework to boost effectiveness in attracting efficiency-seeking FDI. For example:

- Conduct a systematic inventory of incentives.
- Complete a procedural mapping of steps to adjudicate incentives.
- Design incentives to avoid the risk of anticompetitive behavior (potential area of cooperation with the CNDC).
- Continuously assess the effectiveness of investment incentives.

Lower tariffs and NTMs in priority sectors and pursue multilateral tariff reductions through free trade agreements (FTAs). For example:

- Unilateral tariff reduction for final goods: Start with the sectors with the lowest labor adjustment costs (computer central processing units, furniture, home appliances) or the highest impact on GDP (furniture, textiles and apparel).
- Unilateral NTM reforms: Harmonize standards among Mercosur parties; minimize use of nonautomatic licenses.
- Multilateral tariff reduction: Pursue "community reforms" at Mercosur and FTA with the European Union (EU).

prevent the introduction of new policies or regulations that obstruct opportunities for entry and investment, cooperation and interaction among the major institutions in the trade, investment, and competition policy domains are important. The evidence shows that the same barrier can reduce investment, competition, *and* trade. The CNDC, AAICI, and Undersecretariat for Foreign Trade can collaborate to ensure that incentives, standards, statutory requirements, and licenses do not unduly obstruct entry and investment overall.

ACCESS TO EFFICIENT INPUT MARKETS

Domestic and foreign firms do not have access to efficiently priced and reliable energy services. Successive government interventions in all segments of the energy industry have contracted energy supply and affected the reliability and prices of energy services. In the electricity generation segment, the definition of an administrative price that was lower than the marginal cost, together with price caps, in 2001 and the associated introduction of a compensatory mechanism for inefficient plants gradually eliminated the long-term signals in energy and power prices, which contributed to lowering the reserve margin and discouraging more efficient, lower-cost investments. Until 2007, there were practically no new generation plants. In the transmission and distribution segment of the energy industry, the administrative freezing of prices has affected the short-term and long-term sustainability of several enterprises, reducing investment and lowering service quality. In 2004, Argentina created an SOE to provide all electricity services and to exploit and commercialize oil and natural gas resources, which has created additional distortions in potentially competitive segments. As an overall consequence of the government's persistent interventions in electricity markets, the energy sector's commercial balance has changed dramatically. Subsidies to compensate for differences between internal and external prices amounted to 3.5 percent of gross domestic product (GDP) in 2014 (Castro, Szenkman, and Lotito, 2015).

Investors face similar challenges in the telecommunications service sector. Telecommunications penetration is high. In 2015, 69 percent of inhabitants had Internet access, and mobile subscriptions were high, at 67.3 per 100 inhabitants.[11] Argentina lags in infrastructure and quality of Internet service, however, ranking 36th of 50 countries on the 2017 Global Connectivity Index.[12] Broadband speed, measured as the proportion of connections above 4 megabits per second, is low (40 percent) compared to the best performers in Latin American and Caribbean (LAC) (67 percent) and Organisation for Economic Co-operation and Development (OECD) countries (87 percent) (figure 4.9).[13] This outcome is mostly the result of inefficient regulatory design, which has delayed or prevented efficient firms from entering and thriving in the market. For instance, regulatory asymmetries explicitly prohibit participation in certain segments of the telecommunications industry, preventing the provision of converged and better-quality services. Specifically, companies that offer pay television by subscription can offer telecommunications services, but telecommunications companies cannot offer television services. Also, delays in spectrum assignment processes and the absence of rules to protect competitive neutrality have prevented mobile operators from connecting more people at faster speeds. Between 2000 and 2015, there were no auctions for assigning spectrum.

FIGURE 4.9

Broadband speed, April 2017

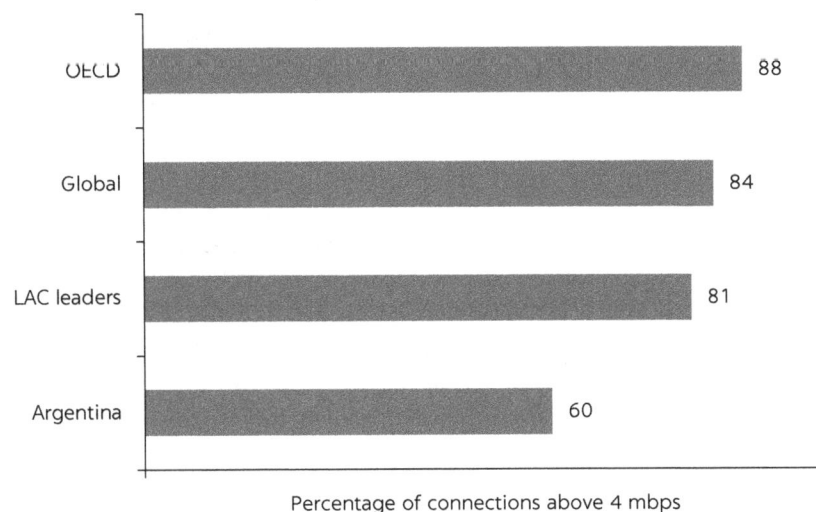

Percentage of connections above 4 mbps

Source: Data from Akamai (2017).
Note: LAC (Latin American) leaders comprise Uruguay (86 percent), Chile (78 percent), and Mexico (78 percent). OECD is an average of OECD member countries (except Iceland).

FIGURE 4.10

Logistics Performance Index vs. GDP per capita (2014–16 average)

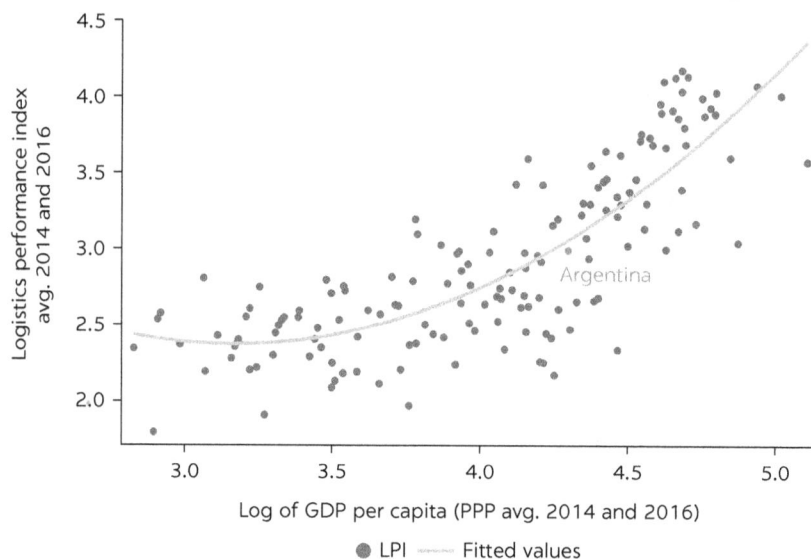

Source: Data from World Bank Logistics Performance Index dataset (https://lpi
.worldbank.org/) and WDI dataset (http://wdi.worldbank.org/tables).

In 2015, 700MHZ spectrum (for 4G) was assigned to Empresa Argentina de Soluciones Satelitales Sociedad Anónima (ARSAT), an SOE that will also administer the fiber optic network and provide it to other mobile network operators. Rules for assuring competitive neutrality are not yet in place. ARSAT is exempt from rules of infrastructure interconnection and sharing.

Firms struggle with high-cost, low-quality transport and logistics services, owing in part to rules that do not induce local providers to operate efficiently. Argentina has a poorer Logistics Performance Index score than would be expected from its per-capita income (figure 4.10). It also underperforms on specific logistic indicators compared to regional peers. For example, the average lead time to import or export in Argentina is seven days, compared to four days for the average LAC country. Logistics costs, adjusted for inflation, have increased by 40 percent since 2003 (Castro, Szenkman, and Lotitto, 2015). In part, the underperformance and high costs of logistics services reflect inappropriate sectoral regulations. For instance, road cargo transport regulations allow truck drivers (represented by the Federación Nacional de Trabajadores Camioneros, or FEDCAM) and transporters (associated through the Federación Argentina de Entidades Empresarias del Autotransporte de Cargas, or FADEEAC) to negotiate jointly salaries applicable to all market participants, including those unaffiliated with FADEEAC or FEDCAM.[14] Such joint negotiation may facilitate or even constitute collusive behavior. In addition, private road freight services (*carga propia*) that want to enter the market and exert competitive pressure on public road freight services must deal with distortive rules: they receive only a 30 percent discount on tolls, while public road freight providers receive a 100 percent exemption.

International evidence suggests that intermediate goods are prone to price-fixing and market-sharing agreements; such cartels have been detected in Argentina in the past and dampen firms' competitiveness. Over the last decade, competition agencies all over the world have been uncovering dozens of cartel agreements in auto parts. In the United States, the Department of Justice, in charge of tackling cartels, has called its efforts in this area the "largest criminal investigation ever," having already issued US$2.9 billion in fines. The turnover of cartels sanctioned in Europe over the last 15 years in products that are typically classified as part of electronics GVCs was US$1.9 trillion.[15] Cement firms have been prosecuted for explicit collusion in at least 14 countries, including Argentina. Factors that are common to standard input products, such as international markets where a few market players have multimarket contact and homogeneous product characteristics, make cartel agreements stable and profitable. Their anticompetitive overcharges, in turn, reduce competitiveness along the value chain.

Firms in Argentina cannot access all input products at competitive prices due to tariff protection and NTMs. The restrictiveness of tariffs and NTMs protects not only final goods manufacturers but also intermediate goods producers. For example, tariffs on aluminum products are as high as 13 percent in an industry that also has a concentrated market structure, which facilitates the exercise of pricing power in domestic markets. In addition, with a tariff equivalence of 17 percent, NTMs in the steel sector reinforce the market dominance of national steel producers and have led to substantially higher prices for producers in the past. Overall, evidence shows that the incidence of NTMs in industrial input-related sectors is particularly high (table 4.1).

Even if tariffs and NTMs were low and products were available at competitive prices, local content rules would potentially hinder investors from sourcing from the most competitive offer. In recent years, the use of local content requirement

TABLE 4.1 **Incidence of NTMs in Argentina**

WITS CATEGORY	NUMBER OF NTMS APPLIED BY CATEGORY (OUT OF 670 NTMS)	NUMBER OF NTMS THAT AFFECT INDUSTRIAL INPUTS
Processed	314	62
Mainly for industry	219	3
Primary	219	11
Mainly for household consumption	210	7
Nondurable	162	13
Capital goods (except for transport equipment)	129	37
Semidurable	97	20
Parts and accessories	67	27
Durable	64	15
Nonindustrial	28	4
Industrial	27	11
Other	21	3
Motor spirit	16	4
Goods not elsewhere specified	16	2
Passenger motor cars	13	2
N/A	5	0

Source: Data from UNCTAD TRAINS dataset (http://unctad.org/en/Pages/DITC/Trade-Analysis/Non-Tariff-Measures/NTMs-trains.aspx) and UN COMTRADE dataset (https://comtrade.un.org/data).

(LCR) policies has increased substantially, part of a trend toward less transparent protectionist measures, including bailouts, tax concessions, and export subsidies.[16] While the use of LCRs may help achieve certain development objectives in the short term, it undermines long-term industrial competitiveness. Investors forced to buy inputs from local sources who do not yet produce the necessary quality and quantity cannot tap into potential efficiency gains that could be available from GVCs. From an overall economic standpoint, the ultimate effect of this type of policy is a negative impact on export competitiveness—not only in those sectors that are targeted directly by the LCR, but in the overall economy. A recent OECD analysis examined a subset of trade-related LCR measures in several countries, including Argentina, and found that LCRs have caused a decline in global imports and total exports in every region. Two LCR measures in Argentina were assessed: one affecting the reinsurance market, introduced in 2011, and the other affecting transportation services in the mining industry, introduced in 2012. The estimated permanent reduction in total exports from Argentina resulting from these measures amounts to 0.3 percent.[17]

Against this backdrop, there is ample space for reforms to streamline firms' access to efficient input markets for firms. Four potential reform areas can be emphasized (box 4.3). The first would be to reinforce procompetition sector regulation in essential input services. The second would be to strengthen anticartel enforcement, especially in homogeneous input products. The third would be to

---

BOX 4.3

Main policy recommendations to enhance access to efficient input markets for firms

Potential reforms to enhance access to efficient input markets for firms include the following:

Reinforce procompetition sector regulation in essential input services. For example:

- Telecommunications: Fully implement Mobile Virtual Network Operator (MVNO) framework to allow MVNOs to provide 4G services and enforce infrastructure access regulation. Implement rules to protect competitive neutrality (ARSAT). Allow pay TV companies to offer telecommunications services.
- Transport: Guarantee effective nondiscriminatory access in rail freight (particularly on tracks operated by bulk users). Review toll exemption rules for public and private providers.
- Strengthen anticartel enforcement, especially in homogeneous input products.
- Introduce a leniency program, under which cartel members can report their infringement to the competition authority in exchange for exemption from fines for the first applicant.
- Further develop and apply techniques for conducting surprise inspections at premises

of alleged cartel members (dawn raids) and IT forensic investigative capacities.

- Increase fines for cartel infringements to effectively deter collusive agreements among competitors.

Introduce effective policies to promote linkages with domestic firms. For example:

- Create an online database of national suppliers.
- Eliminate discriminatory performance requirements and carefully assess existing local content incentives and policies.
- Introduce behavioral incentives aimed at promoting technical training, skill building, and attainment of international certifications.

Impose unilateral NTM reduction:

- Remove import ban on used machinery, equipment, instruments, devices, and parts, and eliminate NTMs for basic industrial inputs (such as plastics, fertilizers, steel, cement, paper and board, and ceramics, among others).

introduce effective policies to promote linkages with domestic firms. The fourth would be to promote a unilateral reduction in NTMs. Ensuring cooperation and interaction among the major existing institutions in the trade, investment, and competition policy domains would be critical in promoting the successful implementation of these suggested reforms. A single NTM, local content rule, or product market regulation can simultaneously reduce competition, export competitiveness, *and* the opportunity to integrate into GVCs. Consequently, the CNDC, AAICI, and Undersecretariat for Foreign Trade must collaborate to ensure that network regulation, NTMs, and investment requirements do not unduly obstruct firms' ability to compete at home and abroad.

ABILITY TO COMPETE ON A LEVEL PLAYING FIELD

Investors in some important sectors (such as air transport and energy) face competition from SOEs that may benefit from undue competitive advantages. SOEs participate in numerous key sectors in Argentina (17, according to product market regulation, or PMR, data), above several regional peers (figure 4.11). While SOE participation is not necessarily distortionary per se, the lack of competitive neutrality principles poses risk to investors of competing operators. Although SOEs and private enterprises receive equal treatment in rules about anticompetitive practices and merger review procedures, in practice the SOEs benefit from advantages compared to their private competitors. For example, Law No. 20,705 provides a special regime to SOEs ("Sociedades del Estado") that does not apply to companies of exclusively private capital ("Sociedades Anónimas"), allowing SOEs to obtain financing that is not available to private competitors. In addition, the government (national, state, provincial, or local) assumes liabilities for the losses of airline and railway SOEs.

FIGURE 4.11

Sectors with state-owned enterprises (SOEs), 2013

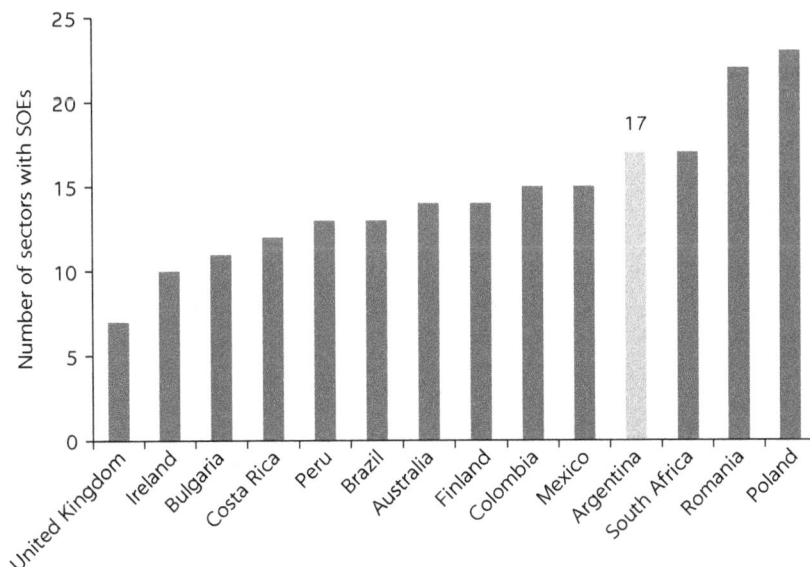

Source: OECD Product Market Regulation database, and OECD-World Bank Group Product Market Regulation database for non-OECD countries 2013, 2016, as of March 2018. (http://www.oecd.org/eco/growth/indicatorsofproductmarketregulationhomepage.htm).

Foreign investors face differential treatment in certain sectors. In principle, the legal regime for investment in Argentina does not discriminate between domestic and foreign investors. Important investment protection provisions are included in the Foreign Investment Law (Law 21.382), including nondiscrimination, expropriation, transparency, and due process of law.[18] However, foreign suppliers receive less favorable treatment regarding taxes and eligibility for subsidies in several sectors, including computers, construction, and telecommunications and business services. In addition, foreign parties and domestic firms do not have equal access to appeal procedures. Unlike in most other economies, foreign firms face unequal chances of winning competitive tenders. Several laws preclude tenders altogether, either by establishing that certain SOEs (such as Repsol, an energy company) are to provide goods and services to public bodies and companies or by favoring Argentine companies even if their prices remain as much as 5–7 percent above those of foreign tenderers.

Argentina has discontinued some policies that could have reduced firms' ability to compete on a level playing field. Overall, the perception of business risk in Argentina has declined, but it is still above levels recorded in comparator countries (figure 4.12). For example, the government of Argentina is phasing out the program "Precios Cuidados," which set prices for a selected list of goods from certain producers. As an alternative measure, it created the website "preciosclaros.gob.ar," which aims to boost transparency for consumers. However, Law 1974 (Ley de Abastecimiento) is still in place and grants the government ample powers to intervene in the economy, including by setting minimum and maximum prices, return margins, and production quotas.

There is space for improvement to level the playing field effectively. There are three main areas for potential reform (box 4.4). The first would be to implement competitive neutrality principles. The second would be to ensure that laws, regulations, and policies apply in a nondiscriminatory way to foreign and domestic firms. The third would be to modify laws that, even though no longer applied, can become a source of limitations to competition. Deploying effective reforms in these areas will depend on how the main institutions in charge of trade,

FIGURE 4.12

Business risks related to weak competition policies by component, June 2017

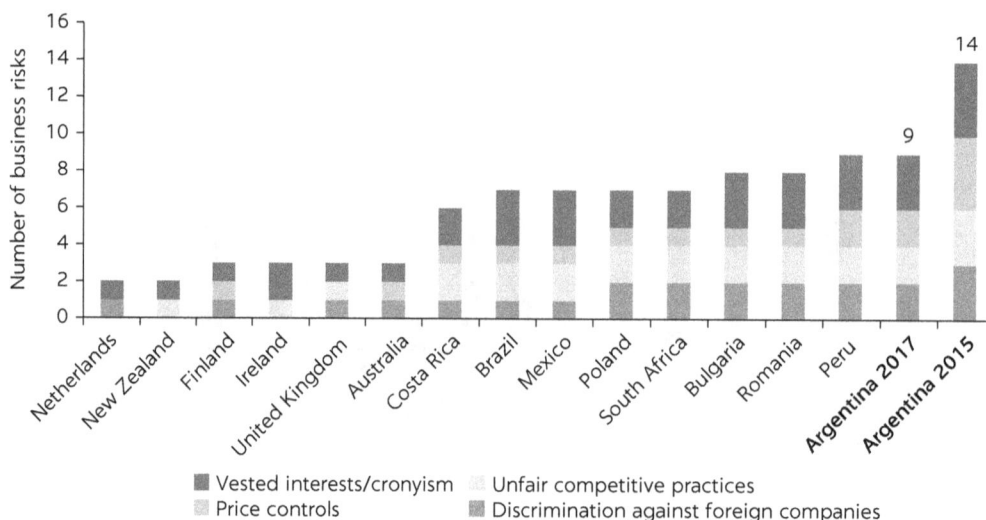

Source: Data from The Economist Intelligence Unit (EIU) Risk tracker dataset (https://www.eiu.com/landing/risk_analysis).

Main policy recommendations to enhance predictability and level the playing field

Potential reforms to boost predictability and level the playing field include the following:

Implement competitive neutrality principles. For example:

- Incorporate SOEs under the same regime as private joint-stock companies.
- Introduce regulatory and tax-neutrality principles for SOEs to avoid undue comparative advantages.

Ensure that laws, regulations, and policies apply in a nondiscriminatory way to foreign and domestic firms. For example:

- Ensure equal treatment for foreign suppliers regarding taxes and eligibility for subsidies in several sectors, as well as equal access to appeal procedures.
- Modify laws that can become a source of limitations to competition. For example, reform or eliminate the 1974 Supply Law that grants the government ample powers to intervene in firms' business decisions.

investment, and competition policy cooperate and interact. Evidence presented here suggests that policies or government interventions that distort the level playing field can not only reduce competition, but also reduce attraction of FDI. To avoid this, the CNDC, AAICI, and Undersecretariat for Foreign Trade could collaborate to ensure that SOE participation in markets and command-and-control regulation do not put global economic integration at risk.

CAPACITY TO EXPAND AND THRIVE IN GLOBAL MARKETS

Investors have not expanded and have often not even been retained, owing to exposure to discretionary or unpredictable government interventions. Investment decisions are influenced largely by transparency, predictability, and stability with respect to government actions. In Argentina, investors' perceptions of the overall quality of regulatory governance are not favorable (figure 4.13), driven essentially by the perception that there is limited transparency in rulemaking.[19] In addition, Argentina's reputation among investors has been compromised by the significant number of investor–state dispute settlement cases triggered after the economic crisis in the early 2000s; at least 57 known treaty-based claims were brought against Argentina in response, all but four of which were lodged under the International Centre for Settlement of Investment Disputes rules (figure 4.14).[20] Since 2009, Argentina has had six cases under the center, with claims focusing mostly on breach of contract, expropriation, and revocation of licenses within the provinces. Although domestic investment dispute adjudication is available through local courts or administrative procedures, the judicial process is lengthy and backlogged. Many foreign investors prefer to rely on private or international arbitration when those options are available in individual contracts.

FIGURE 4.13

Regulatory Governance Index, Argentina vs. selected peers, 2016

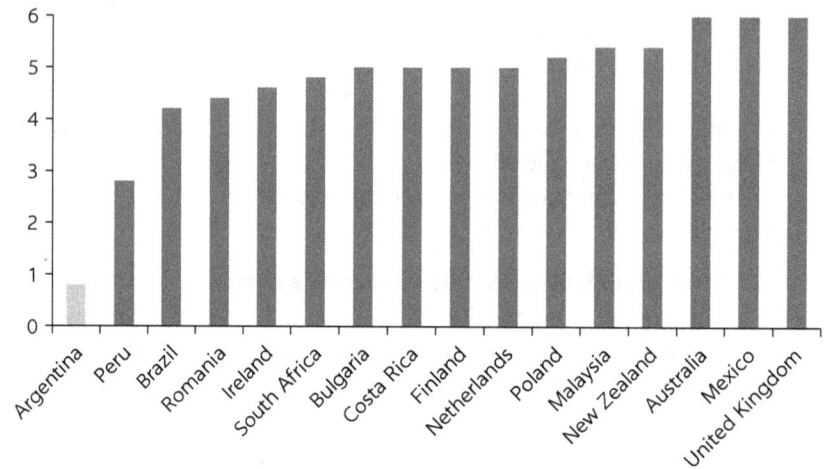

Source: Data from World Bank Global Indicators of Regulatory Governance dataset (http://rulemaking.worldbank.org/data/explorecountries/argentina).

FIGURE 4.14

Investor–state disputes, Argentina vs. selected peers, 2000–17

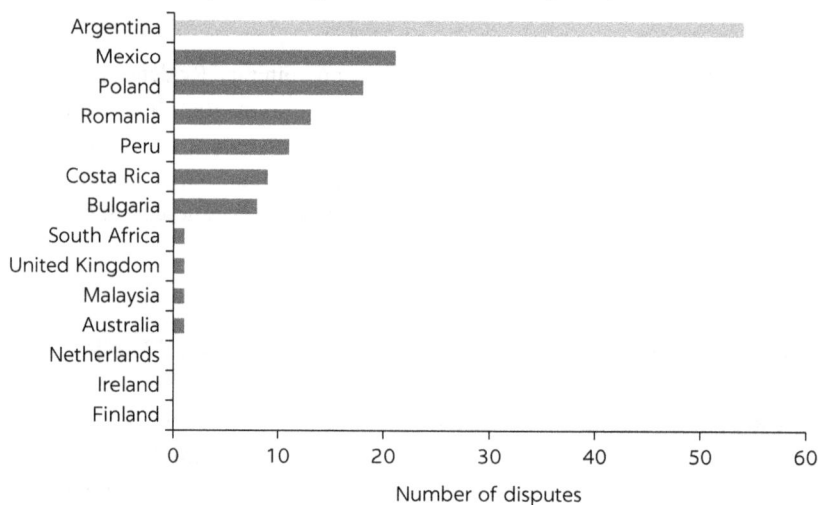

Source: Data from UNCTAD, Investment Policy Hub (http://investmentpolicyhub .unctad.org/ISDS) and ITAlaw (https://www.italaw.com/browse/international -investment-agreement-name).

These types of barriers have negative effects on retention and expansion of all types of FDI, but in particular the "efficiency-seeking" type. Several factors influence foreign investment decisions, often representing a blend among efficiency-, market-, and natural resource-seeking goals. The "efficiency-seeking" investor aims to increase the cost efficiency of the production process by taking advantage of factors that improve the competitiveness of the enterprise. The "market-seeking" investor is almost entirely motivated by the size and characteristics of the domestic market. The "resource-seeking" investor aims to secure access to natural resources in the host country. Market size and the availability of natural resources pull in resource-seeking and market-seeking FDI. By contrast, local authorities need to actively attract efficiency-seeking FDI because the production stages are generally internationally mobile and can thus be located elsewhere.[21] That said, while the existence of barriers triggered by the low predictability of government actions—combined with an investment climate that is not conducive, overall, to the entry and establishment of new firms—tends to hinder the retention and expansion of all types of foreign investments, such barriers are particularly burdensome for efficiency-seeking FDI. In Argentina, the pull factors—mostly the availability of resources and the size of the domestic market—help to counterbalance the burden for "resource-seeking" and "market-seeking" investors, but they are not advantageous enough for "efficiency-seeking" investors.

Firms that are willing to integrate into GVCs continue to face administrative, procedural, and regulatory risks when importing critical inputs. To become full-fledged participants in international production networks, it is essential for firms to be able to import inputs so they can be processed and exported in the form of goods, parts, components, and services.[22] Despite the recent replacement of the Declaración Jurada Anticipada de Importación (DJAI) with the SIMI, as of October 2016, around 1,600 tariff lines remained with import licenses that were not subject to automatic approval, amounting to 25 percent of all imports.[23] Products with licenses not subject to automatic approval included polypropylene, polyethylene and other plastics, and paper and board—all critical for packaging and inputs for typical exporter activities, such as food products and agribusiness.

The government of Argentina has recently improved the consistency and efficiency of procedures that could otherwise delay firms' expansion and growth—notably, by improving the merger review process. The CNDC has reduced the time a merger spends under review by a significant amount. Although the average time for merger review remains high, at 21 months (owing in large part to the many old cases inherited by the new administration), for new cases that have been notified over the last year or so, the average review time is only 4 to 5 months.

As in other policy areas, there is ample space for improvement here, too. Five reforms would be particularly important in enhancing the capacity of firms to expand and thrive in global markets (box 4.5). The first would be reducing regulatory and legal uncertainty through regulatory improvement mechanisms. The second would be overhauling the merger control framework. The third would be to limit the use of licenses that are not subject to automatic approval. The fourth would be to develop a targeted, proactive investment promotion approach by prioritizing a few sectors—potentially the "efficiency-seeking" type of FDI, as it needs a push to be attracted to Argentina. Finally, the fifth key reform would be to enhance investor grievance mechanisms to improve investor protection and confidence. Overall, the evidence shows that policies that generate regulatory risk reduce attractiveness to FDI and limit the potential benefits of trade. This illustrates the need for policy coherence among the trade, investment, and competition policy fronts, which, in turn, depends on effective institutional cooperation and interaction among respective policy actors. For example, the CNDC, AAICI, and Undersecretariat for Foreign Trade could usefully collaborate to minimize regulatory risk through coherent and standardized procedures.

Main policy recommendations to enhance the capacity of firms to thrive and expand

Potential reforms to boost the capacity of firms to thrive and expand include the following:

Reduce regulatory and legal uncertainty through regulatory improvement mechanisms. For example:

- Introduce a legal obligation for regulatory agencies to publish text or proposed regulations before enactment.
- Establish a clear procedural protocol to enforce problems faced by foreign investors and arising from regulatory conduct (federal or subnational).

Overhaul merger control framework. For example:

- Revise notification threshold for companies merging or acquiring another party.
- Clearly define transactions that classify as mergers for the purpose of notification.

- Introduce fast-track procedures for mergers that are unlikely to have anticompetitive effects.
- Improve procedural effectiveness in reviewing mergers.

Remove nonautomatic licenses. For example:

- Limit licenses not subject to automatic approval to the minimum (such as in the case of hazardous imports).

Take a targeted, proactive investment promotion approach:

- Prioritize efficiency-seeking FDI.

Enhance investor grievance mechanisms. For example:

- Establish a systemic investor response mechanism.

NOTES

1. There is substantial empirical evidence on the synergies between trade and investment policies. For instance, Harding and Javorcik (2012) show that attracting FDI inflows can raise the quality of exports in developing countries. Similarly, Halpern, Koren, and Szeidl (2015) and Ahn et al. (2016) show that trade liberalization has a larger impact when combined with pro-FDI measures.
2. Topalova and Khandelwal (2011) show that competition in an industry also influences the payoffs of trade liberalization measures.
3. See, for instance, Gal and Hijzen (2016) and Egert and Gal (2016) for recent empirical evidence on Organisation for Economic Co-operation and Development (OECD) countries.
4. For more details, see IFC and WBG (2018).
5. Not all NTM information is collected for Argentina in this database. For instance, information on temporary barriers such as antidumping and countervailing measures is not collected, although it is available from other sources. Here we focused on two types of measures included in the UNCTAD database: technical measures related to sanitary and phytosanitary and technical barriers to trade and nontechnical barriers in the form of quantity or price controls. The latter are often called "hard" NTMs.
6. In part, this reflects two measures that apply universally or nearly universally across all tariff lines: (1) import licenses that are not subject to automatic approval and (2) a manifest documentation fee, which is a relatively shallow measure that imposes a fee of 90 pesos (less than US$10 at current exchange rates) for air cargo (resolution 3244/2012), which is not likely to affect large commercial shipments in any meaningful way.
7. These measures, and others, could overlap across products, with multiple NTMs affecting the same good.
8. Argentina generally restricts or prohibits the importation of used and remanufactured goods, including agricultural machinery, auto parts, and medical equipment. Capital goods

that may be imported are subject to higher duties than new ones. Recently, in December 2016, the government introduced a program to facilitate imports of used production lines as part of investment projects, subject to approval under certain conditions, including that these production lines are complete and autonomous (decree 1174/2016).

9. These other countries include 50 countries for which NTM data is available in the UNCTAD database for 2015, or for which the latest available year is within the period 2009–15. In the large majority of cases, data are for 2015.

10. The NTM ad valorem equivalent measurement for Argentina follows a price-based approach. This analysis estimates NTM tariff equivalents for goods by looking at detailed, bilateral product price gaps. In practice, international price data are often not very detailed or comprehensive and are often observed at different points of the supply chain. This motivates the use of trade unit values to approximate prices, as they are widely available across imported products (around 5,000 categories at the HS 6-digit level) and many countries. They are also observed before tariffs and behind-border distribution markups, avoiding the need to adjust or proxy for these factors. See Signoret, Rocha, and Molinuevo (2017) for further details.

11. Figures according to International Telecommunications Union database, available at the World Bank WITS website (https://wits.worldbank.org/analyticaldata/e-trade/country/ARG). Internet access numbers for Brazil and Mexico are 59 percent and 57.1 percent, respectively. For mobile subscriptions, Brazil has 88.6 subscriptions per 100 inhabitants, while Mexico has 50.4.

12. The Global Connectivity Index captures adoption of IT (including e-commerce and app downloads), quality (download speeds and affordability), and tech enablers, such as the Internet of things, cloud services, and data centers.

13. According to Akamai (2017).

14. Since 2016, the government has set these rates only if associations of transporters and producers do not come to an agreement in negotiations.

15. Author's calculation based on Global Competition Review data.

16. See Evenett and Fritz (2015) for documentation of the worldwide resort to protectionism in the past decade.

17. See Stone et al. (2015) for further details.

18. The main provisions in the Foreign Investment Law (Law 21.382) are that foreign investors have the same rights and obligations as local investors: (1) foreign investors may transfer abroad-realized profits coming from their investments, as well as repatriate their investments; (2) foreign investors may use any of the legal forms or organization provided within the national legislation; (3) domestic foreign-capital companies may use local credit with the same rights and under the same conditions as domestic national-capital companies; and (4) section 17 of the Argentine constitution affirms the right to private property and states that any expropriation must be authorized by law, and compensation must be provided. See Llobet et al. (2017) for further discussion.

19. According to the World Bank Global Indicators of Regulatory Governance dataset for 2016 (http://rulemaking.worldbank.org/data/explorecountries/argentina), Argentina ranks extremely low in the transparency of rulemaking. There is no legal obligation for regulatory agencies to publish text on proposed regulations before enactment, nor are they required to solicit comments on proposed regulations from the public. Ministries and regulatory agencies do not conduct an impact assessment of proposed regulations. Legislation is not available in one single place for access by the public, and affected parties do not have the right to request reconsideration or appeal to the relevant administrative agency on adopted regulations. See Llobet et al. (2017) for further discussion.

20. Utility operators alone brought 29 cases; the water and sanitation service sector initiated 9; and electricity and gas distributors brought 20 cases. A handful of cases were brought against Argentina in the years preceding the crisis, which revealed to state officials the extent to which the country was ill prepared to address investor claims. See Llobet et al. (2017) for further discussion.

21. See Llobet et al. (2017) for a typology of motivations for FDI.

22. Baldwin and Lopez-Gonzalez (2015) call this process "import to export."

23. As already mentioned, on January 2018, the Ministry of Production issued a resolution that eliminates 314 products from the list of nonautomatic import licenses.

REFERENCES

Ahn, J., E. D. Norris, R. Duval, B. Hu, and L. Njie. 2016. Reassessing the Productivity Gains from Trade Liberalization. IMF (International Monetary Fund) Working Paper WP/16/77. https://www.imf.org/external/pubs/ft/wp/2016/wp1677.pdf.

Akamai. 2017. *Akamai's [State of the Internet] Q1 2017 Report.* https://www.akamai.com/us/en/multimedia/documents/state-of-the-internet/q1-2017-state-of-the-internet-connectivity-report.pdf.

Baldwin, R., and J. Lopez-Gonzalez. 2015. "Supply-Chain Trade: A Portrait of Global Patterns and Several Testable Hypotheses." *World Economy* 38 (11): 1682–1721.

Castro, L., P. Szenkman, and E. Lotitto. 2015. "¿Cómo puede cerrar el próximo gobierno la brecha de infraestructura?" Centro de Implementación de Políticas Públicas para la Equidad y el Crecimiento. Documento de políticas públicas no. 148. https://www.cippec.org/wp-content/uploads/2017/03/1241.pdf.

Égert, B., and P. Gal. 2016. "The Quantification of Structural Reforms in OECD Countries: A New Framework." OECD (Organisation for Economic Co-operation and Development), Economics Department Working Papers, no. 1354. https://www.oecd.org/economy/growth/The-quantification-of-structural-reforms-in-OECD-countries-a-new-framework.pdf.

Evenett, S. J., and J. Fritz 2015. *The Tide Turns? Trade, Protectionism, and Slowing Global Growth: The 18th Global Trade Alert Report.* Geneva: Centre for Economic Policy Research.

Gal, P., and A. Hijzen. 2016. "The Short-Term Impact of Product Market Reforms: A Cross-Country Firm-Level Analysis." OECD (Organisation for Economic Co-operation and Development), Economics Department Working Papers, no. 1311. http://www.oecd-ilibrary.org/economics/the-short-term-impact-of-product-market-reforms_5jlv2jm07djl-en.

Halpern, L., M. Koren, and A. Szeidl. 2015. "Imported Inputs and Productivity." *American Economic Review* 105 (12): 3660–3703.

Harding, T., and B. Javorcik. 2012. "Foreign Direct Investment and Export Upgrading". *Review of Economics and Statistics* 94 (4): 964–80.

World Bank Group. 2018. *Doing Business 2018: Reforming to Create Jobs.* Economy Profile: Argentina. http://documents.worldbank.org/curated/en/899411467995396294/pdf/106122-WP-P156046-PUBLIC-SPANISH-NotasdePol%C3%ADticas-ARGENTINA.pdf.

Llobet, G., V. di Fiori, E. von Uexkull, J. Ramon Perea, D. Gomez Altamirano, and R. Echandi. 2017. "Leveraging Foreign Direct Investment to Transform Argentina's Export to the World: Considerations for the Modernization of Argentina's Investment Policies and Promotion Efforts." Background paper prepared for this report.

Signoret, J., N. Rocha, and M. Molinuevo. 2017. "Trade Policy Reform in Argentina." Background paper prepared for this report.

Stone, S., J. Messent, and D. Flaig. 2015. "Emerging Policy Issues: Localisation Barriers to Trade," OECD (Organisation for Economic Co-operation and Development) Trade Policy Papers, no. 180, OECD Publishing, Paris, http://dx.doi.org/10.1787/5js1m6v5qd5j-en.

Topalova, P., and A. Khandelwal. 2011. "Trade Liberalization and Firm Productivity: The Case of India." *Review of Economics and Statistics* 93 (3): 995–1009.

World Bank Group. 2018. *Doing Business 2018: Reforming to Create Jobs.* Economy Profile: Argentina. http://documents.worldbank.org/curated/en/899411467995396294/pdf/106122-WP-P156046-PUBLIC-SPANISH-NotasdePol%C3%ADticas-ARGENTINA.pdf.

5 Conclusions

Strengthening integration of the Argentine economy into global markets is a primary objective of the new administration. Recently adopted measures have begun to bear fruit. The government has replaced the previous import licensing system, which is expected to boost gross domestic product (GDP) by at least 0.14 percent above baseline projections to 2020. A renewed investment promotion agency, the Agencia Argentina de Inversiones y Comercio Internacional (AAICI), has facilitated investment in at least 539 cases, contributing to 778 new future investment projects announced in the first 24 months of this administration, amounting to a total investment of US$102 billion.[1] The new head and staff at the competition authority, the Comisión Nacional de Defensa de la Competencia (CNDC), have already reduced the time spent on merger reviews by almost 50 percent, presented a new bill to Argentina's Congress, and promoted changes in the card payment market to strengthen competition.

There is still ample space for further reforms, and empirical analyses presented in this report show that both unilateral and multilateral trade liberalization reforms would have the potential to bring substantial payoffs. For example, a comprehensive opening by all Mercosur members to the world could boost Argentina's GDP by at least 1 percent above baseline projections to 2020, and a free trade agreement (FTA) between Mercosur and the European Union (EU) would boost Argentina's exports to the EU by 80 percent above the baseline. Eliminating the remaining nonautomatic import licenses could boost the GDP gains already achieved through the replacement of the Declaración Jurada Anticipada de Importación (DJAI) system from 0.14 to 0.22 over baseline projections to 2020; and eliminating all export taxes would boost GDP by at least 1 percent.

The effects of trade liberalization on employment would differ across sectors. Simulations drawn from the computable general equilibrium (CGE) model suggest that certain sectors would be more susceptible to losing jobs in response to trade reforms. Overall, simulations suggest that sugar, metal products, footwear, auto parts, and other manufacturing sectors would be more susceptible to experiencing large or moderate losses in employment for most of the trade integration scenarios modeled relative to the baseline projections. On the other hand, some sectors emerge as formal employment generators relative to the baseline, regardless of the trade integration scenario under consideration; these include meats, other agriculture, and overall services.

Implementing complementary reforms that tackle anticompetitive business practices and product market regulations that restrict competition could bring further gains to Argentina. Boosting competition in Argentina could generate additional annual labor productivity growth in manufacturing sectors by around 7 percent, on average, and by over 10 percent in the wood, basic metals, and paper products sectors. Simulated scenarios in which Argentina reduces regulatory restrictiveness on competition in service sectors would translate into an additional 0.1 percent to 0.6 percent growth in annual GDP, all else being equal.

The current trade scenario offers opportunities that Argentina could seize. This report highlighted three main opportunities. First, trade in intermediate goods grows faster than trade in final goods, and foreign direct investment (FDI) often plays a crucial role in such global value chains (GVCs). Argentina could thus connect to regional and global value chains by facilitating trade in intermediate goods, attracting strategic FDI, and building on existing capabilities in specific industries. Second, services can be traded by virtually connecting provider and consumer, or by either one moving across borders. Argentina could leverage its comparative advantage in services to increase FDI and exports. Third, information and communications technology (ICT) tools can facilitate cross-border e-commerce and the participation of smaller and new entrants in global markets by boosting their ability to reach a sufficient scale. Argentina could, therefore, foster inclusive trade by facilitating cross-border e-commerce for small and medium enterprises (SMEs).

Argentina could implement key mitigation measures to countervail the transition effects of opening up and integrating into the global economy. International experience suggests that there is no one-size-fits-all strategy for effective mitigation, but that protecting workers instead of jobs is good practice. Both active and passive labor market policies have proved to be effective. Complementary policies and reforms in other markets (such as housing, credit, and infrastructure) play a crucial role in facilitating mobility, thereby reducing adjustment frictions.

Argentina's ability to take advantage of opportunities that have emerged under the new trade landscape will depend on how reforms are designed, sequenced, and managed. International experience with the implementation of reforms in trade, investment, and competition brings valuable lessons. The experience of Australia, Mexico, Poland, and Sweden, for example, highlighted four main lessons. First, reform measures were anchored in broader national policies, and their effective implementation was gradual and took a decade or more. Second, new and existing institutions worked coherently to lead different segments of the overall microeconomic reform program. Third, assessing the impact of reforms, having consistent and corrective monitoring and evaluation regimes, and communicating positive results were critical to sustaining the reform process. Fourth, sequencing and timing were as important as the content of the reforms; in this regard, trade reforms typically combined shock measures with gradualism in sensitive sectors, while investment and competition reforms usually followed a steadier path.

The success and sustainability of reforms will depend on the strength of relevant institutions. This report highlighted international best practices in terms of institutional setup and policy implementation. Three main aspects are noteworthy. First, successful institutions in charge of promoting FDI have certain good practices in common: separate regulatory and promotional functions, a precise mandate that allows effective interaction with investors, and a clear sector strategy. Second, effective competition agencies design and implement enforcement and advocacy tools to ensure the greatest impact on market outcomes; they operate under technical and functional autonomy and work to embed competition principles in broader public policies. Third, the preparation and conduct of negotiations, as well as the implementation of their outcomes, are the core responsibilities of trade institutions.

If properly equipped and supported, these institutions could design and implement specific reforms in the areas of trade, investment, and competition that would bear fruit at the microeconomic level by allowing firms to become more competitive and better integrated into the global economy. This report laid out potential reforms that could be structured around the conditions that firms typically face as they attempt to integrate into the global economy, including (1) opportunities to enter and invest, (2) access to efficient input markets, (3) ability to compete on a level playing field, and (4) capacity to expand and thrive in global markets.

To open up opportunities for firms to enter and invest, Argentina could address red tape and bureaucratic hurdles, open key sectors for investment while improving the incentive framework, and facilitate the entry of foreign providers in priority sectors. Argentina could address red tape and bureaucratic hurdles by setting up one-stop shops, introducing general procedures for regulatory simplification, and introducing a broad application of the silence-is-consent rule. The government could further open key sectors for investment and eliminate barriers that limit market entry (for example, in the air transport sector) and improve the incentive framework by setting up inventories, mapping procedural steps for adjudication, and improving the monitoring and evaluation of incentive schemes. Finally, the government could facilitate entry of firms that organize their activities around imports of final goods, rather than investment in production, by lowering tariffs and nontariff measures (NTMs) in protected sectors, such as furniture and home appliances, and as done recently for computers.[2]

To ensure access to efficient input markets, Argentina could strengthen procompetition regulation in key network sectors, strengthen anticartel enforcement, and promote linkages with domestic firms. Argentina could strengthen procompetition regulation in key network sectors such as transport, electricity, and telecommunications by ensuring effective and nondiscriminatory access to inputs, as well as stimulating competitive outcomes while providing incentives for firms to operate efficiently. It could further strengthen anticartel enforcement, in particular in homogeneous input markets, and simultaneously reduce NTMs, including nonautomatic licenses in input products. Finally, Argentina could actively promote linkages with domestic firms by setting up online databases of national suppliers and redesigning performance requirements.

To strengthen the level playing field and ensure undistorted market conditions, so as to allow the most productive and efficient firms to grow, Argentina could streamline its treatment of state-owned enterprises (SOEs) and remove instruments that distort competition. Argentina could incorporate SOEs under the same regime as joint-stock companies and introduce tax and regulatory neutrality principles for SOEs. It could further eliminate instruments that limit competition, such as the supply law that allows for price controls.

Finally, to help firms expand and thrive in global markets, Argentina could reduce the number of nonautomatic licenses required to import, while also creating transparent procedures for addressing problems faced by foreign investors, overhauling the framework for mergers and acquisitions, and updating the e-commerce framework. By minimizing the use of nonautomatic licenses, Argentina could increase production predictability for exporters. It could also establish clear procedure protocols for addressing problems faced by foreign investors and proactively create a legal obligation for regulatory agencies to publish texts or proposed regulations before enactment. A systematic investor response mechanism would also increase investor confidence. Argentina could further overhaul the framework for reviewing mergers and acquisitions to accelerate efficient firm consolidation. To facilitate e-commerce, it could update the legal framework on e-signatures and strengthen protection for electronic consumers.

All of the above reforms need to be implemented in a coherent way if Argentina is to reap the self-reinforcing benefits of stronger trade, investment, and competition policy. Achieving this objective in any of the policy areas will require effective institutional cooperation and interaction among main policy actors.

NOTES

1. Based on AAICI (2017) and Télam (2018).
2. Import tariffs for certain computer items were brought down to zero in March 2017.

Appendix A
Theoretical and Empirical Links among Trade, Investment, and Competition from the Literature

Among the many policies that can shape the dynamics of resource allocation in the economy, this report focuses on a particular set: product market policies related to foreign direct investment (FDI), trade, and competition. In principle, these three policies share a common attribute: the capacity to shape the incentives of firms to improve resource allocation and to strengthen productivity while integrating into international markets. While foreign investment policy encourages or discourages investment decisions, trade policy shapes the size of the output market and the range of input sources available to firms, and competition policy affects market entry and contestability, as well as incentives to innovate and increase productivity.

The literature identifies several channels through which trade liberalization can boost resource allocation and productivity. The effects of trade policy shocks on productivity can be classified broadly into two main categories: (1) changes within firms that affect firm-level components of productivity and (2) changes that induce intra-industry reallocations of resources toward more productive firms, thereby increasing average industry productivity. Endogenous improvements in firm-level productivity caused by within-firm changes can be triggered by exposure to competition stemming from output tariff reductions and are associated with (observable) actions, such as investment in new technologies, adoption of new management practices, and the decision to export.[1] Within-firm improvements can be also triggered by input tariff reductions and are associated with changes in the level of input expenditures and/or the variety and quality of inputs imported.[2] In the case of multiproduct firms, improvements in firm-level productivity might come from changes in output mix, when firms drop their lowest-expertise products, raise the average productivity of products that survive, and, therefore, raise overall firm productivity.[3] As regards the reallocation (aggregate) effects, trade shocks are expected to reshuffle market shares toward the more productive firms, therefore increasing aggregate productivity; and the extent to which this reallocation process affects aggregate productivity depends on the productivity dispersion of firms prior to the reforms.[4]

Lowering FDI barriers is also expected to bring positive effects to domestic resource allocation and productivity, especially through vertical spillovers. Conceptually, there are two main ways through which lower FDI barriers can affect the allocation of productive resources and productivity (of indigenous firms and of the country as a whole). First, this effect can occur through competitive externalities, which refers to an increase in the competition level of the domestic market. This can affect productivity by inducing within-firm changes in a manner similar to output trade liberalization, as described above, when indigenous firms are pushed to take actions to improve productivity, or by inducing resource reallocation across domestic firms, where less efficient firms are forced to leave and the survivors upgrade their production (or lower their cost base), and, as a result, the average productivity of indigenous firms increases. Second, lower FDI barriers can affect resource allocation through knowledge spillovers, which occur when knowledge created by a foreign firm is used by a domestic company, and this company does not (fully) compensate the multinational firm.[5] This type of spillover typically happens through: (1) the demonstration effect, when local companies obtain knowledge of new products, technologies, and marketing/management strategies by observing foreign competitors; (2) labor turnover, when indigenous firms hire workers trained by multinationals; and (3) knowledge transfer, when foreign affiliates transfer knowledge to their customers or suppliers (and are not compensated for that).

The way in which FDI affects the productivity of local firms and the economy as a whole has been studied exhaustively. As regards the effect of FDI on recipient firms, there is supportive evidence of knowledge transfer taking place between headquarters and foreign affiliates, at least in the context of developing countries.[6] When it comes to the horizontal spillovers (effects of FDI on competing firms within the same sector—the so-called intra-industry spillovers), the empirical evidence is not conclusive, and results are strongly dependent on host country conditions.[7] As for the interindustry (vertical) spillovers, there seems to be stronger evidence about the positive effects of FDI. This can happen through backward linkages, when domestic firms act as suppliers to multinational firms, or mainly through forward linkages, when foreign companies (especially in the service sectors) benefit from local downstream firms.[8]

From the competition side, theoretical and empirical studies provide evidence that greater market competition boosts productivity and economic growth. This evidence falls into two large groups. First, there is a wide variety of empirical studies—on an industry-by-industry or even firm-by-firm basis—providing strong evidence that industries where competition intensity is stronger experience faster productivity growth.[9] The second group of studies uses direct information on the level of competitive pressure faced by firms, rather than the degree of competition itself, to assess the correlation between the level of (or changes in) competitive pressure on productivity (growth). In this regard, see, for instance, Nicoletti and Scarpeta (2003), Conway et al. (2006) and Alesina et al. (2005) for empirical results on the impact of procompetitive regulation on productivity growth.[10] Strengthening competition might drive productivity growth in three main ways: improving allocative efficiency, enhancing productive efficiency, and boosting innovation. First, competition leads to an improvement in allocative efficiency by allowing more efficient firms to enter and gain market share, at the expense of less efficient firms (the so-called between-firms effect). Several studies have attempted to quantify the importance of this market-sorting effect; see, for instance, Syverson (2004) and Arnold, Nicoletti, and Scarpetta (2011). Second, competition leads to an improvement in productive efficiency; it acts as a disciplining device within firms, placing pressure on the managers of firms to become more efficient, which decreases "x-inefficiency"—that is, the difference between the most efficient behavior of which the firm is capable and its observed behavior in practice (the so-called within-firm effect). Bloom and Reenen (2010) examine links between product market competition and quality of management and find evidence that competition is robustly and positively associated with higher management practice scores. Third, competition pushes firms to innovate, which increases dynamic efficiency through technological improvements in production processes, or through the creation of new products and services.

Once properly combined, (foreign direct) investment, trade, and competition polices have mutually reinforcing relationships, in the sense that growth dividends stemming from reforms in one policy area are reinforced when properly combined with reforms in the other two. There are specific mechanisms through which investment, trade, and competition policies can be integrated; see Guasch and Rajapatirana (1994) and Bartok and Miroudot (2008) for an introductory discussion about the three sets of forces at play. In principle, (static and dynamic) gains from trade—from either output or input markets—and FDI reforms rely on price signs that require competitive markets. For example, gains from trade liberalization in terms of lower prices for domestic consumers can be canceled by anticompetitive practices in markets that allow firms to exercise market power. By the same token, opening the market to foreign investors will not benefit consumers if a domestic monopoly is replaced by a foreign monopoly. It is only when domestic markets are competitive and foreign companies have market access that a higher degree of competition can lead to higher productivity and higher income (OECD 2008). The synergies between trade and investment policies, on the one hand, and trade and competition policies, on the other hand, have been widely documented by the empirical literature. For instance, trade liberalization appears to have a larger impact when combined with pro-FDI measures.[11] There is also evidence that the degree of competition in a given industry influences the payoff of trade liberalization measures.[12] More recently, a new research trend in the literature has been to seek to explain the combined impact of reforms in all three of these policy areas.[13]

NOTES

1. See De Loecker (2013) for the case of Slovenia, Lileeva and Trefler (2010) for Canada, and Bustos (2011) for Argentina as examples of studies covering this type of effect.
2. For empirical evidence of these input effects, see Fernandes and Paunov (2012) for the case of Chile; Topalova and Khandelwal (2011) for India; and Halpern, Koren, and Szeidl (2015) for Hungary.
3. See Bernard, Redding, and Schott (2010) for empirical evidence.
4. See Melitz (2003) and Melitz and Ottaviano (2008) for a theoretical and empirical investigation on this aspect and Pavcnik (2002) for empirical evidence on the productivity dividends coming from the reallocation effects caused by trade liberalization in Chile.
5. The idea that FDI inflows are likely to bring new technologies and know-how to the host country is grounded on the argument that multinationals are knowledge producers. Multinationals tend to come from the upper part of the productivity distribution of firms in their countries of origin, since only the most productive establishments can afford the extra cost of setting up production facilities in a foreign country (Helpman, Melitz, and Yeaple 2004). They are able to compete successfully in foreign markets due to their

"ownership advantages" (Dunning 1988), which are strongly determined by their heavy engagement in research and development (R&D), and that are not necessarily codified in proprietary technologies as, for instance, tacit knowledge, know-how, management techniques, and marketing strategies.

6. For instance, Arnold and Javorcik (2009) control for the possible endogeneity of FDI decisions and present results for Indonesia that indicate that foreign ownership leads to significant productivity improvements in the acquired plants.

7. See Javorcik and Spatareanu (2005) for a brief discussion about the countervailing forces stemming from the presence of multinationals within a given sector. A plausible explanation for these mixed conclusions has been proposed by Aitken and Harrison (1999). They postulate that, on the one hand, foreign entry leads to dissipation of knowledge, thus potentially facilitating productivity growth in indigenous firms. On the other hand, increased competition from firms with foreign capital may drive up the average costs of domestic producers in the short run, resulting in lower observed productivity. Since most studies do not include comprehensive controls for the competition effect, they observe the sum of the two forces and, depending on their relative strength, find positive, negative, or no effect.

8. For empirical evidence of the former effect, see Javorcik (2004) and Blalock and Gertler (2004). As regards the forward linkage effects, see, for instance, Arnold, Javorcik, and Mattoo (2011) for the Czech Republic, Arnold et al. (2015) for India, and Fernandes and Paunov (2012) for Chile.

9. See Nickell (1996); Blundell, Griffith, and Van Reenen (1995); Ahn (2002); and Disney, Haskel, and Heden (2003), among many others.

10. In this second group, there are also studies seeking to relate the degree of competition in upstream sectors to productivity performance in downstream sectors. See Barone and Cingano (2011) and Bourles et al. (2013) for OECD countries.

11. See Ramondo and Rodriguez-Clare (2013), Halpern, Koren, and Szeidl (2015) and Ahn et al. (2016).

12. See Topalova and Khandelwal (2011). In this respect, De Loecker et al. (2016) sheds light on how cost reductions and productivity improvements stemming from trade liberalization are passed on to prices (and consumers). They analyze a period of Indian trade liberalization and find that reductions in input tariffs and, therefore, marginal costs are actually offset by firms by raising markups by 11 percent, on average. The incomplete pass-through might be linked with uncompetitive market conditions. Demand conditions could also play a role on this process.

13. Conway et al. (2006), Andrews and Cingano (2014), and Gal and Hijzen (2016), among many others, present evidence of substantial productivity gains from reducing competition-restraining regulations, cutting tariff barriers, and easing restrictions on FDI to "best practice" levels.

REFERENCES

Ahn, S. (2002). "Competition, Innovation and Productivity Growth: A Review of Theory and Evidence." OECD (Organisation for Economic Co-operation and Development), Economics Department Working Papers, no. 317. http://www.oecd-ilibrary.org/docserver/download/182144868160.pdf?expires=1520446788&id=id&accname=guest&checksum=F3302E6D9F7825A4D44CC3D5365F772B.

Ahn, J., E. D. Norris, R. Duval, B. Hu, and L. Njie. 2016. "Reassessing the Productivity Gains from Trade Liberalization." IMF (International Monetary Fund) Working Paper WP/16/77. https://www.imf.org/external/pubs/ft/wp/2016/wp1677.pdf.

Aitken, B., and A. Harrison. 1999. "Do Domestic Firms Benefit from Direct Foreign Investment? Evidence from Venezuela." *American Economic Review* 89 (3): 605–18.

Alesina, A., G. Ardagna, G. Nicoletti, and F. Schiantarelli. 2005. "Regulation and Investment." *Journal of the European Economic Association* 3 (4): 791–25.

Andrews, D., and F. Cingano. 2014. "Public Policy and Resource Allocation: Evidence from Firms in OECD Countries." *Economic Policy* 29 (78): 253–96.

Arnold, J., and B. Javorcik. 2009. "Gifted Kids or Pushy Parents? Foreign Direct Investment and Firm Productivity in Indonesia." *Journal of International Economics* 79 (1): 42–53.

Arnold, J., B. Javorcik, M. Lipscomb, and A. Mattoo. 2015. "Services Reform and Manufacturing Performance: Evidence from India." *Economic Journal* 126: 1–39.

Arnold, J., B. Javorcik, and A. Mattoo. 2011. "Does Services Liberalization Benefit Manufacturing Firms? Evidence from the Czech Republic." *Journal of International Economics* 85 (1): 136–46.

Arnold, J., G. Nicoletti, and S. Scarpetta. 2011. "Regulation, Resource Reallocation, and Productivity Growth." *European Investment Bank Papers* 16 (1): 90–115.

Barone, G., and F. Cingano. 2011. "Service Regulation and Growth: Evidence from OECD Countries." *Economic Journal* 121 (555): 931–57.

Bartók, C., and S. Miroudot. 2008. "The Interaction amongst Trade, Investment and Competition Policies." OECD (Organisation for Economic Co-operation and Development) Trade Policy Papers, no. 60. http://www.oecd-ilibrary.org/docserver/download/241467172568 .pdf?expires=1520447096&id=id&accname=guest&checksum=94823E6890236 B71B711E89FA210CABA.

Bernard, A., S. Redding, and P. Schott. 2010. "Multiple-Product Firms and Product Switching." *American Economic Review* 100: 70–97.

Blalock, G., and P. Gertler. 2004. "Welfare Gains from Foreign Direct Investment through Technology Transfer to Local Suppliers." *Journal of International Economics* 74: 402–21.

Bloom, N., and J. V. Reenen. 2010. "Why Do Management Practices Differ across Firms and Countries?" *Journal of Economic Perspectives* 24 (1): 203–24.

Bourles, R., G. Cette, J. Lopez, J. Mairesse, and G. Nicoletti. 2013. "Do Product Market Regulations In Upstream Sectors Curb Productivity Growth? Panel Data Evidence for OECD Countries." *Review of Economics and Statistics* 95 (5): 1750–68.

Blundell, R., R. Griffith, and J. van Reenen. 1995. "Dynamic Count Data Models of Technological Innovation." *Economic Journal* 105 (429): 333–44.

Bustos, P. 2011. "Trade Liberalization, Export, and Technology Upgrading: Evidence on the Impact of Mercosur on Argentinian Firms." *Amercian Economic Review* 101 (1): 304–40.

Conway, P., D. de Rosa, G. Nicoletti, and F. Steiner. 2006. "Regulation, Competition and Productivity Convergence." OECD (Organisation for Economic Co-operation and Development), Economics Department Working Papers, no. 509. http://www.oecd-ilibrary. org/docserver/download/431383770805.pdf?expires=1520446942&id=id&accname=guest &checksum=2CA976F54702B6B8DAEDCD3D6DD61139.

De Loecker, J. 2013. "Detecting Learning by Exporting." *American Economic Journal* 5: 1–21.

De Loecker, J., P. Goldberg, A. Khandelwal, and N. Pavcink. 2016. "Prices, Markups and Trade Reform." *Econometrica* 84 (2): 445–510.

Disney, R., J. Haskel, and Y. Heden. 2003. "Restructuring and Productivity Growth in UK Manufacturing." *Economic Journal* 113: 666–94.

Dunning, J. 1988. "The Eclectic Paradigm of International Production: A Restatement and Some Possible Extensions." *Journal of International Business Studies* 19 (1): 1–31.

Fernandes, A. M., and C. Paunov. 2012. "Foreign Direct Investment in Services and Manufacturing Productivity: Evidence for Chile." *Journal of Development Economics* 97 (2): 305–21.

Gal, P., and A. Hijzen. 2016. "The Short-Term Impact of Product Market Reforms: A Cross-Country Firm-Level Analysis." OECD (Organisation for Economic Co-operation and Development), Economics Department Working Papers, no. 1311. http://www.oecd-ilibrary.org/economics /the-short-term-impact-of-product-market-reforms_5jlv2jm07djl-en.

Guasch, J., and S. Rajapatirana. 1994. "The Interface of Trade, Investment, and Competition Policies. Issues and Challenges for Latin America." World Bank Policy Research Working Paper No. 1393. World Bank, Washington, DC.

Halpern, L., M. Koren, and A. Szeidl. 2015. "Imported Inputs and Productivity." *American Economic Review* 105 (12): 3660–3703.

Helpman, E., M. J. Melitz, and S. R. Yeaple. 2004. "Export versus FDI with Heterogeneous Firms." *American Economic Review* 94 (1): 300–316.

Javorcik, B. 2004. "Does Foreign Direct Investment Increase the Productivity of Domestic Firms? In Search of Spillovers through Backward Linkages." *American Economic Review* 94 (3): 605–27.

Javorcik, B., and M. Spatareanu. 2005. "Disentangling FDI Spillover Effects: What Do Firm Perceptions Tell Us?" In *Does Foreign Direct Investment Promote Development?* ed. T. Moran, E. Graham, and M. Blomstrom. Washington, DC: Institute for International Economics.

Lileeva, A., and D. Trefler. 2010. "Improved Access to Foreign Markets Raises Plant-Level Productivity . . . for Some Plants." *Quarterly Journal of Economics* 125: 1051–99.

Melitz, M. 2003. "The Impact of Trade on Intra-Industry Reallocations and Aggregate Industry Productivity." *Econometrica* 71: 1695–1725.

Melitz, M., and G. Ottaviano. 2008. "Market Size, Trade, and Productivity." *Review of Economic Studies* 75: 295–316.

Nickell, S. J. 1996. "Competition and Corporate Performance." *Journal of Political Economy* 104 (4): 724–46.

Nicoletti, G., and S. Scarpetta. 2003. "Regulation, Productivity and Growth: OECD Evidence." *Economic Policy* 18 (36): 1–7.

OECD (Organisation for Economic Co-operation and Development). 2008. "Making Trade Work for Developing Countries." *Policy Brief.* May. https://www.oecd.org/trade/40672245.pdf.

Pavcnik, N. 2002. "Trade Liberalization, Exit, and Productivity Improvement: Evidence from Chilean Plants." *Review of Economic Studies* 69: 245–76.

Ramondo, N., and A. Rodriguez-Clare. 2013. "Trade, Multinational Production, and the Gains from Openness." *Journal of Political Economy* 121 (2): 273–322.

Syverson, C. 2004. "Market Structure and Productivity: A Concrete Example." *Journal of Political Economy* 112 (6): 1181–1222.

Topalova, P., and A. Khandelwal. 2011. "Trade Liberalization and Firm Productivity: The Case of India." *Review of Economics and Statistics* 93 (3): 995–1009.

Appendix B
Links between Macroeconomic and Factor Market Policies for Integration

This report discusses microeconomic structural reforms in product markets, and this appendix briefly discusses other complementary policy areas that can be important for success in integrating into the global economy.

An adequate macroeconomic policy also matters because it can help set the right incentives for economic agents. A sound macroeconomic policy—with stabilized inflation and a flexible exchange rate not grossly out of equilibrium—helps bring stability and predictability to economic agents so they can better formulate their production strategies. Macroeconomic stability and appropriate exchange rates matter even more when opening the economy, especially to elicit a robust and strong export response, because imports tend to rise faster than exports in reaction to trade tariff reductions.

Labor market policies must also be favorable to facilitate the resource reallocation movement triggered by pro-opening reforms. Underneath the process of integration into global markets is a turbulent labor reallocation and churning movement. Absent labor market rigidities, opening the economy would cause a smooth reallocation of workers toward more productive activities. This reallocation process does not work automatically, however, owing in part to stringencies created by labor market institutions, such as rigid hiring and firing practices. Evidence suggests that less stringent labor market institutions facilitate the movement of labor to more productive firms and foster firm entry and exit.[1] Impediments to the movement of labor between heterogeneous firms and sectors could undermine both aggregate productivity growth and the benefits from opening the economy. Country-specific studies find that excessive regulation can slow down job creation in global value chains (GVCs), causing countries to miss job-supporting agglomeration effects and knowledge spillovers.[2]

The same applies to credit and financial policies. Allocation of capital across firms (and activities) is another important determinant of aggregate productivity and can shape the effects of international integration. Financial restrictions on the price or quantity of credit can slow down, or even limit, the reallocation process following the economy's opening, because it takes time for productive but low-net-worth firms to accumulate enough assets to operate at full scale.[3] Distortive financial policies can affect misallocation of resources, additional entry, technology adoption,[4] and the ability to cover fixed costs of entry into export activities.[5]

Also instrumental is the combination of significant absorptive capacity and an effective innovation policy to ensure the proper functioning of the "diffusion machine." The gains from further integration into the global economy are conditional on the "absorptive capacity" (for example, human capital) to capture the spillover benefits from trade.[6] In addition, connecting with global markets via trade, FDI, and participation in GVCs provides scope for knowledge diffusion between global frontier companies and national frontier firms. In this regard, the capacity of a country to absorb, adapt, and reap the full benefits of knowledge produced at the frontier depends on strategic investments in research and development (R&D), organizational know-how, and other forms of knowledge-based capital.[7]

Efficient business regulations are another important factor in seizing new opportunities that arise from foreign economic integration while boosting allocative efficiency. Integration into the global economy brings new business opportunities to domestic companies and pushes the reallocation of resources across sectors and firms. The time and financial costs of compliance with business regulations strongly condition the ability of firms to respond to emerging prospects in new sectors. Entry and exit regulations are important. Restrictive entry rules can penalize experimentation, a cost that is disproportionately higher for areas such as information and communications technology (ICT)–intensive industries.[8] Restrictive regulations damage employment growth heavily because young firms are the primary drivers of job creation. Exit regulations (such as bankruptcy legislation) affect how quickly an economy can reallocate resources that are trapped in nonviable firms to more efficient uses.

NOTES

1. See, for instance, Henrekson and Johansson (2010) for an empirical analysis of the role of institutions that encourage the creation of high-growth firms and promote structural transformation.
2. See World Bank (2013) for a detailed discussion on how excessive labor market regulations can offset job creation within value chains.
3. See Buera and Shin (2011) for empirical analysis on the role of financial frictions and resource misallocation in explaining development dynamics.
4. See Midrigan and Xu (2014) for a compelling theoretical and empirical analysis on the impact of financial frictions on total factor productivity (TFP) growth via entry and technology adoption decisions and resource misallocation.
5. See Manova (2013) for a theoretical model and empirical analysis about the detrimental impacts of financial market imperfections for international trade.
6. See Borensztein, De Gregorio, and Lee (1998) for a theoretical discussion.
7. See OECD (2015) for a theoretical and empirical discussion on the role of technology diffusion as a channel to boost productivity growth.
8. See Andrews and Cingano (2014) for empirical evidence.

REFERENCES

Andrews, D., and F. Cingano. 2014. "Public Policy and Resource Allocation: Evidence from Firms in OECD Countries." *Economic Policy* 29 (78): 253–96.

Borensztein, E., J. De Gregorio, and J. W. Lee. 1998. "How Does Foreign Direct Investment Affect Economic Growth?" *Journal of International Economics* 45: 115–35.

Buera, F., and Y. Shin. 2011. "Self-Insurance vs. Self-Financing: A Welfare Analysis of the Persistence of Shocks." *Journal of Economic Theory* 146 (3): 845–62.

Henrekson, M., and D. Johansson. 2010. "Gazelles as Job Creators: A Survey and Interpretation of the Evidence." *Small Business Economics* 35: 227–44.

Manova, K. 2013. "Credit Constraints, Heterogeneous Firms and International Trade." *Review of Economic Studies* 80 (2): 711–44.

Midrigan, V., and D. Xu. 2014. "Finance and Misallocation: Evidence from Plant-Level Data." *American Economic Review* 104 (2): 422–58.

OECD (Organisation for Economic Co-operation and Development). 2015. *The Future of Productivity.* https://www.oecd.org/eco/growth/OECD-2015-The-future-of-productivity -book.pdf.

World Bank. 2013. *Turkey—Reform for Competitiveness Technical Assistance: Fostering Open and Efficient Markets through Effective Competition Policies.* Washington, DC: World Bank.

Appendix C
The CGE Framework

A computable general equilibrium (CGE) model uses economic data and a set of behavioral equations to estimate how an economy might react to changes in policy, technology, or other factors. The model is benchmarked to a starting year dataset that covers the whole economy, tracking the linkages among sectors through input–output or interindustry transaction flow tables, as well as various sources of demand, such as the intermediate demand of enterprises and the final demand of households, government, and investment. It also models the behavior of producers according to the principle of profit maximization and their production functions. Finally, it simulates foreign demand and supply by including equations that explain bilateral trade flows. The analysis using a CGE model starts from the development of a long-term baseline with a set of exogenous variables and parameters (population, productivity growth, and elasticities). Then the counterfactual policy scenario is formulated by changing some exogenous variables or policy parameters. Finally, the impact of a counterfactual policy is assessed by looking at deviations of endogenous variables (that is, those variables that are not fixed or user specified) from their baseline levels—for example, for gross domestic product (GDP), investment, savings, trade flows, sectoral output, employment, wages, household consumption, welfare, relative prices, and so on.

This report presents medium- and long-term scenarios to assess several implications for Argentina of trade liberalization on both unilateral and multilateral integration fronts. These scenarios are based on the World Bank's LINKAGE model—a recursive global dynamic CGE model.

This appendix covers the main features of LINKAGE. A full description is provided by Van der Mensbrugghe (2011). The version of the LINKAGE model applied to Argentina relies on release 9.1 of the Global Trade Analysis Project (GTAP) database. This dataset was customized for Argentina as follows. First, the input–output structure for Argentina was updated from 1997 to 2004 (the latest official tables from Instituto Nacional de Estadística y Censos de la República Argentina, or INDEC). Second, the base year in GTAP (2011) was updated to 2015. Third, 26 regions were identified, including each Mercosur country; the European Union (EU27 + UK); the members of the Pacific Alliance; and other regions with potential for integration, such as Canada, China, the European Free Trade Association,

TABLE C.1 **Sectors identified in the model**

AGRICULTURE/FOOD	NATURAL RESOURCES AND ENERGY	MANUFACTURING	SERVICES
Wine	Biodiesel	Pharma	Communications, financial, and business
Beef	Fuels and fuel products	Computers	Other services
Poultry and swine	Steel	Electronics	
Dairy	Other natural resources	Metal products	
Soybean		Furniture	
Soy meals and oil		Footwear	
Sugar		Vehicles	
Fruits and vegetables		Auto parts	
Corn		Agricultural machinery	
Wheat		Home appliances	
Other food and agricultural products		Other machinery and equipment	
		Textiles and apparel	
		Other manufacturing	

Japan, Korea, and the United States. Fourth, the sectoral dimension in GTAP was expanded to include several new sectors of interest for the Argentine economy (see table C.1 for a final list of sectors).

The core specification of the LINKAGE model replicates largely a standard global CGE model, where production is specified as a series of nested constant elasticity of substitution (CES) functions for the various inputs—unskilled and skilled labor, capital, land, natural resources (sector specific), energy, and other material inputs. The structure of the CES nest characterizes the substitution and complementary relations across inputs.[1] In the labor market at the baseline, the model assumes full employment and allows for internal migration, even though there is no international migration. The model also allows for market segmentation by allowing rural–urban migration of unskilled labor to be a function of relative wages.

Demand on the part of each domestic agent is specified at the so-called Armington level—that is, demand for a bundle of domestically produced and imported goods. Armington demand is aggregated across all agents and allocated at the national level between domestic production and imports by region of origin.[2] Each bilateral flow is associated with three price wedges: the first distinguishes producer prices from the free-on-board price (an export tax and/or subsidy); the second distinguishes the free-on-board price from the cost, insurance, and freight price (an international trade and transportation margin); and the third distinguishes the cost, insurance, and freight price from the user price (an import tariff).

Government income is derived from various taxes: sales, excise, import duties, export, production, factors, and direct taxes. Investment revenues come from household, government, and net foreign savings. Government and investment expenditure are based on CES functions.

Three closure rules are incorporated into the standard scenario. First, government expenditures are held constant as a share of GDP, and fiscal balance is exogenous, while direct taxes adjust to cover any changes in the revenues to keep the fiscal balance at the exogenous level. The second closure rule determines the investment/savings balance. Households save a portion of their income, with the average propensity to save influenced by demographics and economic growth. Government savings and foreign savings are exogenous in the current specification. As a result, investment is savings driven, and the total amount of savings depends on household savings, with the price of investment goods being determined also by demand for investment. The third closure rule determines the external balance. In the current model specification, the foreign savings—and therefore the trade balance—are assumed to be fixed. Changes in trade flows will therefore result in shifts in the real exchange rate.

The LINKAGE model incorporates a few key dynamics in terms of population growth, savings versus investment, capital accumulation, and productivity growth. Population growth is based on the medium fertility variant of the United Nations' population projections. Labor force growth is equated to the growth of the working-age population—defined here as the demographic cohort between 15 and 64 years of age. Investment is equated to savings. Savings are a function of income growth and demographic dependency ratios, with savings rising as incomes rise and dependency ratios decline.[3] Capital accumulation is then equated to the previous period's (depreciated) capital stock plus investment. Productivity growth in the baseline is "calibrated" to achieve a given trend in long-term growth in line with historical growth rates (that is, up to 2015), and then productivity growth remains fixed up to medium- and long-term scenarios (2020 and 2030).

For the baseline scenario of this report, the GDP growth rates assumed for Argentine economy are shown in figure C.1.

Some caveats of the LINKAGE model are worth highlighting. The model does not include some of the features typical for increasing returns to scale with product variety, so the liberalization does not cause dynamic productivity gains and variety effects. However, empirical work supporting this approach is still underdeveloped, and there are no country-specific estimates of elasticity parameters to be applied in global models. The LINKAGE approach is, therefore, based

FIGURE C.1

Annualized real GDP growth in Argentina under the baseline

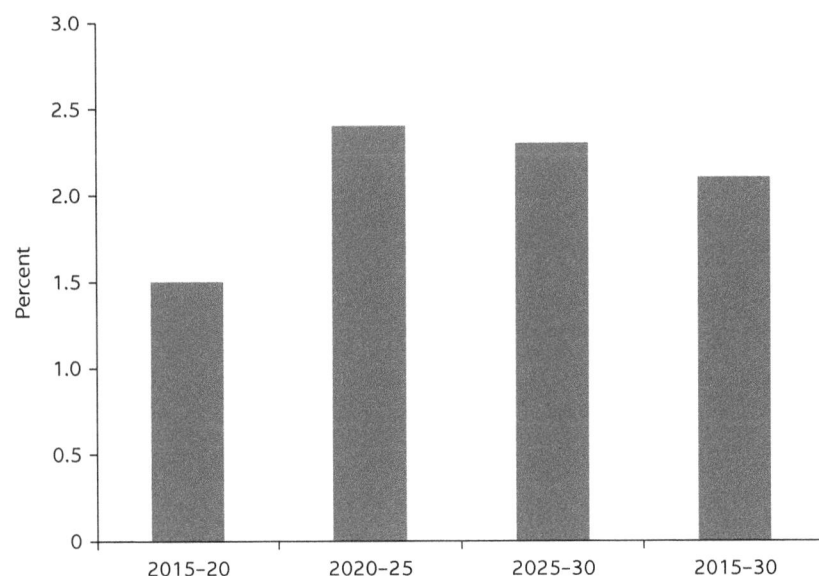

on intersectoral specialization effects alone. In addition, the model does not include other dynamic factors proposed in the literature, such as productivity increases from endogenous growth effects via technological spillovers, "learning by doing," or inflows of foreign technology and investment induced by liberalization. These effects, while possible, are difficult to measure and incorporate in this type of analysis. Moreover, certain policy changes that are often difficult to quantify—such as reforms related to nontariff measures (NTMs) in goods and services and restrictions to investment—present analytical challenges that may affect the estimated economic effects. Owing to these limitations, CGE results presented in the report are likely to be conservative.

NOTES

1. LINKAGE uses a vintage structure of production that allows for putty to semi-putty capital. This means that capital can be either old or new, with new capital being more substitutable with other factors. In addition, it is assumed that old capital is less flexible than new capital.
2. A top-level CES nest first allocates aggregate (or Armington) demand between domestic production and an aggregate import bundle. A second-level nest then allocates aggregate imports across the model's different regions, thus generating a bilateral trade flow matrix.
3. Therefore, countries that have declining youth dependency rates tend to see a rise in savings. This will eventually be offset by countries where the share of the elderly in the population is rising, which will result in a fall of savings.

REFERENCE

Van der Mensbrugghe, D. 2011. *Linkage Technical Reference Document, Version 7.1*. Washington, DC: http://siteresources.worldbank.org/INTPROSPECTS/Resources/334934 -1314986341738/TechRef7.1_01Mar2011.pdf.

Appendix D
The OECD PMR Methodology

The Organisation for Economic Co-operation and Development (OECD) economy-wide and sectoral product market regulation (PMR) indicators measure regulatory restrictiveness with regard to competition. While the economy-wide PMR is a single indicator that summarizes information by regulatory domain, the latter indicators do so by sector. The economy-wide indicator is calculated using a bottom-up approach in which data on regulatory structures and policies are used to assign numeric values to eighteen low-level regulatory domains. These values, or low-level indicators, are then aggregated "up the tree" (figure D.1) to derive seven mid-level indicators, which are, in turn, aggregated to derive three high-level indicators: state control, barriers to entrepreneurship, and barriers to trade and investment. Finally, these three indicators are aggregated to yield the economy-wide PMR.

Sectoral indicators aggregate information by sector. They are based on the same underlying dataset as the economy-wide PMR indicator, and their calculation utilizes a similar bottom-up approach, but the tree structure aggregates numeric values to derive sector-specific indicators.[1] There are three sectoral indicators, corresponding to three sector groups: (1) energy, transport, and communications (ETCR); (2) professional services; and (3) retail distribution. For each group, computing the corresponding sectoral PMR indicator aggregates lower-level scores into an indicator for each sector in the group. For example, in computing the ETCR, we obtain indicators for the electricity, communications, and transport sectors. These are finally aggregated to obtain the ETCR indicator. Figure D.2 shows the tree structure of the ETCR and professional services nonmanufacturing regulation indicators.

FIGURE D.1

OECD PMR indicator

```
                        ┌─────────────────────────────┐
                        │  Product market regulation  │
                        └─────────────────────────────┘
        ┌───────────────────────────┬───────────────────────────────┐
  ┌─────────────┐         ┌───────────────────────┐      ┌─────────────────┐
  │ State control│         │ Barriers to            │      │ Barriers to trade│
  └─────────────┘         │ enterpreneurship       │      │ and investment  │
                          └───────────────────────┘      └─────────────────┘
```

Public ownership	Involvement in business operations	Complexity of regulatory procedures	Administrative burdens on startups	Regulatory protection of incumbents	Explicit barriers to trade and investment	Other barriers to trade and investment
Scope of SOEs

Government involvement in network sectors

Direct control over enterprises

Governance of SOEs | Price controls

Command and control regulation | Licenses and permits system

Communication and simplification of rules and procedures | Administrative burdens for corporations

Administrative burdens for sole-proprietor firms

Barriers in service sectors | Legal barriers to entry

Antitrust exemptions

Barriers in network sectors | Barriers to FDI

Tariff barriers | Differential treatment of foreign suppliers

Barriers to trade facilitation |

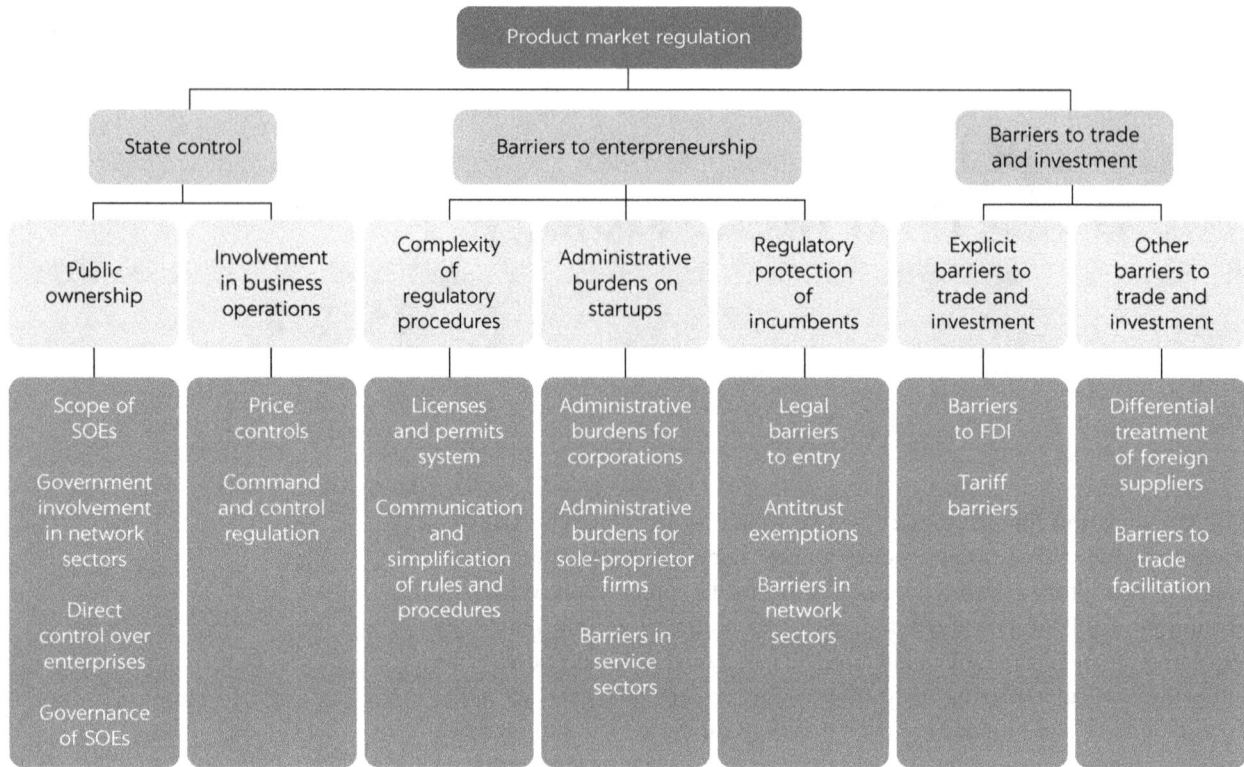

Source: Koske et al. (2015).
Note: SOE = state-owned enterprise; FDI = foreign direct investment.

FIGURE D.2

OECD Nonmanufacturing indicators in energy, transport, and communication sectors

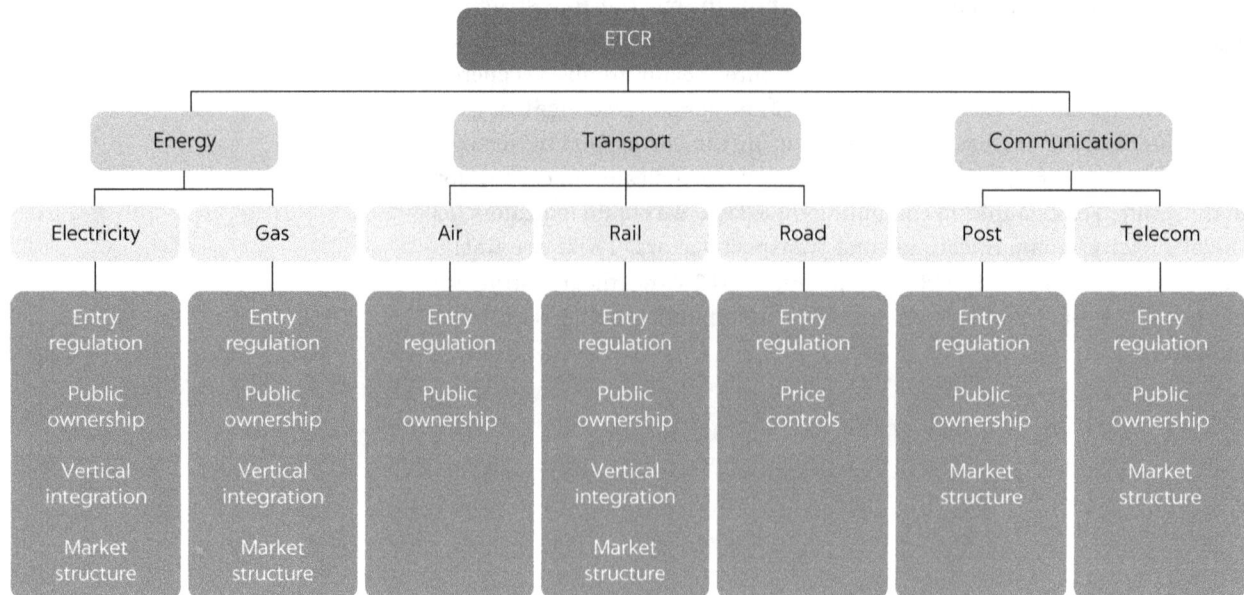

```
                        ┌─────────────────────────────┐
                        │            ETCR             │
                        └─────────────────────────────┘
        ┌───────────────────────┬───────────────────────────┐
   ┌──────────┐           ┌──────────┐              ┌──────────────┐
   │  Energy  │           │ Transport│              │Communication │
   └──────────┘           └──────────┘              └──────────────┘
```

Electricity	Gas	Air	Rail	Road	Post	Telecom
Entry regulation

Public ownership

Vertical integration

Market structure | Entry regulation

Public ownership

Vertical integration

Market structure | Entry regulation

Public ownership | Entry regulation

Public ownership

Vertical integration

Market structure | Entry regulation

Price controls | Entry regulation

Public ownership

Market structure | Entry regulation

Public ownership

Market structure |

Source: Koske et al. (2015).

NOTE

1. For example, data on the requirement of membership in a professional organization enter the calculation of the economy-wide PMR indicator via the "barriers in service sectors" subcategory within the "administrative burdens on startups" category. However, the same data enter the calculation of the professional services PMR indicator via the "compulsory chamber membership" subcategories within the "entry-regulation" categories for each of the four professional services.

REFERENCE

Koske, I., I. Wanner, R. Bitetti, and O. Barbiero. 2015. "The 2013 Update of the OECD's Database on Product Market Regulation: Policy Insights for OECD and Non-OECD Countries." OECD (Organisation for Economic Co-operation and Development), Economics Department Working Papers, no. 1200. http://www.oecd-ilibrary.org/docserver /download/5js3f5d3n2vl-en.pdf?expires=1520448144&id=id&accname=guest&checksum =C9B7289FC51F2C4DBED4AC5E9320994A.

Appendix E
Calculation of the Potential Impact of Reforms Associated with Less Restrictive Service Regulations

This appendix presents an ex ante calculation of the potential impact of service sector reforms that would reduce restrictive product market regulations on value added and associated gross domestic product (GDP) growth. The exercise follows the existing literature on the effects of restrictive product market regulation reforms on growth,[1] notably Barone and Cingano (2011), Conway et al. (2006), and Arnold, Nicoletti, and Scarpetta (2011).

Based on the World Bank Group's Markets and Competition Policy Assessment Tool, four scenarios are calculated:

- Scenario 1: The simulation is based on the differential of the reform effect between service-intensive and non-service-intensive sectors as a proxy of the size of the reform effect for only above-average service-intensive sectors.[2] The analysis identifies Argentine sectors with above-average technical coefficients of service inputs based on the input–output tables for Argentina (for 2011)[3] as intensive in all services combined (telecommunications, transport and storage, electricity, gas and water supply, and other business activities that capture professional services).[4] In this scenario, additional value added is calculated using data on 2011 value added in sectors intensive in services,[5] and the additional GDP growth is calculated based on the share of additional value added in 2017 GDP.

- Scenario 2: Includes the same assumptions as in Scenario 1 and takes into account the reform effect for only above-average service-intensive sectors. In this scenario, additional value added is calculated using data on 2011 value added in sectors intensive in services, and the additional GDP growth is calculated based on the share of additional value added in 2011 GDP.

- Scenario 3: Includes the same assumptions as in Scenario 1 and takes into account the reform effect for only above-average service-intensive sectors. In this scenario, additional value added is calculated using 2011 value added in sectors intensive in services, and the additional GDP growth is calculated based on the share of gross value added in 2011 GDP.

- Scenario 4: Takes into account the reform effect for *highly* intensive service sectors. Highly intensive sectors are those whose technical coefficients for services inputs exceed the 75th percentile of the technical coefficients for services across all sectors. In this scenario, additional value added is calculated using data on 2011 value added in sectors that are highly intensive in services, and the additional GDP growth is calculated based on the share of additional value added in 2017 GDP.

Table E.1 presents the results of the sensitivity analysis using these four alternative calculation methods. The results are robust to the assumptions presented above and suggest that if Argentina undergoes reforms that decrease the regulatory restrictiveness of the service sector, growth in value added in service-intensive industries would translate into an additional 0.1 percent to 0.6 percent growth in annual GDP, all else being equal.

TABLE E.1 **Sensitivity analysis of impact calculation**

CALCULATION METHOD		ADDITIONAL VALUE ADDED (US$ MILLIONS)	ADDITIONAL GROWTH OF ANNUAL GDP (%)
ADDITIONAL VALUE ADDED	**ADDITIONAL GROWTH OF ANNUAL GDP**		
Scenario 1. Calculated using data on 2011 value added in sectors intensive in gas, electricity and water supply, telecom, transport, and other business services	Based on the share of additional value added in 2017 GDP	1,394.8	0.26
Scenario 2. Calculated using data on 2011 value added in sectors intensive in gas, electricity and water supply, telecom, transport, and other business services	Based on the share of additional value added in 2011 GDP	1,394.8	0.35
Scenario 3. Calculated using data on 2011 value added in sectors intensive in gas, electricity and water supply, telecom, transport, and other business services	Based on the share of additional value added in 2011 gross value added	1,394.8	0.59
Scenario 4. Calculated using data on 2011 value added in sectors that are *highly intensive*[a] in gas, electricity and water supply, telecom, transport, and other business services	Based on the share of additional value added in 2017 GDP	607.9	0.097

Source: Data from OECD Input-Output table for Argentina (https://stats.oecd.org/Index.aspx?DataSetCode=IOTS) and IMF World Economic Outlook database, April 2017 (https://www.imf.org/external/pubs/ft/weo/2017/01/weodata/index.aspx)

[a] Highly intensive sectors are those whose technical coefficients for service inputs exceed the 75th percentile of the technical coefficients for services across all sectors.

NOTES

1. See Kitzmuller and Licetti (2012) for a literature review.
2. Based on Barone and Cingano (2011), the differential of growth in value added of industries at the 75th and 25th percentiles of intensity in services was calculated to be approximately 0.75 percentage points higher in a country at the 25th percentile than a country at the 75th percentile of regulatory restrictiveness. Fixed prices and no supply constraints are assumed.
3. All calculations presented here are conservative, as the input–output table is endogenous to the current restrictive service-sector regulation, and, as a result, the contribution of service-intensive industries in the current economy is likely to be biased downward.

4. In the case of Argentina's 2011 input–output table, available from OECD, the industries C73 (R&D) and C74 (other business activities) are reported jointly. Excluding this sector entirely does not change the results substantially.

5. The sectors that use services intensively in Argentina are the following: food products, beverages, and tobacco; pulp, paper, paper products, printing, and publishing; chemicals and chemical products; other nonmetallic mineral products; basic metals; computer, electronic, and optical equipment; electricity, gas, and water supply; wholesale and retail trade; repairs; transport and storage; post and telecommunications; financial intermediation; computer and related activities; R&D and other business activities; and other community, social, and personal services.

REFERENCES

Arnold, J., G. Nicoletti, and S. Scarpetta. 2011. "Regulation, Resource Reallocation, and Productivity Growth." *European Investment Bank Papers* 16 (1): 90–115.

Barone, G., and F. Cingano. 2011. "Service Regulation and Growth: Evidence from OECD Countries." *Economic Journal* 121 (555): 931–57.

Conway, P., D. de Rosa, G. Nicoletti, and F. Steiner. 2006. "Regulation, Competition and Productivity Convergence." OECD (Organisation for Economic Co-operation and Development), Economics Department Working Papers, no. 509. http://www.oecd-ilibrary.org/docserver/download /431383770805.pdf?expires=1520446942&id=id&accname=guest&checksum=2CA976F54702B6B8D AEDCD3D6DD61139.

Kitzmuller, M., and M. Licetti. 2012. *Competition Policy: Encouraging Thriving Markets for Development.* Public Policy for the Private Sector; note no. 331. Washington, DC: World Bank. http://documents .worldbank.org/curated/en/778181468328582034/Competition-policy-encouraging-thriving-markets -for-development.

Appendix F
Specifications of the Price Regressions

TABLE F.1 **Price comparisons analysis: Buenos Aires, Argentina, vs. cities in all other countries (with Numbeo data)**

	(1)	(2)	(3)	(4)	(5)
Argentina	0.138***	0.141***	0.330***	0.323***	0.319***
	(0.022)	(0.024)	(0.022)	(0.032)	(0.040)
Log of GDP per capita PPP (2011 international $)	—	—	0.409***	0.410***	0.416***
			(0.026)	(0.026)	(0.034)
Log of cost of import	—	—	—	0.014	0.011
				(0.046)	(0.046)
Tariff rate, applied	—	—	—	—	0.003
					(0.010)
No. of observations	17,724	17,724	17,542	17,542	17,482
R-squared	0.615	0.616	0.756	0.756	0.756
Product fixed effects	Yes	Yes	Yes	Yes	Yes
Year fixed effects	No	Yes	Yes	Yes	Yes

Source: An elaboration using Numbeo data.

Notes: Results are from an OLS regression using data from Numbeo. The dependent variable is the logarithm of market prices (US$/kg) of the following products: milk (regular, 1 liter), loaf of fresh white bread (500 g), rice (white, 1 kg), eggs (12), local cheese (1 kg), chicken breasts (boneless, skinless, 1 kg), beef round (1 kg, or equivalent back leg red meat), apples (1 kg), bananas (1 kg), oranges (1 kg), tomatoes (1 kg), potatoes (1 kg), onions (1 kg), lettuce (1 head). Standard errors clustered at the city level are in parentheses. Significance is indicated by ***, **, and * at 1 percent, 5 percent, and 10 percent, respectively.

TABLE F.2 **Price comparisons analysis: Buenos Aires, Argentina, vs. comparator cities in Latin America (using the prevailing EIU market exchange rate to convert local currencies into US$)**

	(1)	(2)	(3)	(4)	(5)
Argentina	0.231***	0.231***	0.196***	0.164***	0.165***
	(0.040)	(0.040)	(0.034)	(0.029)	(0.028)
Log of GDP per capita PPP (2011 international $)	—	—	0.272*	0.290*	0.272*
			(0.143)	(0.142)	(0.137)
Log of cost of import	—	—	—	0.114**	0.090
				(0.049)	(0.093)
Tariff rate, applied	—	—	—	—	0.006
					(0.018)
No. of observations	1,176	1,176	1,176	1,176	1,176
R-squared	0.782	0.786	0.795	0.798	0.798
Product fixed effects	Yes	Yes	Yes	Yes	Yes
Year fixed effects	No	Yes	Yes	Yes	Yes

Source: An elaboration using EIU data.
Notes: Results are from an OLS regression using data from the Economist Intelligence Unit (EIU) dataset (http://www.eiu.com/site_info.asp?info_name =EIUcityData&entry1=DataServicesNav&entry2=DataServicesNav2&infositelayout=site_info_nav). The dependent variable is the logarithm of market prices (US$/kg) of the following products: apples (1 kg), bananas (1 kg), beef (roast, 1 kg), cheese (imported, 500 g), chicken (fresh, 1 kg), eggs (12), lettuce (1 head), milk (pasteurized, 1 liter), onions (1 kg), oranges (1 kg), potatoes (2 kg), tomatoes (1 kg), white bread (1 kg), and white rice (1 kg). Standard errors clustered at the city level are in parentheses. Significance is indicated by ***, **, and * at 1 percent, 5 percent, and 10 percent, respectively. The comparator countries in Latin America with available data include Belize, Bolivia, Brazil, Chile, Colombia, Costa Rica, Ecuador, Guatemala, Mexico, Panama, Peru, Uruguay, and Venezuela.

TABLE F.3 **Price comparisons analysis: Buenos Aires, Argentina, vs. comparator cities in Latin America, using PPP conversion factor**

	(1)	(2)	(3)	(4)	(5)
Argentina	0.137**	0.136**	0.139*	0.084	0.090
	(0.059)	(0.059)	(0.070)	(0.118)	(0.114)
Log of GDP per capita PPP (2011 international $)	—	—	−0.023	0.008	−0.054
			(0.182)	(0.202)	(0.179)
Log of cost of import	—	—	—	0.183	0.096
				(0.201)	(0.165)
Tariff rate, applied	—	—	—	—	0.021
					(0.020)
No. of observations	1,162	1,162	1,162	1,162	1,162
R-squared	0.783	0.787	0.787	0.794	0.795
Product fixed effects	Yes	Yes	Yes	Yes	Yes
Year fixed effects	No	Yes	Yes	Yes	Yes

Source: An elaboration using EIU data.
Notes: Results are from an OLS regression using data from the Economist Intelligence Unit (EIU) dataset (http://www.eiu.com/site_info.asp?info_name =EIUcityData&entry1=DataServicesNav&entry2=DataServicesNav2&infositelayout=site_info_nav). The dependent variable is the logarithm of market prices (US$/kg) of the following products: apples (1 kg), bananas (1 kg), beef (roast, 1 kg), cheese (imported, 500 g), chicken (fresh, 1 kg), eggs (12), lettuce (1 head), milk (pasteurized, 1 liter), onions (1 kg), oranges (1 kg), potatoes (2 kg), tomatoes (1 kg), white bread (1 kg), and white rice (1 kg). Standard errors clustered at the city level are in parentheses. Significance is indicated by ***, **, and * at 1 percent, 5 percent, and 10 percent, respectively. The comparator countries in Latin America with available data include Belize, Bolivia, Brazil, Chile, Colombia, Costa Rica, Ecuador, Guatemala, Mexico, Panama, Peru, Uruguay, and Venezuela. — = not available.

Appendix G
Detailed Matrix of Policy Recommendations

SHORT TERM			MEDIUM TERM			LONG TERM		
CONTENT OF REFORM	RESPONSIBLE INSTITUTION	REQUIRES	CONTENT OF REFORM	RESPONSIBLE INSTITUTION	REQUIRES	CONTENT OF REFORM	RESPONSIBLE INSTITUTION	REQUIRES
Open up further opportunities to enter and invest								
Lower tariffs and NTMs in priority sectors								
Limit nonautomatic licenses to the minimum (hazardous imports)	ComEx	New decree	**Unilateral tariff reduction for high protected sectors**	ComEx	New decree	**Harmonize standards among Mercosur parties**	Foreign Affairs, ComEx, CNDC	Negotiations within Mercosur
			Pursue FTA with EU	Foreign Affairs, ComEx	International agreement	**Pursue "community reforms" at Mercosur**	Foreign Affairs, ComEx	International agreement
Improve incentive framework to attract efficiency seeking more effectively								
Introduce a systematic inventory of incentives	AAICI	Coordination federal–state	**Procedural mapping of steps to adjudicate incentives**	AAICI	Coordination federal–state			
			Strengthening monitoring and evaluation of incentives	AAICI	New program			
Open key sectors for investment and eliminate barriers that limit market entry								
Limit GoA's liability for losses of Aerolineas Argentinas	Advocacy by CNDC, AAICI	Change in law (Ley 26466, Art. 3)	**Eliminate "public hearing" for granting new licenses for air transport services**	Advocacy by CNDC, AAICI	Change in law (Ley 17285, Art. 102)	**Open domestic air transport market to foreign carriers**	Advocacy by CNDC, AAICI	Change in law (Ley 19030, Art. 3)
Address red tape and bureaucratic hurdles that affect ease of doing business; particularly in the entry phase								
Better regulation efforts to improve in the areas of doing business	Advocacy by AAICI, CNDC	New law and institution	**Broad application of "silence-is-consent" rule**	Advocacy by AAICI, CNDC	Change in law (Código Civil, Art. 919)	**General procedure for regulatory simplification**	Advocacy by AAICI, CNDC	New law and institution
Enhance access to more efficient input markets for firms								
Unilateral NTM reduction in input products								
Remove import ban on used machinery, equipment, instruments, devices, and their parts	ComEx	New decree	**Reduce NTMs for key industrial inputs**	ComEx	New decree			

continued

	SHORT TERM			MEDIUM TERM			LONG TERM		
CONTENT OF REFORM	CONTENT OF REFORM	RESPONSIBLE INSTITUTION	REQUIRES	CONTENT OF REFORM	RESPONSIBLE INSTITUTION	REQUIRES	CONTENT OF REFORM	RESPONSIBLE INSTITUTION	REQUIRES
Introduce effective policies to promote linkages with domestic firms									
Develop a central (online) database of national suppliers		AAICI	New program	**Redesign performance requirements and local content rules, e.g., revise tax benefits in auto industry**	Advocacy by AAICI	Change in law (Ley 27263)			
				Introduce behavioral incentives for firms to enhance capacities	AAICI	New program			
Strengthen anticartel enforcement, especially in homogeneous input products									
Strengthen cartel investigation techniques (IT forensic capabilities)		CNDC	Increase in budget and training	**Elevate sanctions for cartels**	CNDC	Change in law (Ley 25156, Capítulo VII)			
				Introduce leniency program	CNDC	Change in law (Ley 25156)			
Strengthen procompetition sector regulation in key input services									
Implement rules to protect competitive neutrality in the telecom sector		Advocacy by CNDC	Change in law (Ley 26092)	**Fully enforce MVNO framework**	Advocacy by CNDC	Implementation	**Allow pay-TV companies to offer telecommunication services**	Advocacy by CNDC	Change in decree (Decreto 267)
Guarantee effective non-discriminatory access in rail freight		Advocacy by CNDC	New policy	**Review toll-exemption rules for private ('self'-) cargo transport and public cargo transport (to third parties)**	Advocacy by CNDC	Change in Decree (Decree 455/2007, Art. 1 and Joint Resolution 111/2011)			
Enhance predictability and a level playing field for the private sector									
Implement competitive neutrality principles and eliminate instruments that can limit competition									
Eliminate the government's ability to control prices		Advocacy by CNDC	Change in law (1974 Supply Law)	**Incorporate SOEs under the same regime as private joint-stock companies**	Advocacy by CNDC	Implementation/ potential change in Ley 20705 and company-specific laws	**Introduce regulatory and tax-neutrality principles for SOEs**	Advocacy by CNDC	New law

continued

	SHORT TERM			MEDIUM TERM			LONG TERM	
CONTENT OF REFORM	RESPONSIBLE INSTITUTION	REQUIRES	CONTENT OF REFORM	RESPONSIBLE INSTITUTION	REQUIRES	CONTENT OF REFORM	RESPONSIBLE INSTITUTION	REQUIRES
Enhance the capacity of firms to thrive and expand								
Remove nonautomatic licenses to increase predictability								
			Ensure that nonautomatic licenses are set to the minimum	ComEx	New decree			
Reduce regulatory and legal uncertainty through broad regulatory improvement mechanisms								
Introduce a clear procedural protocol to solve problems faced by foreign investors and arising from regulatory conduct	AAICI	New secondary legislation/ guideline						
			Legal obligation for regulatory agencies to publish text or proposed regulations before enactment	AAICI	New legal provision			
						Establishment of a systemic investor response mechanism	AAICI	New law and institution
Strengthen the legal framework for e-commerce								
Remove exemptions to e-signatures and e-documents; give validity to all types of e-signature	AAICI and ComEx	Change in law (Ley 25506)	Strengthen consumer protection specific to electronics consumers	AAICI and ComEx	New law			
Overhaul merger control framework								
Raise notification threshold for mergers	CNDC	Change in law (Ley 25156, Art. 8)	Introduce fast-track procedures for mergers unlikely to have anticompetitive effects	CNDC	Change in law (Ley 25156, Capítulo III)			
			Improve procedural effectiveness in reviewing mergers	CNDC	Secondary legislation			

Notes: ComEx = Sub-Secretaría Comercio Exterior; CNDC = Comisión Nacional de Defensa de la Competencia; FTA = free trade agreement; EU = European Union; AAICI = Agencia Argentina de Inversiones y Comercio Internacional; MVNO = Mobile Virtual Network Operator; SOE = state-owned enterprise.

www.ingramcontent.com/pod-product-compliance
Lightning Source LLC
Chambersburg PA
CBHW080424270326

41929CB00018B/3151

9 781464 812750